THE RETREAT FROM MOSCOW

R. F. DELDERFIELD

THE RETREAT FROM MOSCOW

ATHENEUM

NEW YORK

1967

DEDICATED TO THE OFFICERS, N.C.O.'S AND MEN

OF THE GRAND ARMY OF THE YEAR 1812

Copyright © 1967 by R. F. Delderfield
All rights reserved
Library of Congress catalog card number 67-25469
Printed in the United States of America by
The Murray Printing Company, Forge Village, Massachusetts
Bound by H. Wolff
First American Edition

CONTENTS

ILLUSTRATIONS

MAPS

THE RETREAT
FROM MOSCOW

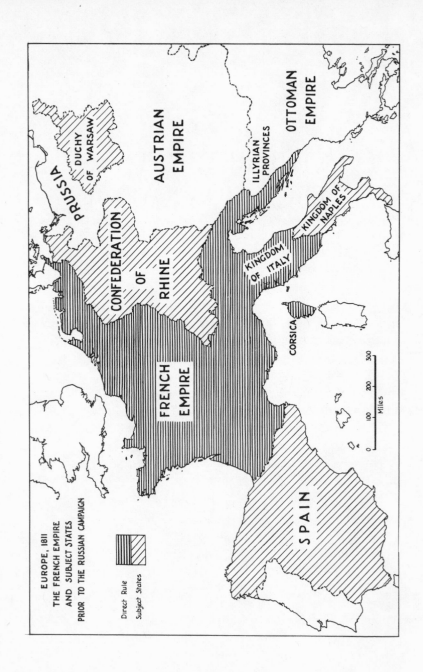

EUROPE, 1811
THE FRENCH EMPIRE
AND SUBJECT STATES
PRIOR TO THE RUSSIAN CAMPAIGN

Direct Rule
Subject States

PRUSSIA

DUCHY OF WARSAW

AUSTRIAN EMPIRE

OTTOMAN EMPIRE

CONFEDERATION OF RHINE

ILLYRIAN PROVINCES

FRENCH EMPIRE

KINGDOM OF ITALY

KINGDOM OF NAPLES

CORSICA

SPAIN

100 200 300
Miles

12

CHAPTER ONE

'WHICH IS THE WAY TO MOSCOW?'

'My ears will ever be open to negotiations for peace ...'
Napoleon at Vilna

1

ON June 30th, in the year 1812, a small group of professional soldiers and diplomats assembled in a room of a
house in the ancient city of Vilna, then the capital of
Russian Lithuania. One was a Russian, the other five were
French. The Russian was a nonentity, there on behalf of
his sovereign to ask why a huge French army, the largest
force ever assembled in modern times, had invaded Russia.
Of the five Frenchmen present all had acquired inter-
national reputations, but one of them, Napoleon Bonaparte, was the most celebrated man in the world. He at
once set the tone of the conference by smashing the loose-
fitting ventilator of the window because its persistent rattle
in the breeze irritated his nerves. The frame cracked and
the glass tinkled to the ground.

Nobody paid much attention to the incident. A man
who had mastered Europe in sixteen years was entitled to
break a window if the act released his tensions. In his time
he had broken a great many windows, including those of
palaces occupied by hereditary kings.

Presently the six men sat down at a table and began to
talk. Marshal Berthier, celebrated Chief of Staff of the
Grand Army, said nothing and neither did Marshal Bes-
sières, once a hairdresser, now Commander of the Old
Guard. They were there, as usual, to listen, not to talk.
Duroc, the amiable Palace Marshal, probably said little,
and if Caulaincourt, former French Ambassador to the
Court of Alexander of Russia, contributed anything of im-

portance to the discussion it was not recorded in the envoy's notes.

Such intercourse as there was passed between the Russian General and the Emperor of the French Empire, in personal command of nearly 400,000 armed men at that moment lapping over Russia's western provinces. He asked a number of questions and received as many polite answers. He wanted to know how many people lived in Moscow and how many houses and churches it contained. Told there were 340 churches he was scornful, remarking that people nowadays were not religious. The Russian, General Balachov, demurred. 'It varies,' he said, quietly, 'they may not be religious in Germany or Italy but they are in Spain and Russia!'

It was a barbed gibe. At that moment a hundred thousand Frenchmen were being herded back across the Spanish peninsula by a small British army and the world was laughing into its sleeve. One of the main reasons for the French failure in Spain was the fanatical religious faith of the Spanish peasant. Balachov was implying that Napoleon was opening another running sore in the East before there was any prospect of the wound in the West being healed, or even staunched.

Napoleon was silent for a moment, measuring his man and perhaps his chances. Then he asked, abruptly, 'Which is the way to Moscow?'

This time it was the Russian who considered. 'I find that a puzzling question,' he said at length. 'In Russia we say, as you do, that all roads lead to Rome. The way to Moscow is a matter of choice. Charles XII was going by way of Poltava.'

Charles XII had been a King of Sweden who invaded the realm of Peter the Great one hundred and four years before. At Poltava, a town in the Ukraine, he had been disastrously defeated and had fled back across the River Niemen almost alone. [1]

*   *   *

When this exchange of views took place the French invasion of Russia was six days old. On June 22nd war had been declared. On June 24th the vast host of the French, and their numerous contingents of allies, had crossed the Niemen on three pontoon bridges and set out along the dusty road to Vilna, without meeting any opposition. The greatest gamble of modern history up to that time had begun.

As a military adventure it was to have no rival in size and scope for another 102 years, when Von Moltke's army of a million Germans developed its historic right-hook at Paris, in the long, hot summer of 1914. But even that gigantic manoeuvre—the famous Schlieffen plan designed to capture Paris in six weeks—was not such a spectacular failure as Napoleon's thrust at Moscow, in the summer of 1812. In 1914 the Germans, although repulsed on the Marne, were able to dig in and hold on for another four years; the French invasion of Russia was seen to be abortive in less than four months, and six weeks after that it was recognised throughout the Chancellories of Europe as the greatest military disaster of all time.

Of the half-million men and camp-followers who crossed the Niemen on June 24th, 1812, no more than one in ten returned, except as released prisoners of war. Of one hundred thousand odd who actually reached Moscow, only a few thousand half-insane fugitives recrossed the Kovno bridge in mid-December. In terms of military achievement even the Nazi invasions of 1941 were more positive than that.

No one will ever be able to measure the full cost to France and the French-dominated Europe of that time of what has been called, not altogether justly, Napoleon's ultimate madness. The casualties were enormous on both sides. For months after the issue of the Emperor's brutally frank 29th Bulletin, acquainting Paris with the débâcle, almost every family in the capital wore black. Yet accurate estimates of the cost in lives and material are very difficult to assess. Napoleon minimised his, the enemies of France magnified them, and Russian statisticians kept no tally of the hundreds of thousands of Russian soldiers and non-combatants who died contesting the ground over the 1,100-mile route between Kovno and the capital, and back to Kovno again. All that can be said without fear of contradiction is that of the hundred thousand who went the full distance fewer than ten thousand returned and with them perished the legend of Napoleon Bonaparte's invincibility. Never again, despite many victories obtained against impossible odds, did the veterans of Egypt, Austerlitz, Jena, Friedland and Wagram, or the conscripts of 1813 and 1814 who replaced them, fight with the élan that had made post-Revolutionary France the most formidable military power in the world. The heart had gone from the senior commanders, the faith from the junior officers and old moustaches. With very few exceptions all ranks had entered Russia confident of victory on a grand scale. The stragglers who survived carried the virus of defeat into the newly-raised armies that were to fight holding actions against a confederation of European powers during the twenty months before Parisiens watched Cossacks ride down the Champs Elysées. They marched in as conquerors. They returned knowing that the Empire was doomed.

It was a gamble on which Napoleon himself staked everything acquired since his first victories in Italy, sixteen years before, but in June 1812 he did not see it as such and neither, for that matter, did anyone else. He and Europe, allied and hostile, looked upon it not so much as a war but as a huge punitive gesture, executed for the purpose of demonstrating the might of regenerated France, and Napoleon entered upon it with no thought of territorial ambitions. It was an attempt to prove to his one dangerous rival on the European mainland that Russia would have to fall into line with every other state and accept the fact of French hegemony. Yet it was very far from being a reckless gamble, made on impulse. He had prepared for it over a period of eighteen months and his planning, having regard to the fact that this was an age before railways, preserved rations or any form of intelligence communications better than the heliograph, was as thorough and imaginative as any task he had set himself in the past. His army was the finest fighting machine ever assembled under a single commander for a single campaign. His staging depots were well-sited and his magazines were full. Provision was made for advanced bases, for recruits and remounts, for a steady flow of grain, ammunition and everything else necessary to maintain a huge army in the field. His overall strategy was simple, direct and was, in the main, applied with efficiency. For all that he failed, as few military men have failed and on a scale that made even the cynical gasp.

This is the story, fragmentary but terrible, of what overtook the Grand Army during a period of one hundred and seventy-nine days, between June 24th and December 19th, the date on which the hero of the retreat, Michel Ney, fired a last contemptuous shot at his pursuers on the wooden bridge that crossed the Niemen at Kovno. Its dominant theme is one of horror and butchery on an unprecedented scale, but it has undertones of self-denial, physical hardihood and courage on a heroic scale.

2

The two adversaries who resolved to measure their strength in June 1812 had been nominal allies up to the moment of the declaration of war.

For a period of almost exactly five years—ever since the signing of the Treaty of Tilsit after Russia's spectacular defeat at Friedland in 1807—Tsar Alexander had stood aside and watched the high tide of Imperial France lap across Europe, rolling across the plains and down into the remote peninsulas of the Continent, engulfing all islands of resistance, large and small, including territories owned by members of every royal family and every petty potentate from Lisbon to Moscow. This was the price Russia paid for her failure to avert the overthrow of the Habsburg Empire at Austerlitz in 1805, when she had been Austria's ally in the field, and for her tardiness in going to the assistance of Prussia when that state challenged the French at Jena the following year. [2] In February 1807 Russia had imposed a severe check on the Grand Army at Eylau, but four months later, at Friedland, she was decisively beaten and the celebrated meeting between the two most powerful men in Europe took place on a raft, moored in the centre of the Niemen.

Under the terms of this Treaty Alexander virtually gave Napoleon a free hand to consolidate his conquests, some of which, like the newly-created Grand Duchy of Warsaw carved out of a subject Poland, would almost surely encourage the Tsar's Polish subjects to secede. Yet it was not disputed territory that decided Alexander and his advisers to tear up the Treaty of Tilsit, and goad Napoleon into invading Russia. Neither was resistance symptomatic of a wish on the part of the Russian aristocracy to avenge the humiliations of Austerlitz, when they had encouraged the Tsar to make peace rather than risk exposing their serfs to the temptation of embracing the Revolutionary creed. The rupture was caused—as it usually is when nations make war—by the stresses of dislocated trade, and by Russia's tacit and finally flagrant defiance of the Berlin Decrees, Napoleon's method of destroying the British by denying her shipping in Continental ports and thus ruining her commerce. For alone among the nations of Europe Britain had continued to wage war on France. With one brief interval of peace she had been doing this since the week the head of Louis XVI fell into the basket in Place de la Révolution. She would continue to do it, directly and indirectly, until the last discharge of grapeshot at Waterloo three years in the future. She not only blockaded France and opposed her in the field in Spain and Portugal, she let it be known that she was prepared to finance any nation who would join her in fighting Napoleon. The cost of her unflagging effort, of a war that had now been waged for half a generation, was ruinous, but she had far too much at stake to leave Europe to its fate, and confine herself to exercising undisputed sea-power won at the Nile and underwritten at Trafalgar. She saw the vast Empire of the Tsar as the widest chink in the wall that Napoleon had built round Europe. It was comparatively easy for French customs officials to ensure that the Berlin Decrees were observed (apart from a little, well-regulated smuggling) in places like Copenhagen, The Hague and Trieste. It was quite another thing to close Russian markets to all British merchandise and Russian merchants took full advantage of their relative immunity. Ever since the Treaty of Tilsit had been signed a steady flow of British goods had reached Continental countries through Russia, and Tsar Alexander, despite a professed admiration for Napoleon, did little or nothing to stop this flow. Thus Napoleon's entire policy of bringing Britain down was jeopardised from the beginning. By 1812 it was in tatters and nothing would make it good again except a dictated peace on Russian soil.

There were other, minor, causes of mutual irritation. The Tsar had just imposed an import tax on French goods. Resentment of the mismanagement of the previous war still rankled with some of Russia's professional soldiers. The territory of Oldenburg, owned by the wife of the Russian heir-apparent, had been annexed by the French. All three issues contributed to the quarrel, but the principal supplementary cause was the cavalier manner in which Napoleon had switched his policy after making up his mind to divorce Josephine and marry a wife capable of bearing him an heir.

At that time, in the summer of 1809, there had been serious talk of him choosing the Tsar's sister, Anne, then only fifteen years of age, but the project found no favour among the Russian nobles and the Tsar procrastinated with the result that Napoleon, to whom the word patience was a blasphemy, dropped his suit and married the daughter of Francis, Emperor of Austria. He gave as his official reason the fact that the Russian Grand Duchess was too young to be likely to bear a son whereas Marie Louise, then eighteen, came from more promising stock. Her mother had borne thirteen children, her great-grandmother twenty-six.

Alexander shared the reluctance of his advisers to promote a marriage alliance between the House of Romanoff and the House of Bonaparte but was none the less extremely piqued by Napoleon's hasty marriage to the complacent Austrian girl. It was just one more discord in the one-sided duet the two autocrats had been playing at Europe's expense for the last five years. When the best of the French battalions and their brilliant leaders appeared to be bogged down in the Spanish peninsular Alexander's approach to his friend and ally grew increasingly cool. More and more forbidden British goods leaked into Europe. More and more adjustments and amendments were sought to the provisions of the Treaty of Tilsit. Alexander quibbled and Napoleon, enjoying domestic peace for the first time in his life, humoured him, but by the middle of 1810 everyone engaged in this game of double bluff could see that it would eventually lead to war. The year 1811 was one of preparation and embassies continued to post between St. Petersburg, Moscow and Paris right into the spring of 1812. By then, however, a confrontation was inevitable. It amounted to this: either Napoleon would have to admit the Tsar as an equal partner in the task of dismembering and completely reorganising Europe, or Alexander would be obliged to wriggle back into favour by severing all communication with the British, by condoning the presence of French garrisons in Prussia and by facing up to the prospect that, sooner or later every Pole under his dominion would enlist under the tricolour banner of France as their one hope of resurrecting the ancient kingdom of Poland.

On the 1st of July, shortly after the polite rebuff he received from the Tsar's envoy, General Balachov, Napoleon was writing to the Tsar in the spirit of a sad, indulgent father reasoning with a wilful son. '...*I marched on the Niemen profoundly convinced that I had done all I could to spare mankind these fresh misfortunes, whilst satisfying my own reputation, the honour of my people, and the sanctity of treaties... We are at war then. God himself cannot undo what has been done. But my ears will ever be open to negotiations for peace...'*

To this unctuous appeal Alexander returned no answer. With nearly half-a-million men a week's march inside his frontier he had obligations that must have seemed to him more immediate.

.　　.　　.

3

Large armies, wholly barbarous or semi-civilised, had been ranging the Continent since the dissolution of the Roman Empire but there had never been an occasion such as this, with one man in control of the military reservoirs of France, the Lowlands, Italy, Germany, the multi-racial Habsburg Empire, part of Poland, part of Spain and spheres of influence far beyond these open frontiers, a leader whose Imperial device, the bronze eagle, was planted outside Cadiz, in Pomerania, in Lithuania and as far south as Calabria, in the toe of Italy. Kings, princes, dukes, counts, local despots and office-holders high and low had been bribed, bullied or bundled out of their territories and offered a choice of returning as minor satraps or seeking permanent refuge across the Channel or the Atlantic. Italy was subjected, Spain and Portugal overrun. Holland and Saxony were reduced to the status of recruiting depots for the Grand Army. Prussia, with its military legacy of Frederick the Great, had been eliminated as a fighting power in a single brief campaign. The sprawling empire of the Habsburgs, acquired over six centuries, had been defeated in a hundred battles and half-a-dozen major clashes and had bought peace at the price of a dynastic alliance. French troops garrisoned the eastern shores of the Adriatic as far as the borders of the half-defunct Ottoman empire. Only in the Spanish peninsula were the eagles on the defensive.

Nor was this all. The task of consolidation had advanced at a breakneck pace. Two of Napoleon's brothers had sat upon emptied thrones and a third had had a kingdom created for him. His three sisters ruled elsewhere, one sharing a throne with a French marshal, the others with husbands who were figures of fun. What we now know as Western Germany became the Confederation of the Rhine and its natural leaders received their orders from Paris. A record of French triumphs since 1792 could be read in the titles of some of Napoleon's ex-Jacobin comrades-in-arms— the Duke of Istria, the Duke of Danzic, the Duke of Albufera, the Prince of Wagram. 'If they have sonorous titles of their own,' Napoleon had said, only half in jest, 'how can they object to mine?'

The very vastness and variety of a military empire acquired in sixteen years goes far to explain the fiendish complexity of the army that entered upon the Russian adventure that sultry June day in 1812. It was composed of at least eighteen national groupings, some there from personal choice, some at the command of their reduced but not unwilling overlords, the rest grudgingly contributed by former enemies. At least half this host was composed of dubious fighting material but there was nothing lacking in the men who led them. Without exception their commanders were brave, intelligent men, and most of them had enormous experience in war for this was how the army had been planned and assembled. Marching over the pontoon bridges that day were Swiss, Austrians, Prussians, Poles, Illyrians, Rhinelanders, North Italians, Neapolitans, Saxons, Bavarians, Westphalians, Portuguese, Spaniards, Lithuanians, Hungarians, Dutchmen and Croats, but the hard core was French. Napoleon and his Chief of Staff, Berthier, had made certain of that.

Like the ultimate casualty figure the original strength of the army is difficult to estimate. A "state" supplied by General Gourgaud, one of Napoleon's aides, quotes a figure as low as 350,000 with 984 guns, but other estimates are much larger, sometimes getting on for double the

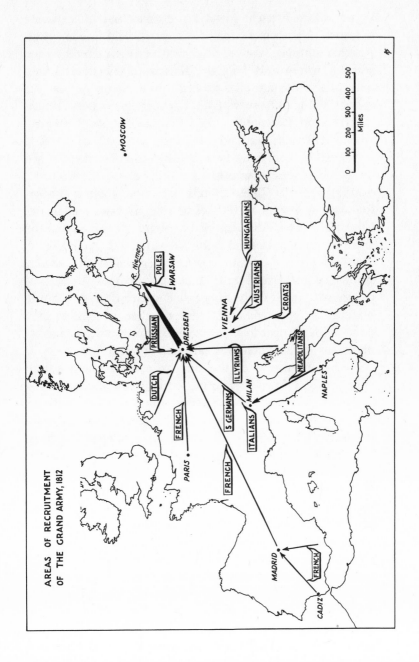

AREAS OF RECRUITMENT
OF THE GRAND ARMY, 1812

23

figure. One French historian claims that there were 355,000 infantrymen, 59,000 cavalry and 1,200 guns. Another estimate arrives at a total of just under 500,000 men, of whom only half are designated effectives. When one surveys the national groups, however, the figures are more reliable. There were approximately 145,000 Frenchmen, 30,000 Prussians, 45,000 Italians, 25,000 Germans, 30,000 Austrians and 70,000 other nationalities merged together; in addition (and not included in the French total), there was a large cavalry reserve and the Old and Young Guard. These totals do not include campfollowers so that it would seem, after averaging estimates from all sources, that the actual fighting strength of the original army exceeded 350,000 men, with well over a thousand guns and about 150,000 noncombatants, mostly sutlers, teamsters and tradesmen for work upon the lines of communications. Only about one quarter of this horde marched as far as Moscow. Large numbers of fighting men and civilians operated north and south of the line of march, or were detached as garrisons en route.

As has been stated, the quality of these men varied enormously. Of the French more than half, and including the entire Guard, were veterans, some of them only recently withdrawn from Spain or from comfortable German garrisons. They were, in the main, men who had fought in Napoleon's Italian campaigns and had marched across the Sinai desert to besiege Acre as long ago as 1799. Hardly one of them had not played some part in the series of brilliant victories of which Marengo, Austerlitz, Jena, Friedland and Wagram were but five. Among them, notwithstanding their age, there was to be a high proportion of survivors, men like Bourgogne of the Old Guard, whose account of this campaign is the most graphic war memoir ever written by a non-commissioned man in any army. These grognards had learned the tricks of survival. Physically they were almost indestructible and although many of them had scant respect for authority, including that of the Emperor, they had a profound attachment to their regiment and their comrades. It was said of the *Grande Armée* that even the rats starved when the veterans passed that way, and this is not an exaggeration. These men could march and fight for a week on the yield of a looted cabbage patch. They had no family ties outside the barracks. They lived for fighting and looting and their record of unbroken success went right back to the days when Danton and other Republican orators had recruited them as boys to rout the professional armies of kings challenging the Revolution. Their loyalty, such as it was, belonged to the Emperor, but they were not above criticising him when things went wrong or when they doubted the wisdom of his dispositions. This group, the kernel of the host, was reinforced by another cadre of equally tough fighting material, younger officers like Marbot, who had grown to manhood under the eagles of Napoleon and whose experience in war at the age of twenty-five was superior to that of most senior officers in any other army in history. There were many such men in the line regiments and their presence was an example and a rallying point to young conscripts making their first campaign.

Of the allied contingents the quality varied a very great deal. By far the most loyal and aggressive were the Poles, many of whom had been fighting alongside the French since Napoleon entered Warsaw in 1807, and whose lancers were reckoned among his best troops. Next to the Poles in the enthusiasm they brought to the enterprise were some of the South Germans who preferred the French to their Prussian cousins in the North. Then came some of the Italians under Napoleon's stepson, Prince Eugène. Against all probability these men were to stand the rigours of a Russian winter more successfully than many of the Northerners, and on the whole they were dependable troops. Low down on the list came the Austrians, present because Napoleon had recently married their Emperor's daughter, and smaller minorities like the Spaniards, whose Government was at war with France on the far side of Europe, the Portuguese, whose Government was actively helping Wellington in the Peninsula, and the Dutchmen, who had seen their homeland annexed to France and their King, Napoleon's brother Louis, disgraced for intervening on their behalf. Perhaps the weakest spot in the Imperial Army, however, was where the 30,000 Prussians were stationed on the extreme left, for Prussia, still smarting under her catastrophic defeats at Jena and Auerstadt, [3] was slowly re-emerging as a nation and looking forward to the day when she could regain her independence. A tepid patriotism was stirring among civilians in Prussian towns and villages. The Tugendbund, a national liberation movement, was already embarked upon a policy of murdering Frenchmen whenever it could be achieved with safety. A courier who rode alone across Prussia in 1812 did not take his life in his hands, as did any Frenchman moving between occupied posts in Spain, but the risks increased every day.

The magic of Napoleon's reputation, however, kept this polyglot army together up to the moment of defeat. Nobody could foresee that a fighting machine of this size and quality would disintegrate in a matter of weeks; when this happened the lukewarm allies fell away like so many rotten branches. Within five months of Napoleon's return to France survivors of allied contingents were in arms against him, or planning to desert on the battlefield, as many did in the campaign of Saxony the following year.

Napoleon at this time was almost forty-three years of age and his physique was largely unimpaired by the tremendous exertions of his life. He suffered from occasional bouts of dysuria but he could still ride all day and dictate most of the night. His mental faculties were alert to any contingency and the only deterioration that revealed itself in his judgment was a tendency to avoid risks it might have paid him to take. One such moment of caution coinciding with, and perhaps caused by, his bladder trouble was to cost him the fruits of a major success later in the campaign.

Operating directly under Napoleon were some of the most brilliant warriors of all time, men whose names were already a legend and whose personal valour and tactical skills were unchallenged by their enemies.

Heading the First Corps in the centre was Marshal Davout, a dour professional soldier whose obstinacy, severity towards recalcitrant civilians and humourless devotion to duty, had earned him the soubriquet of "The Iron Marshal". Fanatically loyal to Napoleon he was a brilliant strategist, rare among the Marshalate. His personal honour was never questioned, not even when Napoleon was toppled from power. He was the only high-ranking officer in France who could return to the eagles with clean hands after the Emperor's escape from Elba in 1815.

Commanding the Second Corps, soon to be detached from the main body to fight an independent war against Wittgenstein on the extreme left, was Marshal Oudinot, a brewer's son who had once been a grenadier. He was lion-hearted but impulsive when removed from under the guiding hand of his chief. The success of operations out here on the left was due to the fact that he was wounded early in the campaign and his command passed to the brilliant but unlikeable St. Cyr, a former jack-of-all-trades who won his baton in Russia, itself a unique achievement.

The incomparable Michel Ney commanded the Third Corps, also with the centre and spearheading the infantry advance. Ney was a sound tactician but lacked the cool head necessary for objective planning. He was usually right up in the skirmishing line and thus out of touch with overall strategy, but as a leader and inspirer of fighting men he had no equal. This campaign was to earn him the unstinted admiration of friend and foe.

Prince Eugène, the sober and admirable stepson of Napoleon, commanded the Fourth Corps, made up of Italians. He was brave, intelligent and utterly dependable. He too emerged from the campaign with credit. Prince Poniatowski, the Polish patriot, commanded the Fifth Corps and, at the outset, St. Cyr led the Sixth. General Reynier, a great friend of Ney and another hard-fighting veteran, was in command of the Seventh, and the pleasure-loving youngest brother of Napoleon, Jerome, King of Westphalia, was a bad choice as commander of the Eighth, out on the right of Grand Army. Jerome did not last very long. He was soon withdrawn and sent home in disgrace, followed by the ravings of his terrible brother.

Marshal Victor, an ex-drummer boy and pre-Revolution N.C.O., commanded the Ninth Corps. Victor was a pompous, excitable man whom nobody liked, but his reputation as an aggressive fighter went back a very long way. So did his reputation for abandoning colleagues in trouble.

Marshal Macdonald, son of a Scots clansman, commanded the unreliable Prussians on the left but took no active part in the campaign as a whole. Marshal Augereau, ex-footman and military adventurer, was in command of the Eleventh Corps but he remained garrisoned in Germany when the main body advanced. Marshal Murat, brother-in-law of the Emperor and the most famous cavalry leader in the world, commanded the Twelfth Corps in the centre and was constantly in action all the way to Moscow. Murat was perhaps the most colourful of all the men around Napoleon. He was celebrated for his brilliant showmanship, manifested in the extraordinary uniforms he designed and the panache he displayed in the field. He led many of his own charges, armed with a gold wand and before the army had advanced as far as Vilna his circus tricks were being discussed in the bivouacs of the Cossacks to whom he made instant appeal.

Schwartzenberg, the Austrian general, was out on the extreme right with his reluctant Thirteenth Corps, all Austrian subjects. He was to betray the French within months. In a little over a year he would be leading Habsburg troops in the new Coalition assembled to break the Imperial grip on Europe.

With the Old and Young Guard, some forty thousand moustached veterans, were three other famous leaders, all marshals and all highly-trained commanders in the Napoleonic style of making war. Bessières commanded the Old Guard, a quiet, cautious and polite man, utterly devoted to his chief. Mortier, son of a small farmer, led the Young Guard and was to emerge with honour from the graveyard of reputations along the road home. Mortier was a huge, genial man, who never made an enemy and was much admired by the British, who paid him the kind of compliments Montgomery's Eighth Army accorded General Rommel over a century later. Both he and Bessières were much beloved by their men. For the third marshal riding with the Guard, fifty-six-year-old Lefèbvre, once a Royalist sergeant-major and now a Duke, the veterans had respect and affection. In the worst days of the retreat the marshal was to show courage and initiative that would have been a credit to much younger men.

With the army went six bridging trains and one siege train, under the command of General Eblé, an extremely able Sapper, hurried up from Spain for the occasion. Senior to all these men, and working day and night as Napoleon's nerve centre, was the famous Marshal Berthier, who had been at the Emperor's side since his first Italian campaign in 1796.

Berthier's reputation as a Chief of Staff has still never been equalled, much less surpassed. He had a phenomenal memory and an executive ability superior to Napoleon's own. Berthier's position as Chief of Staff was a very difficult one, for many of the marshals disliked one another and not one of them took kindly to fighting under the command of another. Thus Berthier was a kind of referee between the rivals competing for the Emperor's ear. His physical stamina matched his brilliant talent for staff work. Small, neat and fastidious in dress and bearing, he could go for days without rest yet remain as clearheaded as the hour he first went on duty. Berthier, so long as he co-ordinated the policy of others and was not required to initiate one of his own, was irreplaceable.

To oppose this enormous host led by the most able group of professional soldiers ever produced by one nation in a single generation, were three Russian armies, already widely separated from one another and amounting, all told, to about 200,000 men.

They were led by three Russian generals acting independently of one another and in such a way as to imperil their chances of resisting this tide of invasion unless a unified command could be established without delay. This eventually happened, but not before they came within an inch of being destroyed piecemeal in the best Napoleonic tradition.

Russian armies of the period were usually led by the sovereign in person. This had been the case, with disastrous results, seven years earlier at Austerlitz, and perhaps it was the memory of what occurred on this occasion that led Tsar Alexander I to yield to the persuasions of his advisers and retire to St. Petersburg for the duration.

The history of the Romanoff dynasty is rich in bizarre and enigmatic Tsars, but perhaps Alexander was the greatest enigma of them all inasmuch as nobody, not even the master psychologist Napoleon Bonaparte, was able to take his measure, from the time of their first meeting on the raft at Tilsit, to the day Alexander led his victorious squadrons into Paris and paid a polite call upon his adversary's divorced wife. Ever since succeeding generations, Russian, French and British, have been attempting to assess the moral and intellectual worth of the handsome, graceful, powerfully-built man who exercised despotic sway over millions of Russians when their homeland was invaded in 1812. He remains a question mark, idealist, hero, part weakling, a man of enormous promise who is yet as ineffectual as a middleclass intellectual in a play by Chekhov, a figure with the physique and mystique of a Bayard, whose achievements had no substance and therefore no permanency.

On the surface he was impressive in every way. Contemporaries describe his eyes as being "a heavenly blue" and his Wurttemburg mother bequeathed to him, and to several of his successors, a magnificent stature that combined robust strength with unusual, narrow-waisted grace. At any moment, it was said, Alexander could fall into a pose that was negligently statuesque and standing thus could charm a highly intelligent man like Talleyrand or, if necessary, a half-savage Cossack partisan.

His father, Paul, had been a Tsar in the old tradition, a half-crazy martinet, whose policy was dictated by mood. It was said of Paul that officers setting out for the parade ground to await a review by the Tsar took the precaution of stuffing their pockets with money in case a minor infringement of martial etiquette led to them being banished to Siberia on the spot. They might also be promoted. It depended very largely upon the Tsar's digestion.

Paul went the way of a number of Russian rulers. He was knocked on the head and strangled by his Palace Guards and there is a suspicion amounting almost to certainty that his heir was a tacit accomplice to the murder. He was never quite able to escape from the shadow of parricide and perhaps one must look here, as well as in his liberal education by the French tutor Laharpe, for the curious complexity of his character throughout his spectacular reign. On the surface he was an earnest idealist with (for a Russian Tsar) extremely liberal ideas. He had been taught to regard the French Revolution as a progressive and welcome event and on his father's death he surrounded himself with young men eager to reform Russia from top to bottom and bring it in line with the more constitutional monarchies of the West. Under their influence Alexander pledged himself to give Russia a constitution, free the serfs, found innumerable universities and schools and make himself the most beloved monarch in Russian history. He even talked of freeing Poland. He also talked of retiring and studying nature. But somehow none of these worthy projects was ever achieved. He did, it is true, found a few educational establishments, but Russia had to wait until 1917 for its short-lived constitution, whereas the serfs were not even free on paper until 1856. And yet there was something very appealing and genuinely paternal about his attitude to the Russian people as a whole. He never ceased to try, here and there, to create an educated class, capable of supporting a constitutional government and of his patriotism, which most Russians have in great abundance, there was never a doubt.

He had, of course, the thirst for martial glory that was the inheritance of all Romanoffs, but it was glory as a libertarian that he really coveted and the traits of the martinet were happily missing from his character. He was a consummate actor and therefore a natural diplomat. Napoleon called him the "Talma of the North" or "The Sphinx". [4]

It was soldierly ambition that led him into his first conflict with Napoleon ending on the Pratzen heights at Austerlitz where, seeing his army cut to pieces, he sat down on the ground, burst into tears and cried, 'We are babies in the hands of a giant!' Yet he was not without the ability to learn from experience and in the next seven years, during his tortuous dealings with the French, he learned a great deal more about Napoleon's psychological make-up than did any other European autocrat, so much, indeed, that on his arrival in Paris two years after the invasion of Russia, he remarked, a little smugly, 'And they said I was a fool!' He was by no means a fool. In many respects he was an astute, patient, resolute man, and his overall behaviour during the next few months establishes this. He was to play Napoleon like a great stranded fish and once he had decided upon a policy, and absorbed the initial shock of invasion, his determination to pursue that policy to its logical end was expressed in a remark he made to someone who suggested he should sue for peace. 'I would sooner,' he said quietly, 'grow a beard and live on potatoes in Siberia for the rest of my life!' The beard in Russia signified serfdom.

Only peasants serving as soldiers were allowed the privilege of shaving.

From the moment of invasion, however, Alexander's part in the campaign was limited to ignoring Napoleon's overtures to come to terms. The actual conduct of the defensive campaign was left, in the first instance, to Wittgenstein, commanding the small northern army covering St. Petersburg, to Barclay de Tolly, commanding 120,000 men in the approximate centre, and to Prince Bagration, with another small army in the south. A fourth army, under the impetuous Tchichagoff, was engaged with the Turks on the Danube and was to play a dramatic part in events later on.

Of these four men Barclay de Tolly and Bagration are the most interesting and their characters could hardly have been in greater contrast, which was a source of trouble until unified command came with the appointment of Kutusoff, "the old fox of the North" as he was delighted to be called.

Barclay's ancestry was Scots and he was a Lithuanian, an excessively cautious man and a scientific fighter. Bagration had learned warfare under the savage Suvorov, whom Byron once described as "hero, buffoon, half-demon and half-dirt!" It was a not inaccurate description of the man, but he was a terrible opponent in war who could inspire his men to perform impossible feats of valour and hardihood and whose tactics were limited to frenzied assault wherever the enemy presented himself. Bagration had been with Suvorov when the demon general had cleared Northern Italy of the French while Bonaparte was in Egypt, and he had accompanied Suvorov's fantastic cross-country march over the Alps, after Masséna had destroyed the Russian's allies at Zurich.[5] Bagration was contemptuous of Barclay de Tolly's caution. He wanted to sally across the Russian frontier and create a diversion that would halt the French in their advance on Moscow, perhaps make them double on their tracks. In the event he was extremely lucky not to be surrounded and annihilated and he would have been had General Junot, one of Napoleon's closest personal friends, been in good mental health, or Jerome, Napoleon's playboy brother, been any use as a soldier.

As it was the Russians fought delaying actions all the way from Vilna to Borodino, not far short of Moscow itself, and at Smolensk the main Russian armies (apart from Wittgenstein's covering St. Petersburg and opposed to the French left wing) were united under Kutusoff. In the great battle before Moscow Prince Bagration was killed.

By that time Alexander was committed to a scorched earth policy and the French were hopelessly strung out over a devastated route of five hundred miles. Perhaps Napoleon reflected on a remark made by the French swashbuckler, General Rapp, at a little dinner party in Danzic shortly before the invasion began, Napoleon had asked of Berthier, his Chief of Staff, and of Murat, his brother-in-law, 'How many leagues from Cadiz to Danzic?' The marshals were too discreet to answer but Rapp answered for them. 'Too many!' he said.

CHAPTER TWO

THE RELUCTANT DON QUIXOTE

'Oh, this splendid people...!'—*The Tsar's mother in
1812*

1

In his eminently readable *Napoleon Bonaparte, His Rise
and Fall*, the historian J. M. Thompson provides an interesting parallel of the march in terms of distances between modern towns in Britain. He compares the route to
a journey made between Brighton, on the south coast, to
Edinburgh, a few marches north of the Scottish border. In
place of the main stops on the inward journey he pinpoints
London, York, Darlington and Berwick, as representing
Vilna, Vitepsk, Smolensk and Borodino, where Kutusoff
made his one determined stand.

One is inclined to think of any journey made inside
Russia as one on which a traveller would guard against
falling temperatures, forgetting that in the months of
June, July and August, a footslog across the great Russian
plains can be as gruelling as a march in parts of the
tropics. Napoleon's veterans and conscripts certainly found
it so from the moment they filed across the Niemen and
headed due east for Vilna, arriving there in force about
five days later.

Heat and the choking clouds of dust were the main
enemies and when a cooling thunderstorm broke the tracks
disintegrated under the impact of so many feet and so
much wheeled traffic. The strain on the infantry, bowed
under the dragging weight of uniform, musket, cartridges,
sword-bayonet, knapsack and cooking utensils, began to
show almost at once and they took it out in grumbling. For
a large number of horses the ordeal proved fatal, for fodder

was in short supply and many died from eating unripe rye. Soon men too began to sicken with acute colic and from the very first bivouac inside Russia there seems to have been a spirit of indiscipline that had been absent from the previous thunderflash campaigns of the Imperial Army. This was possibly induced by the Russian withdrawal, miles ahead of the French skirmishing line at this stage.

The vanguard, under Ney and Murat, was spoiling for a fight and for a long time saw no Russians in any great numbers. Indiscipline was also due to the large number of foreigners in the ranks and attendant language difficulties, as well as rivalries. Sergeant Bourgogne of the Guard crossed the river on June 24th but he did not hear the sound of gunfire until the night of the 28th–29th. Major Marbot, commanding a cavalry regiment out on the left flank under the old grenadier Oudinot, went into action a day later, when his corps clashed with the small, hard-fighting army of Wittgenstein at Wilkomir, on the road to St. Petersburg.

In the meantime the usual crop of omens had not been lacking. The night before the general advance Napoleon, disguised as a Polish officer, suffered a heavy fall from his horse when a hare made the animal swerve, whereas the Emperor Alexander, then at Vilna, came close to being seriously injured when the floor under his chair gave way. At the time nobody read very much into either accident. Napoleon had a notoriously bad seat on a horse, and many of the timber buildings in Russian provincial cities were gimcrack.

The first French to cross into Lithuanian Russia were members of a sapper patrol, sent across the Niemen to work on the bridgehead. To oppose the advance of 400,000 men they found a single Cossack who was sufficiently curious, or coolheaded, to ask them what they were doing there. The sappers told him they had come to fight the Emperor Alexander and capture Vilna and this, it seemed, finally convinced him of their hostile intent. He turned and trotted off and three of the sappers discharged their muskets into the wood. They were the first shots of a gigantic and almost nonstop conflict that was to rage between Moscow and the Portuguese frontier for the next twenty-two months and engage millions of Europeans in war on a scale unknown since the barbarian invasions of the fifth century. In another sense those three shots were the forerunners of the millions of salvoes to be exchanged at Verdun and Stalingrad more than a century later, for, unlike any previous campaign of Napoleon, this was to prove a national war, fought for motives of patriotism and on a scale far exceeding the so-called people's war now being fought in the Spanish peninsula. It is true that patriotism was closely involved in Spain, but without the nucleus of Wellington's superbly trained army popular resistance would have died away in a matter of months. This was not the case in Russia. Here the moujik voluntarily enlisted with the cause of his hereditary ruler the moment the first French shako showed over the western horizon. His stubborn opposition to the invader not only endured until the last Imperial marshal had recrossed the Niemen, but followed the beaten army right across Poland, over the Elbe, across the Saxon plains, and over the Rhine to Paris.

In the absence of any large army to oppose the advance there was little the Russian peasant could do at the moment but that little he did very willingly, and with a thoroughness and despatch that moved the Tsar to tears. As soon as Russia proper was reached resistance stiffened with every mile covered by the French. The inhabitants burned their villages, laid waste the countryside, drove off livestock, and then dispersed to join one or other of the resistance groups, already forming in the vast birch forests of the plain.

The scorched earth policy had been tried, very successfully, in Portugal, when Wellington retreated to Torres Vedras in September 1810, but here was stubbornness of a far greater scale, and involving millions rather than thousands of peasants living off the land. 'Oh this splendid people!' the Tsar's mother was to exclaim. 'It has shown plainly what it really is!'

2

Anyone attempting the impossible—that is, anyone who attempts an invasion of Russia—has a choice of two plans and there is no room to manoeuvre outside them, despite the vastness of the terrain. He can either bring the Russian armies to bay before his portable supplies fall too far in the rear, and hope, by beating them, to negotiate a peace; or he can set a strict limit on his objectives, occupy a specified area and hope in time to detach the people of that area from their allegiance.

The latter plan is one Hitler might have followed in the Ukraine in 1940–41, and it is what Napoleon should have done in Russian Poland in 1812, in order to achieve a limited success. Hitler, by treating the Ukrainians as allies or even as human beings, might have stood his ground in the south for some considerable time. Napoleon, a far better pacifier, would have almost surely rallied every Pole to his eagles and presented Alexander with a choice of accepting the fait accompli of a regenerated Poland, or wasting his strength in attempts to expel the French from territory that was only nominally Russian. The mistake Napoleon made was not in invading Russia at all. If British trade was to be ruined, and if the Eastern borders of the French Empire were to be safeguarded, he had no option but to bring Alexander to battle. His mistake lay in his failure to specify his intentions, even to himself, and in the policy of drift and opportunism that characterised every league of his penetration into Russia. His indecisions, his needlessly long delays at stages on the march, belong in later chapters of this story. At this point, during the first week of the invasion, it is only necessary to read his correspondence written at the time in order to understand the dilemma in which he found himself as soon as it became clear that Barclay de Tolly could not be brought to action, and that

38

the rash Bagration was going to fight his way clear of the trap the French were baiting for him.

The French advance guard reached Vilna on June 28th, the main body two days later. Yet, on July 1st, Napoleon was writing to the Tsar, '*If Your Majesty wishes to end hostilities you will find me ready to do so. If Your Majesty wishes to carry on, and would like to draw up an agreement on liberal lines, such as that men in hospital shall not be regarded as prisoners (then neither side need evacuate in a hurry—always a cause of heavy losses) or such as a fortnightly exchange of prisoners ... or any other stipulations that the rules of war commonly allow between civilised nations, then Your Majesty will find me ready for anything...*' Strange proposals from a man at the head of a victorious and advancing army.

The appeal to reason resulted in nothing. From then, until the French began their retreat three and a half months later, every Imperial messenger to St. Petersburg returned empty-handed and yet, with incredible obstinacy, Napoleon continued to try and bargain with Alexander, first from a position of strength, finally from a position of extreme weakness. He seems never to have given serious thought to a realistic alternative, that of creating a permanent buffer state in Poland. 'I have no wish to become a Polish Don Quixote!' he is said to have remarked, when this policy was urged upon him. From the French viewpoint it was a tragedy. Don Quixote was overthrown by the windmills but generations of Europeans still think of him with affection. Napoleon could have had the affection of Poland for nothing and perhaps the entire subsequent relationship of east and west up to our time would have been very different.

The Headquarters of the Grand Army remained fixed at Vilna for seventeen days. There did not seem to be all that urgency to push on across the steppe to Vitepsk, to Smolensk, to Moscow. Oudinot, far out on the left wing, was more than holding his own against the Russian army guarding St. Petersburg under Wittgenstein and had, in-

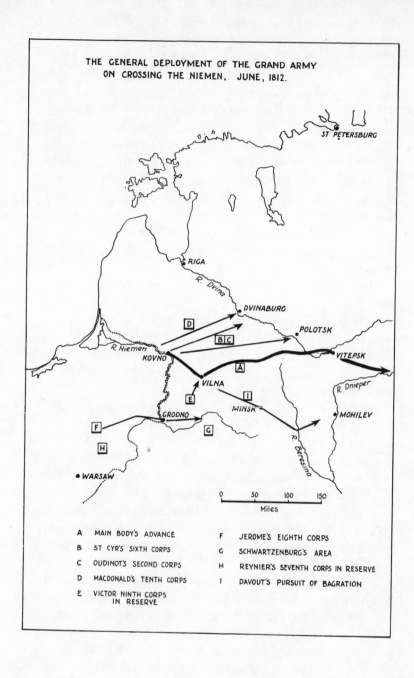

THE GENERAL DEPLOYMENT OF THE GRAND ARMY
ON CROSSING THE NIEMEN, JUNE, 1812.

A MAIN BODY'S ADVANCE
B ST CYR'S SIXTH CORPS
C OUDINOT'S SECOND CORPS
D MACDONALD'S TENTH CORPS
E VICTOR NINTH CORPS
   IN RESERVE

F JEROME'S EIGHTH CORPS
G SCHWARTZENBURG'S AREA
H REYNIER'S SEVENTH CORPS IN RESERVE
I DAVOUT'S PURSUIT OF BAGRATION

deed, inflicted a crushing defeat on him the day Napoleon entered Vilna. Far to the south the impulsive Bagration was now, it appeared, hopelessly separated from the main army of Barclay de Tolly still steadily retreating east, perhaps for the entrenched camp at Drissa on the Dwina where there was fleeting talk of forming a Russian Torres Vedras,[1] perhaps still hoping for a junction with the isolated Bagration at Smolensk or somewhere west of Smolensk. Napoleon was not sure. There were so many confused reports. It was such a huge country and summer thunderstorms had reduced the wretched roads to mud tracks. He was, however, certain of one thing; the extreme vulnerability of Bagration and his forty thousand, now eighty leagues behind the main line of retreat, and it was Suvorov's pupil whom he watched, a spider waiting for an enterprising fly to penetrate the web. Clearly there was no hope for Bagration.

In the meantime there was much to be done and the Lithuanian capital bustled with activity. Diplomats consorted there and couriers galloped in and out of the old city carrying despatches to every part of Europe and bringing reports from Paris, Vienna, Naples, Milan, Berlin and even, through the medium of British newspapers, the latest news from the embattled Spanish peninsula.

Napoleon's couriers, rich in experience of how best to cover enormous distances at a rattling pace, made the trip from Paris to Vilna in ten days. Today, with so many frontiers to cross, and so many bureaucrats to parry, it would take almost as long in a jeep. Under the Empire the right priorities were observed. Despatch riders were not bothered by red tape. At every posthouse their path was made swift and easy and some of Napoleon's young horsemen, six-campaign men at twenty-five, could travel day and night for a week almost without rest. It was imperative that they did; the Emperor might be engaged in a campaign that was to take him 550 miles inside Russia but he still had to keep the threads of European government in his hands. Even at this distance from his capital all major decisions were his. To him came the embassies, the concessionaires, the importunate, picking their way among the 25,000 sick who cluttered the town, and occasionally getting an audience in advance of impatient soldiers with messages from outlying corps, but all the time the major part of his mind was pondering two factors: how and when could Barclay de Tolly's main force be brought to battle; how soon would Bagration be driven into the web?

He made the less urgent decision the moment he heard his brother Jerome was at Grodno, on the Niemen. Jerome did not write to ask for instructions (he was the kind of young man who made his own decisions, almost invariably wrong-headed ones) but rather to complain that General Vandamme, one of the toughest senior officers in the Grand Army, had been committing brigandage. Napoleon was irritated by the complaint. He knew Jerome and he knew why Jerome hated Vandamme as wholeheartedly as he hated Marshal Davout. When Jerome had been given the bankrupt kingdom of Westphalia some years before Davout had driven him to despair with his merciless demands for contributions to the Imperial Treasury, but the quarrel with Vandamme went deeper than this, touching the young man's honour. During the 1806 Prussian campaign General Vandamme had seen King Jerome pottering about the trenches outside Neiss and a shower of cannon balls had fallen near them, spattering them with dirt. A master of ironic invective Vandamme had remarked, 'These devils of bullets! They have no respect for strangers!'[2] Jerome had never forgiven him for the remark, and now, representing the southern prong of the trap Napoleon had set for Bagration, Jerome was in command of 60,000 men and Vandamme was attached to him. It was something that should have been foreseen, and so should the difficulties arising from expectations of a working partnership between Jerome and Davout, now waiting at Minsk, a hundred miles south-east of Vilna, to pounce on Bagration as he withdrew. There was nothing wrong with this prong of the trap. The Iron Marshal's corps was

the best disciplined in the Grand Army and it had a reputation for marching and fighting remarkable even
among the veterans of the Guard.[3] Bagration had only to
appear within striking distance and he was netted. The
single flaw in this piece of Napoleonic strategy was the fact
that Jerome's army, dawdling at Grodno, was commanded
by a vain, inexperienced young idiot.

All his life Jerome, the pampered baby of the Bonaparte
family, had been a spectacular failure. Alone among his
brothers and sisters he had never known the pinch of
poverty and from his boyhood there had never been a time
when statesmen, pretty women and even soldiers possessing
more tact than Vandamme and Davout, had not deferred
to him, knowing that Napoleon regarded the young scamp
with great affection. The result of all this cosseting was
that Jerome grew from spoiled brat to pleasure-loving
egotist, utterly unable to take orders from anyone much
less someone he actively disliked. He had arrived at
Grodno from Warsaw on June 30th, the day Davout left
Vilna for Minsk, preparatory to pouncing on Bagration as
he fell back before Jerome's onslaught. The onslaught did
not come. Jerome remained at Grodno until July 4th, giving as his reason that his men needed a rest. He also sent
off some high-toned suggestions to Davout that 'they
should co-operate!'

Davout, who had once out-fought an entire Prussian
army with a single corps and thus made Napoleon's victory
at Jena possible, was not the kind of man to accept suggestions, good or bad, from an amateur. He at once
appealed to Napoleon and Napoleon, making another
psychological slip, placed Jerome under Davout's command but told the marshal to keep the matter quiet for the
time being. At the same time he wrote to his brother, *You
are jeopardising the whole success of the campaign on the
right wing. It is not possible to carry on war in this way!*
Davout thought precisely the same. He was very devoted to
Napoleon but extremely jealous of his reputation as a
soldier. He sent off a despatch to Jerome informing him

that he was now a subordinate, giving him orders to advance at once and drive Bagration into the trap.

Jerome was furious. He would not have taken orders from Berthier, senior marshal of the army; how was it possible that he would obey a man who had repeatedly dunned him for money, and had kept him so short of cash in Westphalia that he was heavily in debt before he had issued a single royal edict? Writing an indignant letter to Napoleon he did not wait for a reply but threw up his command and retired to Warsaw.

Napoleon's rage was terrible. For years now Jerome's folly and extravagance had put an immense strain upon his patience, but here was a member of his own family retiring from the field in the face of the enemy. He packed Jerome home to Westphalia and replaced him by Junot, giving that General orders to advance upon Bagration within the hour. He should have spared a little of his rage for himself. Any commander, and certainly the greatest in the world, should have known that his youngest brother was not fit to command a platoon in the field and the situation should never have arisen.

His choice of substitute was another blunder. Junot, a hard-fighting soldier, was one of Napoleon's oldest friends. At the siege of Toulon, when Napoleon was an unknown artillery officer and Junot a volunteer sergeant, a shell had scattered earth on a despatch Junot was writing at Napoleon's dictation. Junot had remarked, with a chuckle, 'We shall not need sand to dry this one!', and those nine light-hearted words laid the foundations for his career. He had been with his chief in Egypt, in all the great victories from Marengo to Wagram, and had even survived personal failure against Wellington in Portugal, but now he was a used-up man, with a wound in his head that put his judgment in jeopardy. He made no more haste than Jerome and Bagration withdrew on the Upper Niemen, without any pressure from the west.

Even so he was lucky to escape. Davout, despairing of co-operation, chased after him with 12,000 men and flung himself on Bagration's rearguard on the road to Mohilev. The Russian then had 36,000 men under his command but he was badly mauled by Davout's audacious attack and crossed the Beresina and the Dnieper cured of his hunger to go over to the offensive. Hearing that he was safe, Barclay de Tolly continued his steady retreat, hoping to make a stand when he found favourable ground.

3

In the meantime the main advance had been resumed, generally headed for Vitepsk. The Guard moved out on July 16th and the army plodded after the elusive Barclay, rank and file longing to bring him to bay in this wilderness of dust and depopulated steppe. Discipline continued to deteriorate, eroded by sultry heat and the deaths of 10,000 horses that had stranded commissariat waggons far behind the line of march. Men dispersed in every direction in search of food and forage. The number of sick increased to figures regimental commanders would expect to see on their parade-states after a major battle.

Captain Franz Roeder, an officer of the Lifeguards of the Grand Duke of Hesse, has left us an interesting account of this section of the advance, from Vilna to Vitepsk. The heat and the dust-clouds, he says, were terrible, and every now and again he came upon dying stragglers abandoned by those following in the rear. One such infantryman, a private of the Young Guard, had been dying for three days beside the road and they could do nothing for him. Looting as well as foraging broke up the formations and at one point an officer of Roeder's regiment raided the château of a French sympathiser, purloining his chaise and pair and seventy-five bottles of his best French wine! There were frequent quarrels between the French and their allies. Roeder's Lifeguards were ordered to hand over their transport horses to a French unit but managed to avoid the requisition. Horse, foot, guns and a horde of camp-followers trudged eastward. The only inhabitants of the region were Jews, who struck lucrative bargains with men like Sergeant Bourgogne of the Guard for gin, vodka and flour. These were the principal inhabitants of Russian Lithuania and they were old and wise in the ways of dealing with invaders. They let war, any war, lap over them, and when the troops moved on they counted their profits.

By now nearly one-third of the enormous host that had crossed the Niemen had melted away for one reason or another. Detachments and dismounted cavalrymen accounted for a large proportion and at every sizeable village men had to be left to guard the communications against marauding Cossacks, many of whom, unattached to the main Russian armies, roved the plain in search of stragglers and the pickings they represented. Nobody, not even Napoleon himself, could be sure of the ultimate terminus of the main Russian contingents, but it was known that a group of foreign advisers were urging the Tsar to make a permanent stand in a fortified camp at Drissa, on the Dwina, and employ Wellington's brilliantly successful tactics at Torres Vedras. To test this, perhaps, Napoleon made a feint north-eastward above Glubokoe, but then he switched south-eastward for Vitepsk, reasoning that even if Bagration's army had escaped his purpose should be to deny both Russian commanders the main road to Moscow.

Outside Vitepsk, occupied by the French on July 28th, exactly one month after they had reached Vilna, the Russian rearguard made a stand and the first serious engagements of the campaign took place. They were sharp and bloody.

The heroes of the fighting at Ostrowno, outside Vitepsk, were the dashing Murat, heading the cavalry advance guard, and a body of two hundred Parisien Voltigeurs that Murat's furious charges had caused to be isolated among a welter of Russian lancers and cuirassiers.

All this time, to the disgust of Marshal Ney and his foot-slogging Third Corps, Murat had been behaving as though he was a star performer in a circus rather than a responsible commander of the army's eyes. The Cossacks in particular were delighted with his tricks when he thundered over the plain in sky-blue coat and pink breeches, seated on a leopard-skin saddle cloth and waving, instead of a sabre, a gold wand. He was a heroic if a slightly ridiculous figure, but his charges usually went home. Men like Ney complained that he wore out his horses and called on the infantry only when he ran into trouble and this actually occurred outside Vitepsk, when the French cavalry advanced at a canter and retired at a gallop on finding unexpected resistance, abandoning the two hundred skirmishers to be slaughtered by the enemy.

Several accounts of this tiny engagement have come down to us from the pens of eye-witnesses. Because of the nature of the ground, a flattish piece between two elevated points, it seems to have been closely observed by both armies, who were equally astonished at the result. The two hundred, men of the 9th regiment of the line, were entirely separated from their comrades and when a large body of Russian cavalry swept down on them they were given up for lost. When the dust settled, however, it was seen that they had formed platoon and then square and were calmly fighting their way back to the main French body. Round them, as they moved in a compact group, rose ramparts of dead lancers and cuirassiers, and when the dead were counted it was seen that these two hundred marksmen had emptied three hundred saddles. Napoleon, always quick to exploit a chance to improve morale, sent his personal congratulations and awarded the coveted Legion of Honour (a decoration much debased by Napoleon's successors) to a large number of men whose names were submitted by their officers.

The little action proved a fillip to the army. In these actions the Russian rearguard lost ten cannon, 1,500 prisoners and upwards of 6,000 men, killed or wounded. At one time it looked very much as though Barclay was going to stand and fight and Napoleon himself expected a major battle. It did not come. By the 28th the Russians had again withdrawn and the French entered their third major town in Tsarist territory, a city of 30,000 inhabitants, most of whom had disappeared.

Here was a second chance to halt and form an advanced winter base well inside enemy territory and Napoleon, urged to do this by several of the marshals, hesitated for another fortnight. At one time it seemed as though he was almost convinced. 'This is likely to prove a three-years' war,' he said, but in the end confidence in his ability to compel Alexander to sue for peace prevailed. On August 13th the Grand Army, now a more closed-up body of 144,000 men, filled knapsacks with what provisions were available and set out on the road to Smolensk, the largest city between Vitepsk and Moscow, but still more than two hundred miles short of the old capital.

At least one man in the Grand Army marched eastward with a sense of achievement. Quartered on a family of Jews in Vitepsk Sergeant Bourgogne had acquired a supply of hops and persuaded one of his comrades, an ex-brewer, to make five barrels of excellent beer which were placed in the care of the company cantinière. A soldier of Bourgogne's experience should have known better. When the Guard set out for Smolensk there were two barrels left, but Madame Dubois, the cantinière, remained behind and sold the beer to thirsty men of the rearguard while the men who made it were tortured by thirst.

CHAPTER THREE

'EVERYTHING GOES WELL...!'

Napoleon to Marie Louise, July, 1812

1

NEAR Kamen, some fifty miles west of Vitepsk, the River
Dwina, flowing generally south-west, takes a broad, north-
westerly sweep to flow into the Gulf of Riga. At Orcha,
some sixty miles south of Vitepsk, the other great river, the
Dnieper, takes an equally broad southerly sweep to flow
across Russia to the Black Sea. The Grand Army was now
entering the zone between these two mighty streams, and
their route between Vitepsk and the next major halt at
Smolensk, lay across seventy-odd miles of the plain en-
closed by these rivers.

It was a thinly populated strip of featureless country,
half-covered with vast thickets of birch and elder, and such
villages as existed in this virtually roadless country were
composed of squalid huts from which the peasant families
who had remained were ejected to provide some kind
of shelter for the swarm of invaders pushing east and
south-east in the hope of bringing the Russian army to
battle.

Captain Roeder, the Hessian Lifeguard, has left us a description of the kind of hospitality he found in these dwell-
ings when he followed the path of the Grand Army from
Vitepsk to Smolensk, then known as "The Bulwark of
Moscow", although it was about two hundred miles west of
the capital. The huts, he says, were small and a limited
amount of light entered them from narrow, slitted windows. He could not imagine what they would be like in
winter, when these slits were shuttered and the stoves were
kept going day and night. In high summer they stank so

49

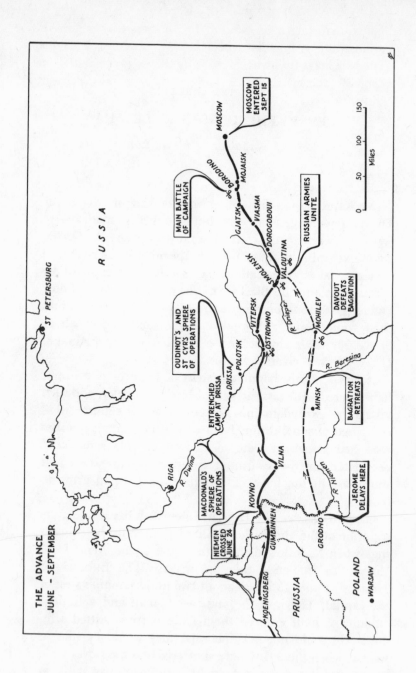

THE ADVANCE
JUNE – SEPTEMBER

RUSSIA

ST PETERSBURG

MOSCOW
MOSCOW ENTERED SEPT 15

BORODINO
MOJAISK
VIASMA
DOROGOBOUI
GJATSK
MAIN BATTLE OF CAMPAIGN

SMOLENSK
VALOUTINA
RUSSIAN ARMIES UNITE

VITEPSK
OSTROWNO
R. Driepa
MOHILEV
DAVOUT DEFEATS BAGRATION

OUDINOT'S AND ST CYR'S SPHERE OF OPERATIONS

POLOTSK
DRISSA
ENTRENCHED CAMP AT DRISSA

R. Dwina
RIGA

R. Beresina

MINSK
BAGRATION RETREATS

VILNA

MACDONALD'S SPHERE OF OPERATIONS

KOVNO
NIEMEN CROSSED JUNE 24

GUMBINNEN

R. Niemen
GRODNO
JEROME DELAYS HERE

KOENIGSBERG

PRUSSIA

POLAND
WARSAW

0   50   100   150
Miles

50

badly that cartridges had to be burned to sweeten the atmosphere. A hut that Roeder's party occupied was populated by horse-flies who "get inside like lice and once there conduct themselves with considerable activity". There were also armies of cockroaches where his men bedded down on a cement floor covered with straw. For company, once the family was ejected, they had a goat.

Over this cheerless terrain tramped Ney and his indomitable Third Corps, crossing the Dnieper on August 10th and engaging the Russian rearguard at Krasnoi, about thirty-five miles from Smolensk. Napoleon, who left Vitepsk on August 13th, wrote home to his Empress, Marie Louise, "Everything is going well..." but he could not have believed it. No major battle had been fought but the wastage continued relentlessly. One Bavarian general reckoned his losses from exhaustion, dysentery, desertion and other causes, at 900 men a day. Left behind in Vitepsk Captain Roeder collected figures that go some way to corroborate this appalling estimate. After the engagement at Smolensk, where losses on both sides were considerable, a Wurttemburgher major told him that four regiments of the line and four battalions of light infantry, together totalling some 7,200 men, were reduced to 1,500 before the city was stormed. Afterwards they mustered 900! In the meantime Roeder himself had seen hundreds of dismounted cavalry trekking westwards in the hope of finding remounts.

Visual evidence of what was happening to the magnificent army Napoleon had led across the Niemen less than two months before undoubtedly hastened demoralisation, which was something quite new in a Napoleonic army. In Egypt, at crisis points such as the retreat from Acre, or, only three years before, when the Grand Army crossed the Sierras in a blinding snowstorm, morale had remained high and the desertion rate was negligible but here, in fine weather, a prolonged advance was having a more damaging effect upon morale than the near-disasters of Eylau and Aspern-Essling in 1807 and 1809. The garrison at Vitepsk showed a nervousness that had never before revealed itself in an assembly of Napoleonic troops. On several occasions after the Guard had left on August 13th, the entire contingent left behind to guard the city stood to arms in the middle of the night to resist the attacks of a few dozen stray Cossacks. What was going wrong? What factors contributed to this unsoldierly slackness and jumpiness? Rations were short, the conditions of march desperately tiring, and there had been no opportunity to take it out on the enemy—but all three circumstances had been present during previous campaigns. There is a possible solution. The very vastness and emptiness of the terrain over which they were advancing had a depressing effect on men accustomed to be fêted by civilians and received either as liberators or warriors it was wise to propitiate. No such demonstrations were to be found here where the monotony of the skyline was broken only by a posting-stage, a few huts or a trackless wilderness of conifers. Rank and file felt isolated and remote from the civilisation of the West. And every step they trudged took them further from their bases, their women and wineshops.

On August 15th the main body of the French celebrated Napoleon's forty-third birthday and Ney and Murat discharged a hundred cannon in salute. Both marshals were sharply reprimanded for wasting powder but explained that it was powder recently captured from the Russians. Napoleon saw the joke and nothing more was said.

On the following day the main body came within sight of the old, Spanish-looking city of Smolensk on the banks of the deep, narrow Dnieper. It looked a hard nut to crack. Its fortifications were defended by some 30,000 of the Russian rearguard and the main army of Barclay de Tolly was bivouacked just across the river and in touch with the western suburbs by bridges. The place itself was strong, with thirty twenty-five-foot towers built partially of wood, a rampart-crowned fifteen-foot thick wall, and a citadel that could be supplied and reinforced from over the river, but to add to this the western suburbs had been fortified and would have to be stormed by house-to-house fighting.

General Eblé, an extremely able officer, advised Napoleon to turn the position by sending the Polish Corps over the river, but Ney preferred a bombardment and a frontal attack and he had his way, although as a concession to the more cautious Napoleon ordered the town to be all but encircled and the attack delivered from three sides.

Ney went in from the west, Davout from the south and Poniatowski's Poles were sent up the river bank to move in from the east. Formidable batteries of artillery were brought up, including three batteries of twelve-pound howitzers for the task of breeching. At six o'clock the cannonade began and the infantrymen opened their murderous assault on the suburbs.

The Russian rearguard fought doggedly. Dokhturov, their commander, directed the defence from a gatehouse although he was in a high fever at the time and at every barricade the infantry fought with bayonet and clubbed musket. All day and all night the batteries thundered and fighting at close quarters was resumed on the 17th. The damage done to the town was immense and soon fires began to blaze in many quarters, a dress rehearsal for what was soon to occur at Moscow. It looked as if here, at last, the Russians would be brought to bay, but the sober-minded Barclay de Tolly soon showed that he had no intention of tying up six divisions in the beleaguered city. During the night of the 17th he began to withdraw. And why not? His main object had been attained. Bagration's hard-pressed 35,000,. hounded all the way from the Niemen, had now joined the main army east of Smolensk and the two commanders (intriguing furiously against one another in the best traditions of the French marshalate) were united at last. At two a.m. the next day French grenadiers of the assault column mounted the ramparts to find them undefended. All the Russians who had survived the bombardment were gone and three parts of the town was in flames. Twelve thousand corpses blocked the narrow streets.

Napoleon moved into the burned-out shell. Of grain and other stores he had expected to find there were none. Everything likely to be useful to the famished army had either been carted off by the Russians or destroyed in the flames. Veterans in search of loot were lucky to find a few bottles of local gin in the cellars. There were cannon and prisoners in plenty but the French did not have sufficient teams to drag their own guns and most of the prisoners were abandoned wounded.

It was a victory of sorts but it hardly justified the Emperor's jubilant despatch to Maret, the Foreign Minister, that night, when he wrote: *'We have captured Smolensk without the loss of a man ... the Russian army is marching on Moscow in a very discouraged and discontented state...* Was it any more discouraged or discontented than the French wounded, lying in the shattered suburbs of the city and reflecting on the deaths of eight thousand of their comrades?

The Russian armies, now united east of the burning town, were at last under a single commander. Both Barclay and Bagration had been superseded, despite the former's patient and brilliant handling of the situation. Barclay, as a Lithuanian of foreign descent, had never been popular with the Russian aristocracy for this, they argued, was a People's War and a Russian patriot should direct it. They felt shamed by Barclay's endless withdrawals and his sacrifice of so many Russian towns and villages. At Austerlitz the French mounted grenadiers had ploughed through the Russian Noble Guard shouting, 'We'll give the ladies of St. Petersburg something to cry about!' but the young men around the Tsar still regarded themselves capable of defeating the upstarts from the West and bundling them back across the Niemen after a single resolute engagement. Urged from all sides to make a change in command Tsar Alexander, now permanently in St. Petersburg, gave way. He chose the elderly General Kutusoff, another pupil of the mad Suvorov, but grown so unwieldy that he had to be driven about the field in a carriage. Age and increasing girth, however, had not dulled the faculties of the man who had fought Napoleon at Austerlitz seven years before. He was still the old fox from the north and although he did not say so he still believed implicitly in Barclay's strategy of withdrawal, of tempting the French farther and farther from their Polish and German bases until they were hopelessly isolated in the loneliness of the Russian plains and forests. He was to make a stand outside the Holy City of Moscow. Morale alone justified this, but he had every intention of playing the game much as Barclay had played it and in the end he was seen to be right.

For Napoleon, looking at the smoking embers of Smolensk, the choice was not so simple. Charred as it was, Smolensk could be converted into a winter base and the campaign renewed in the spring, after reinforcements, winter clothing, remounts and provisions had been brought up along the line of march. Even the impetuous Ney counselled this and so, surprisingly, did Murat, who had already pranced his way hundreds of miles inside Russia. Napoleon hesitated, as he had hesitated at Vilna and again at Vitepsk. There was a great deal to be said for digging in but, in a sense, the choice was dictated for him. He thought of himself, as others thought of him, as the master of Europe, the source from which all modern ideas, all reorganisation of antiquated systems of government stemmed. As a general he could accept the dictates of commonsense but as an Emperor prestige prevented him from doing so. None of his appeals to Alexander had been heeded. All moderate suggestions that they should come to terms had been met with silence and he was now more than 300 miles inside Russian frontiers, with very little to show for enormous expenditure of men and materials. Even so, when every aspect had been weighed and considered, he was inclined to listen to the voice of reason, to draw some stark conclusions from the parade-states handed him every day by his Chief-of-Staff. Strategically there was something to be said for pushing on. Prestige might be salvaged by the occupation of the enemy's capital and, if the Russian conservatives had their way, there was a good chance of a major battle and perhaps another Austerlitz. There was, however, even more to be said for staying where he was, or for withdrawing to Vitepsk and fortifying it against next year's campaign, or even for turning on St. Petersburg which was still a long way from home but nearer his sources of supply than Moscow. He might tell Maret, his Foreign Minister, that he had captured Smolensk without the loss of a man but Maret was unlikely to believe it and the news from central Europe was not encouraging. The British had now succeeded in forming another alliance with the Tsar. Sweden, whose Crown Prince Bernadotte had once been a French marshal, was considering enlisting his Swedes against his old comrades.[1] Austria, guided by Metternich, was restive. The Tugend-bund in Prussia was gaining more support every day, and down in Spain Wellington was trouncing every French army he encountered, although the news of his recent victory over Marmont at Salamanca was not yet known at Imperial headquarters. Surely, in view of all this, it was time to stop, time, perhaps, to compromise in some way.

Then some good news came in, so good in fact that it was enough to tip the balance in favour of a continued advance. Up in the north-west, where he had been success-fully operating since June against the St. Petersburg army of Wittgenstein, Marshal Oudinot, the ex-grenadier, had just won a shattering victory at Polotsk that secured the French flank from any interference in that quarter and boosted French prestige throughout the entire north-west.

Oudinot, a gallant but unimaginative general, had not really won a battle. He had been wounded on the evening of the first day, the day Napoleon sighted Smolensk, and had retired with a bullet through his arm. He was to take another bullet out of Russia before the retreat ended. In the wars of the Empire he was wounded thirty-four times. In his absence command devolved upon the brilliant, moody St. Cyr, the most contradictory and puzzling personality of all the Napoleonic marshals. An artist, an actor, a musician, an architect, he had graduated to high rank without making a single friend, arriving there by the exercise of his own self-contained genius in the fields of higher strategy. His own men disliked him. He was known, but not derisively, as 'The Owl'. He was also reckoned, alongside Marshal Masséna, the finest defensive soldier in Europe.

The town of Polotsk lies on the Dwina and on August 16th Wittgenstein attacked it with 60,000 men. It was defended by the Second and Sixth Corps, respectively commanded by Oudinot and St. Cyr, with Oudinot as supreme commander and during the first day's fighting the Russians made excellent progress. Oudinot, worried about his dispositions, continually asked St. Cyr for advice but all he got by way of response was a deferential repetition of the words 'My Lord Marshal!' Major Marbot, who was there with his chausseurs, interpreted this to mean, 'In view of the fact that the Emperor has seen fit to make you a marshal you must know better than I!' Towards dusk, riding at a walk along his lines, Oudinot was hit by a Russian sharpshooter and St. Cyr took his place as commander. He at once set about ensuring victory, calling in his skirmishers, clearing the town of wounded and keeping open his line of retreat over the single bridge. Then he used a friendly Polish landowner to get some last-minute information of Russian strength, the Pole sending his bailiff into the Russian camp with a load of forage. By this means he discovered that Wittgenstein was expecting considerable reinforcements the following day, among them the Cossacks of the Guard. St. Cyr determined to strike at the earliest possible moment and at six a.m. a single cannon-shot signalled the advance all along the line. By evening the Russians were in flight and a delighted Napoleon sent St. Cyr his marshal's baton. He was the only man to win one in Russia.

General Junot, the Emperor's oldest comrade in the

field, was not so lucky. Junot, it will be recalled, had replaced Jerome in command of the Eighth Corps, and after Smolensk this unlucky man had yet another chance to write his name in history as one of the Empire's fighting marshals. He lost it, perhaps through sloth but more likely through what we should now call shell-shock or combat fatigue. He had been in the field since 1792 and had seen as much active service as Ney and Murat, but he lacked the stamina of one and the self-confidence of the other.

Established in Smolensk, or rather in the ruins of Smolensk, Napoleon gave Ney a free hand to advance and pin down the retreating Russians. Ney came very close to doing it, engaging them on a plain between two masses of high ground at Valoutina, east of the city. A terrible encounter took place here and General Gudin, one of Marshal Davout's three 'Immortals', was killed. The plan was for Ney and Murat to engage the enemy at close quarters until Junot's corps could take them in the flank from the north but Junot failed to appear. Murat, furious at the delay, dashed off and found him, urging him to attack at once. Junot said his Westphalians were tired and Murat, recalling perhaps that for years Junot had had the coveted baton within his grasp, led a charge himself and told Junot that the baton was his at last. It slipped away again, just as it had when Junot led his army down into Portugal in 1808 and was shipped home again by the obliging British. The main body of the Russians closed up and marched away, leaving the defile between the two heights choked with the dead and wounded of both sides. Barclay de Tolly had escaped again.

The news made Napoleon have second thoughts and it was during his week's stay in Smolensk that he went to extraordinary lengths to bring the war to an end by negotiation. He asked a captured Russian general to write to the Tsar and when the officer said that this was not possible he suggested that the prisoner should write a personal letter to his brother, then in service at St. Petersburg, stressing the fact that the French Emperor was eager to compromise. The officer obliged but the letter made no impression. It must, in fact, have provided additional proof of Imperial weakness and encouraged Alexander to hold on. The incident was another curious psychological error on the part of a man who had been bullying and wheedling kings and diplomats since he was twenty-six years of age.

When no reply came to any of his messages Napoleon doubled the stakes and told Bessières and Mortier of the Guard to continue the advance in the wake of Ney and Murat. In conversation with the frank Alsation, General Rapp, the aide-de-camp who had advised against the campaign at the Danzic supper party, he said, 'A capital which has been in possession of the enemy is like a woman who has lost her honour. The wine is poured. I have been playing at Emperor too long. It is time I became a general again!' Unable to reassure others he was now hard at work reassuring himself.

2

The Guard marched out on the 25th, but by then the vanguard, under Davout and Murat, were well on their way to Viasma. The two marshals were in truculent mood and soon began to quarrel furiously. At one point they came within an inch of fighting a duel.

Most of the marshals disliked Murat, whose marriage to Napoleon's youngest sister, Caroline, in the days of the Consulate, had given him precedence over all but Berthier, Chief of Staff. Marshal Lannes, killed at Aspern, had hated the sight of him and after the battle of Eylau is reported to have said, in the Emperor's presence, that Murat was 'a dancing dog who belongs in a pantomime'. Perhaps Davout recalled this comment as he watched Murat exhausting the cavalry by a variety of brilliant but unnecessary manoeuvres as the vanguard headed east. Having, as usual, advanced too far and too fast, Murat found himself in a tight spot and sent an appeal to Davout for help but Davout, who would have gladly seen him dead or captured, refused to send infantry to his assistance. As it happened the cavalryman fought his way clear unaided, but there were bitter complaints to Imperial headquarters and counter-complaints to match them. Murat had to be restrained by his Staff Officers and Napoleon had to exercise all his tact to smooth ruffled plumes. Finally the vanguard pushed on, through Viasma, another blazing town, through Gjatsk and into a country of marshy ravines and hillocks around the villages of Shevardino, Seminovskoi and Borodino, where the Russians appeared to be digging in for a major stand.

The main body, perhaps 50,000 strong, toiled behind, finding a little brandy in the pillaged towns but no food. Davout and Ney were obliged to fan out in order to find forage and every day bands of Cossacks swooped on stragglers so that Napoleon, furious at losing men to these savages, wrote the Corps commanders a stiff letter telling them that on no account were they to detach foraging parties without cavalry escorts. Napoleon also complained to Davout about the tardiness of his advance; the comment must have infuriated a man who, with Ney as his principal partner, had now fought his way 300 miles into Russia without, in his view, any appreciable support.

The Guard reached Viasma on the 29th and Gjatsk on September 1st. Four days later the main body caught up with the advance guard in front of Shevardino, where Kutusoff had converted a hillock rising to about 150 feet into a formidable redoubt, obviously intending to use this outwork to gain time while completing a more extensive system of earthworks south of the main Moscow road at Borodino.

Here, on a ridge intersected with ravines and wooded towards the south, the one full-scale engagement of the campaign was to be fought. It was to prove the bloodiest battle of the Napoleonic wars and provide carnage on a scale that until then, had seldom been matched in history.

The hillock had to be stormed before the two armies could come to grips and in this kind of country a knoll of this height was a small mountain, much as rising ground was to prove on the Flanders plain in the great battles of 1914–18. It was stormed at high cost to the French, and the Russian infantrymen who died there may have been satisfied by the knowledge that they had gained Kutusoff a day in which to perfect his fortifications. By the evening of the 6th he was ready to fight, his line hinged on a great redoubt, his left and right wings covered by smaller earthworks. Only a vast turning movement could dislodge him and open the way to Moscow, and Napoleon did not have sufficient men for such a turning movement. There remained no alternative to retreat but a frontal attack, cost what it may.

Barclay de Tolly held the Russian right, and a general called Tuchkov, one of three brothers to die in this campaign, was holding the wooded country on the Russian left. In the centre, buttressed by the Grand Redoubt bristling with heavy-calibre guns, was the old veteran Kutusoff and with him Bennigsen, the Russian general whom Napoleon had defeated at Friedland five years before. It was Bennigsen who had chosen the ground.

The armies were about equal in strength but any advantages there might have been in numbers lay with the Russians who had been constantly reinforced by small detachments as they fell back towards the capital. The French army now numbered round about 140,000, roughly one quarter of the host that had crossed the Niemen seventy-four days earlier. The position was surveyed and, in spite of its obvious strength, the French welcomed the prospect of a battle. Defeat for the Russians here, about seventy-five miles from Moscow, meant an end to this punishing crawl across devastated country. It also ensured the occupation of Moscow, with dazzling prospects of peace and loot.

The sun went down and a chill wind swept over the bivouacs, a foretaste of the Russian winter. Bourgogne describes how, in anticipation of the next day's fighting, the Guard set about cleaning their arms, some of them quartered round and about the Imperial tent. There was an air of confidence among the veterans but it did not seem to have penetrated inside the tent where Napoleon was suffering from the effects of a chill and was unable to get much rest. Evidence that he was not himself had been available earlier in the day when Count de Segur observed him pause during a reconnaissance and cool his forehead on the barrel of a field-gun. In the evening his servant had applied a hot poultice to his belly. He remained restless, and even the arrival of despatches from the west did not succeed in rousing him.

For three days, at this most critical phase of the campaign, Napoleon's health, ordinarily so robust, failed him to a degree that clouded his judgment. In addition to a sharp bout of his old complaint, dysuria, damp bivouacs had left him with a dry cough and loss of voice. On account of the dysuria he had extreme difficulty in passing water and when his personal physician, Mestivier, arrived to treat him he said, wryly, 'You see, Doctor, I am getting old!' He was certainly in no condition to direct a major battle. Mestivier later recorded that he had a 'persistent dry cough, difficult irregular breathing, his urine came only in drops and with pain and was thick with sediment'. He went on to say, 'His legs and feet were extremely oedematous, the pulse febrile in type and intermittent every twelve beats or so' and that 'these symptoms suggested the presence of oedema of the chest'. Doctor Yvan, who was also making the campaign, reports that the symptoms were sufficiently severe to cause some fever and that he found the Emperor 'exhausted physically and mentally'.

Great physical discomfort was distraction enough. Loss of voice, preventing dictation of orders, made matters a great deal worse, particularly as Napoleon's handwriting had never deserved to be called legible. It is ironic that Captain Favrier, the despatch-rider from the far west, should have found him here, shivering and ailing, on the eve of the bloodiest battle of his career, for Favrier's news was of another battle in far off Salamanca, where the

French suffered their greatest defeat in Spain up to that time.

The Captain's presence in the bivouac that evening represented a near-miracle in the field of improvised transportation. Thirty-two days before he had been in Central Spain and the speed at which he rode the length of Europe justified good news, not bad. His despatches told how Marshal Marmont, the Emperor's oldest friend, had been severely wounded but they probably did not add that, but for the skill and coolness of General Clausel, who replaced the Commander-in-Chief, the French army might have been utterly destroyed. Napoleon did not comment on the news. He seemed more interested in something else Favrier had brought in his despatch bag, the latest portrait of the infant King of Rome, by-product of Napoleon's marriage to the bovine Austrian girl, Marie Louise. The portrait was propped outside the Emperor's tent and the veterans of the Guard stared at it with interest. To them at least it represented continuity.

. . .

All around, the dusty, footsore men of Davout, Ney, Poniatowski and Prince Eugène were taking their rest before the bivouac fires, or under roughly built arbours of boughs. Among them, scattered evenly among the various divisions, was an élite whose names would arouse the fleeting interest of twentieth-century tourists, making a sightseeing tour to the Arc de Triomphe. These men, most of them in their mid-thirties although they already ranked as colonel or above, were the survivors of nearly twenty years' continuous warfare, and of this single group no fewer than forty-three were to be carried from tomorrow's field dead, dying or severely wounded. It is worth studying them for a moment. They represent, in themselves, the very essence of the Napoleonic saga.

They had enlisted as half-grown youths in the patriot armies of Danton and Carnot, when the Revolution was being challenged by an alliance of kings and princes. To

Frenchmen, even at this distance, their names have a heroic ring—Compans, Morand, Huard and Marion; Bruyère, Lepel, Plauzonne and Caulaincourt; Rapp, Anabert and Dessaix; Delzons, Gerard, Grouchy, Nansouty, Latour-Maubourg and Montbrun. The oldest among them had helped to smash the Prussian invasion at Valmy and the Austrian invasion at Jemappes. They had ridden across the ice to capture the Dutch fleet in the Texel, and later stormed down into Italy to make their young commander-in-chief, whom some called Hop-o'-my-Thumb and others Longboots, the most famous soldier of all time. Among them were men who had held Switzerland against the assaults of Suvorov or had marched and fought on the banks of the Upper Nile and across the Sinai Desert to Acre and back. They had crossed the Alps to defeat the Austrians at Marengo, practised invasion-drill on the coasts of Northern France, and afterwards swung south-east halfway across Europe to shatter another coalition at Ulm and Austerlitz. They had destroyed other Prussian armies at Auerstadt and Jena, crossed the bogs of Poland to engage the Russians at Eylau and vanquish them at Friedland, and then recrossed Europe and ridden down into Portugal or over the mountains to Corunna to see what could be done about driving the British into the sea. Then they had turned about and returned to the Danube, finding fresh glory and more wounds at head-on clashes like Aspern and Essling, and had again triumphed at Wagram and after that, seeking no more than rapid promotion and a chance to add lustre to the eagles, they had ridden back to the Peninsula with Masséna and followed Wellington all the way to Torres Vedras. All of them had been wounded, some very severely, but they left their garrison towns and hospitals when the Emperor summoned his court of subject kings to Dresden and announced his intention of invading Russia. And here they were, on a marshy strip of land west of the fabulous city of Moscow and for many of them it was the end of the road.

Night fell and the chilling wind continued to blow. In

the Imperial tent Napoleon rose at three-thirty and asked for hot punch. It was brought him and he shared it with General Rapp, his aide-de-camp, asking him what he thought of the day's chances. Accustomed to yes-men he valued, was perhaps amused by, the gruff Alsatian's bluntness of speech. Rapp had been wounded twenty-one times in the service of France. Tomorrow he was to be wounded again. 'We are obliged to win!' Rapp told him briefly. It was as simple as that.

Ney came in for orders and at the sight of him some of Napoleon's lassitude disappeared. 'March on!' he said. 'Open the gates of Moscow for us!' Ney had never needed complicated orders. He always preferred the simple directive—attack!

3

The cannonade began at six o'clock and was to continue, unabated, for the next twelve hours. There was to be some attempt at turning after all. Poniatowski was sent into the wooded country on the Russian left with orders to fight his way towards the centre and here, for a time, the fighting attracted a major share of attention. Then the central attack of Davout and Ney on the redoubts developed, and with it a supporting movement by Prince Eugène and his Italians on the French left. Soon the entire battle line was joined and 1,200 pieces of artillery were belching round-shot, grape and canister at close range.

There was no doubt that Kutusoff was making his stand. Tuchkov, on the left, disputed every coppice, every dip in the ground, and the slaughter among Poniatowski's men was terrible, one regiment, the 57th, losing 1,500 men. General Compans was wounded and succeeded by Dessaix. Dessaix was wounded and succeeded by Rapp; after a brief interval Rapp was wounded and replaced.

It was the same, or worse, in the centre, where the Russian batteries tore gaps in the advancing infantry. Davout's horse was shot under him but the attack was pressed home,

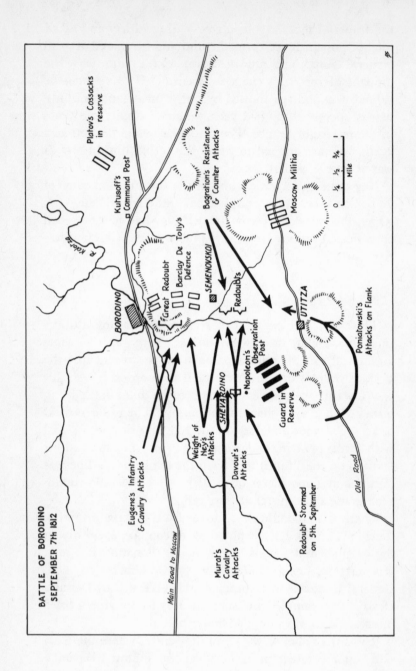

BATTLE OF BORODINO
SEPTEMBER 7th 1812

Platov's Cossacks
in reserve

Kutusoff's
Command Post

R. Kolotza

BORODINO

Great Redoubt

Barclay De Tolly's
Defence

SEMENOVSKOI

Bagration's Resistance
& Counter Attacks

Moscow Militia

0 ¼ ½ ¾ 1
Mile

Redoubt's

UTITZA

Napoleon's
Observation
Post

Poniatowski's
Attacks on Flank

Weight of
Ney's Attacks

SHEVARDINO

Davout's
Attacks

Guard in
Reserve

Eugene's Infantry
& Cavalry Attacks

Redoubt Stormed
on 5th September

Murat's Cavalry
Attacks

Old Road

Main Road to Moscow

66

Alexander I, Emperor of Russia

From the drawing by L. de St. Aubin, engraved by Vendramini

Napoleon at the time of the invasion of Russia

From the "Corpus Imaginum" of the Photographic Society, Charlottenburg

and at last the French grenadiers stormed into the redoubts, Ney sending furious messages back for reinforcements but getting none, or getting them too few and too late. Salvoes of Russian cannon killed or disabled three-quarters of the storm column. Russian cavalry rode in and drove the survivors out and then, in turn, were themselves overthrown by one of Murat's furious charges. Infantrymen, gunners, cuirassiers and dragoons surged to and fro over the trampled earthworks and all the time the guns thundered right, left and centre, every discharge dealing death, sometimes to friends.

For an eye-witness account of what the Grand Redoubt looked like at this moment we have a lively picture from Labaume, who was attached to Prince Eugène's corps on the French left. Describing Murat's counter-attack he says, 'The whole eminence which overhung us appeared in an instant a mass of moving iron; the glitter of the arms, the rays of the sun, reflected on the helmets and cuirasses of the dragoons, mingled with the flames of the cannon that on every side vomited forth death, gave to the redoubts the appearance of a volcano in the midst of the army.' Again the French were ejected and again they returned to the attack, infantry supported by Third Corps cavalry, who overturned everything standing in their way. The best of the Russian cavalry, Cuirassiers of the Guard, tried yet again and there was another melée of horsemen in the ruined redoubt. The Russians fought to the last man. 'In the midst of this scene of carnage,' says Labaume, 'I discovered the body of a Russian cannoneer decorated with three crosses. In one hand he held a broken sword and the other grasped the carriage of the gun at which he had so valiantly fought. All the Russian soldiers in the redoubt chose rather to perish than to yield.'

By now, however, Poniatowski, reinforced by Ney, was making progress on the French right. General Tuchkov was dead and Bagration mortally wounded, together with many other Russian generals. Prince Eugène, taking advantage of the moment, brought up more artillery and pounded the enemy centre; slowly, without panic or even haste the Russians began to give ground.

This was the critical juncture of the day and Ney, in the thick of the fight, realised as much. Turning aside from the battle he wrote an impassioned despatch to Napoleon, asking him to order the immediate advance of the Old and Young Guard. With this matchless reserve, he declared, victory could be converted into triumph and the war ended on the spot. But the moment passed, as the Russian withdrawal became general, and the bearskins of the Guard did not appear through the drifting smoke. Realising that all this slaughter had availed nothing Ney lost his temper, raving like a lunatic at the misdirection of the battle. 'If he is no longer a general,' he is reported to have shouted, 'let him go back to the Tuileries and leave the fighting to us!'

Ney had no means of knowing the mood that pervaded at headquarters, where a curious lassitude, so uncharacteristic of Napoleon in action, continued to clog the workings of the Imperial brain. It had never happened before. It was to happen twice in the future, once at Dresden, again at Waterloo. In all the hours the battle had raged the Emperor had only ascended the observation knoll twice. His share in the tremendous struggle had been that of an elderly eighteenth-century general, operating at extreme range. He made only minor decisions, like the replacement of a dead general by an on-the-spot promotion, taking little or no part in the strategical or tactical direction of the battle as it was fought. Too ill to ride he spent the time walking to and fro, or lying on a black bearskin spread on the ground and with him, awaiting orders, were 20,000 of the best troops ever fielded by any army in any age. What were they doing all this time? Standing to arms in full-dress uniform, listening to their band playing Republican marches, the blare of their brass drowned by the roar of artillery and the outcry of 200,000 men locked in combat. Yet Napoleon was not out of range, although he could only overlook a third of the battlefield. Bourgogne, who was close to him at the time, says that Russian balls fell around him all day. At Toulon, many years ago, he had received a bayonet thrust in the thigh, and at Ratisbon, three years ago, he had received a musket ball in the foot, but now, on this day of decision, neither the threat of personal injury nor the frenzied pleas of Ney and Davout could persuade him to throw off his mental lethargy and make a gambler's decision. When Ney's final message asking for the Guard was given to him he hesitated and Marshal Bessières, Commander of the Guard, made a remark that changed the course of the war, possibly the course of nineteenth-century history. 'Will you risk your last reserve 800 miles from Paris?' Napoleon thought a moment and shook his head. 'No,' he said, 'suppose there is another battle to-morrow?' He seemed to be talking to himself. The band of the Imperial Guard played on.

Ney did not get his reinforcement and the Russians withdrew, terribly mauled but in excellent order. Down the years military historians have argued interminably about this decision, but was it so foolish as it appears today, as indeed it did appear to Ney, to Davout and to Eugène at the time? Paris was 800 miles distant. The French losses had been appallingly high. By late afternoon one in four of the men engaged had been killed or wounded, and Moscow still had to be reached. Deep in his own country Kutusoff could rely upon ever-increasing numbers of peasants and Cossacks to fill the gaps torn in his ranks, but where was the source of French reserves? Every gap in the French ranks would have to be made good by a trickle of men moving along a thinly-held line that stretched all the way back to the Niemen, a route devastated by the advance and signposted by burned-out towns and villages. Cossacks were already moving freely between the captured cities. Every caisson of ammunition had to be dragged over tracks for hundreds of miles, and in all that vastness there was nothing to eat outside the magazines of Vilna, Vitepsk and Smolensk.

The army never forgave Bessières for the advice he gave

Napoleon on that day but it was, after all, the counsel a prudent man might be expected to give. There is also another way of looking at it; without the Guard as a rallying point nobody at all would have returned from Russia. Napoleon's career and Imperial France would have been snuffed out like a candle by the end of December 1812.

．　　　．　　　．

Gradually the firing died down. There could be no question of immediate pursuit. North and south of the Grand Redoubt something approaching 60,000 dead or broken men littered the ground and among them were upwards of 25,000 horses. Debris of every description cluttered every yard of the field, overturned gun carriages, shattered arms of all kinds, drums, helmets, knapsacks and innumerable items of personal kit, including love letters and treasured locks of hair from all corners of France and Russia. On the Russian side Bagration was dying and Tuchkov was dead, together with over forty other leaders and 30,000 men. On the French side the losses were finally computed at 28,000 and included in them was the flower of the army. Montbrun, the blackbearded leader of heavy cavalry, was dead, and so was Caulaincourt, brother of the Emperor's friend and former ambassador to the Court of St. Petersburg. Huard, Marion, Lepel, Plauzonne, Bonami and Compere lay out there, and among the severely wounded were Friant, Latour-Maubourg, Bruyère, Morand, Gerard, Grouchy and Nansouty. One man was to die who had held the active rank of general for exactly fifteen minutes. Colonel Anabert had ridden to Imperial headquarters during the heat of the action and told Napoleon that his commander had been killed. 'Take his place!' was the command, and within a quarter of an hour the aide-de-camp of General Anabert, of the Foot Chasseurs, galloped up to report that his chief was mortally wounded. He died eight days later, after holding the rank for just over a week.

Ammunition had been expended on a stupendous scale.

The French fired 90,000 rounds from their cannon and the cartridge pouch of every infantryman, who had gone into battle with upwards of a hundred rounds, was empty. Guns were taken but many of them were shattered. Few prisoners and no standards were left behind by the retreating Russians. Yet Napoleon made the most of this Pyrrhic victory, walking over the ground and remarking there were five dead Russians to every Frenchman. 'He must,' says a cynic, 'have mistaken Germans for Russians!' His despatches home were even more laconic than the bulletin sent from Smolensk. In a letter to Marie Louise he described the battle and claimed 30,000 casualties. 'I had a number of men lost,' he adds, almost as an afterthought.

As soon as news of the engagement reached St. Petersburg it was hailed as a victory and the Tsar ordered a Te Deum to be sung in the cathedral. There was one sung in Paris too, to give thanks for the same battle. But nobody stayed to bury the dead.

4

An epilogue to the battle comes down to us from Sergeant Bourgogne and concerns the irrepressible King of Naples, perhaps the only man in either army whose spirits were not blighted by the carnage. Bourgogne, being in the Guard, had not fired a shot on September 7th, but he lost many old friends and wandered across the field the following day to draw his own conclusions of what had happened. Here, where the fighting had been thickest, he passed the tents of Murat pitched in a ravine, and there he saw the marshal himself superintending the amputation of the legs of two Russian gunners, an operation performed by Murat's personal surgeon. When it was over he gave each sufferer a glass of wine and then walked to the edge of a wood to take a closer look at the ground over which he had ridden at the head of his cavalry the day before. Even a veteran like Bourgogne was impressed by his bearing. 'He was splendid to look at—so distinguished by his gallantry, his cool courage and his handsome appearance,' says the Guardsman who had often seen him in action. In the eyes of an N.C.O. who made six campaigns, a man who could lead charges as Murat led them could be forgiven his vanity.

Murat and Bourgogne were not the only men of the Grand Army who spent the day wandering about the battlefield. Along the lengths of the ravines, choked with dead, wounded and debris, survivors moved in search of pickings or fallen comrades or both. Cantinières searched among the dead for their protectors. Surgeons did their best to cope with an impossible number of amputations, giving friend and foe what treatment was available. Labaume, of the Fourth Corps, remained behind to help destroy the half-shattered redoubts. Many of the wounded asked him to put them out of their misery, as though they had been injured animals awaiting a farmer's mercy-shot through the head. Behind the Russian positions Labaume saw the terrible effect of the French heavy artillery. Every available building over a wide area was converted into a hospital, but there were few surgeons and fewer drugs. Only the toughest of the wounded survived the next few days.

In the meantime, even for the hale, there was practically nothing to eat and morale could only be lowered by contemplation of the price the Grand Army had paid for the battle it had sought since crossing the Niemen. The shrunken squadrons of the King of Naples set out after the Russians who had taken the road to Mojaisk and within twenty-four hours the bulk of the army were trailing after them. The road to Moscow was open.

Mojaisk, when Murat reached it, was in flames, one more charred town on the endless road from the west. There was some sporadic fighting with the Russian rear-guard but no resistance that could not be brushed aside by the cavalry. Murat pushed on into the Sparrow Hills and the main body followed, leaving Mojaisk on the 12th, five days after the battle. In the early afternoon of the 13th the advance guard topped the last fold of ground buttressing the city in the west and there, below them, was Moscow, its hundreds of onion domes and spires reflecting the bright September sunshine. It was a prospect that caused the most hardbitten dragoon to pause and stare and wonder.

The main body now closed up and climbed the western slopes of Mont du Salut (the sacred hill upon which every good Muscovite stops and crosses himself) on the afternoon of the 14th. Here again the magic of the moment ran through the dusty columns like a summer wind stirring a field of corn. Leading files began to prance and shout and behind them men who had, as yet, not glimpsed the prospect, caught their mood and quickened their step until the entire Guard was shouting 'Moscow! Moscow!' Here is Sergeant Bourgogne's recorded memory of that summer afternoon when the end of the eighty-two-day march was sighted.

'It was a beautiful summer's day; the sun was reflected on all the domes, spires and gilded palaces. Many capitals I have seen—such as Paris, Berlin, Warsaw, Vienna and Madrid—they only produced an ordinary impression on me. But this was quite different; the effect was to me—in fact to everyone—magical. At that sight troubles, dangers, fatigues, privations were all forgotten, and the pleasure of entering Moscow absorbed all our minds. To take up good quarters for the winter, and to make conquests of another nature—such is the French soldier's character; from war to love, and from love to war! While we were gazing at the city the order was given to appear in full uniform!'

So it was to be a triumphal entry of the kind most of the capitals of Europe had witnessed since the French armies swept into Milan in 1796. Bandsmen unwrapped their instruments and bearskins were donned. The Emperor rode up to do his share of gazing, but his mood, although one of relief, was not ecstatic. He said, as to himself, 'There it is at last! It is high time!'

The Guard moved down towards the Dorogomilov Gate in the wake of Murat's advance guard and there, until

73

three p.m. they halted. Years of despotic power had made Napoleon a stickler for the conventions. Now was the moment when respectful boyars should make their appearance, presenting him with the keys of the city and humble requests for clemency, in the tradition of barbarian chiefs submitting to a Roman General. Two hours passed but no boyars appeared. The silence was oppressive. In all that great city no column of smoke rose from a chimney. All that could be seen in motion was the coming and going of aides, riding to and from the advance guard now established in the suburbs. All that could be heard was the far off murmur of the Russian rearguard leaving the town by the eastern gates and marching on Kalouga, thirty leagues distant.

Presently a Russian officer appeared, purporting to come from Kutusoff and proposing a truce that was half a threat. 'Give us time to evacuate,' he said in effect, 'or we will burn the city down!' Napoleon, still far from well, was in no mood to protest. The Russians were allowed to withdraw unmolested and the unofficial truce led to an extraordinary scene of fraternisation in the eastern sector of the city. It concerned, as might be expected, the first senior officer to enter, the pantomimic King of Naples.

Murat had set out to impress when he led the vanguard over the bridge and down the broad thoroughfare towards the administrative centre of the great city. Always flamboyantly uniformed he now looked like the Prince in a fairy-tale, riding to claim the hand of an Oriental beauty. His high collar and sword belt were thickly encrusted with gold embroidery. His riding-breeches were pink and his boots bright yellow. In his cap, in addition to the usual ostrich plumes, he wore an aigrette of heron's feathers. Everything about him shone and twinkled in the strong afternoon sunlight.

The Cossacks, whom he met when the French advance guard caught up with the evacuating rearguard, were delighted. They forgot he had harried them over 550 miles of their devastated homeland and gathered round him uttering shouts of admiration and calling him their *hetman*. Murat preened himself in their approval and then, feeling no doubt that the occasion merited a munificent gesture, he collected the watches of his staff and distributed them among the wonderstruck Cossacks. He was always an open-handed man, with other people's property as well as his own. The Cossacks trotted off like children leaving a Christmas party and Murat hunted up comfortable quarters.

News of this astonishing scene did not reach the western approaches at the time. Napoleon was still waiting for his deputation of burghers and when it did not arrive he expressed the opinion that 'the poor devils were probably so terrified by his approach that they were hiding in their houses!' Officers came out to assure him that the city was deserted. He refused to believe them until one aide-de-camp, bent on pleasing his master at all costs, rounded up half-a-dozen local strays and drove them in front of the Emperor like a small flock of lost sheep. Napoleon stared down at them and the truth began to dawn. He shrugged his shoulders and issued the order to begin the march. The Guard formed in three columns and the bands struck up *La Victoire est à Nous*. It was indeed, but nobody was there to cheer.

There had never been a conquest remotely resembling this. The oldest man in the Guard could not recall an occasion when the Grand Army had marched into a huge, empty city and nobody at all had lined the footwalks or peeped from the windows. It was a sombre experience, but not without its touch of farce.

As the Guard band marched over the bridge spanning the river at least one Muscovite made an appearance, emerging suddenly from under the bridge just as the drum-major drew level. Bourgogne, who was close to the drum-major at the time, described the incident that gave everyone who witnessed it an indication of the kind of welcome the French were likely to get. The man wore a sheepskin cape and a thick white beard that fell to his waist. His three-pronged fork and general air of venerability gave him the appearance of Neptune rising from the sea. Without the slightest hesitation he walked up to the drum-major and aimed a blow at him with his trident. The N.C.O. ducked, snatched the weapon and pitched the old fellow over the parapet into the water. Shortly afterwards the column came up with shaggy characters of a similar stamp, some of them brandishing flintlock muskets which they attempted to use but which did no harm. Guardsmen relieved them of their weapons and let them go, even though one had already attempted to stab one of Murat's officers.

It did not take the army long to realise that any Muscovite who had remained behind when the city was evacuated was almost surely hostile. Murat sent word that a group of these wild-looking men had barricaded themselves in the Kremlin and refused to open the gates. The gates were blown with cannon and everyone inside was driven out and allowed to disperse. If Murat's men had taken the trouble to question them before they scattered a great deal of grief might have been avoided, but as it was the men of the Grand Army, in tolerant mood after reaching the end of their interminable journey, did not even bother to keep them under arrest. After an hour's marching the Guard reached the first enclosure of the Kremlin and then, swinging left, the street leading to the Place de Gouvernement, where stood the empty palace of Moscow's Governor, Rostopchin. Here it was quartered under strict orders not to disperse but this was too much to ask of men who had marched 550 miles across a wilderness. In less than an hour the entire area was stacked with loot, including choice wines, liqueurs, preserved fruits, sweet cakes and enormous quantities of flour. Every house at which the Guardsmen called was empty, so the veterans walked in and helped themselves. A few scared French and German refugees crept out of hiding and reported that, before leaving the city, the Governor had released all the gaolbirds, which explained the presence of so many curiously-attired vagabonds. Apart from these ruffians and a few police there was not a Russian left in the city.

Napoleon quartered himself in the Kremlin and his first thought—as though he had been a young husband parted from his bride and set down in a foreign showplace—was to send someone in search of views of Moscow! We are not told whether his emissary was successful in finding any in that vast, empty city, but by evening Napoleon had settled down to work and was studying his muster-rolls. He was never without these; Berthier saw to that and among the staff they were known as "the Emperor's Bible". 'I could get together a quarter of a million men here,' he mused, 'but what about feeding them? This place seems to have been set down in the middle of a desert!'

.   .   .

According to Bourgogne the first fire-alarm was raised within an hour of the Guard reaching the Governor's palace. He himself saw a pall of smoke and a whirl of flames issuing from a bazaar, but put it down to the carelessness of freebooters. Deliberate incendiarism was not suspected for a moment and fire-squads were despatched to deal with the outbreak.

By seven o'clock, however, other outbreaks were being reported and one fire had gained a firm hold at the rear of the Governor's palace. Bourgogne took a squad of eighteen men to deal with it but was fired on from an alley. Having traced the source of the shots the French broke open the door of a house to find nine convicts, all armed and all wearing the belted sheepskin cape of the kind worn by the man who had attacked the drum-major. The convicts were very drunk on brandy and a tremendous fight ensued, eight of the nine being despatched and the last retained as a guide. Bourgogne then attempted to return to his billet, but during the fight the fire had spread so rapidly that a direct return was impossible. The whole area was now in flames and a high wind carried the blaze from house to house with terrible rapidity.

At last the veterans began to get an inkling of what was happening and any convicts they caught (some were arrested with British-made torches in their hands) were shot or bayoneted. Caught in the act of setting a house or a church on fire some of the convicts dropped their torches and ran away. Others paid no attention to the French but went doggedly about their task until they were knocked on the head. Frenzied efforts were made to control the fires that had been started in all parts of the city and to stop new ones breaking out, but the French were totally unfamiliar with the layout of the city and the incendiaries so bold and so numerous that they had the initiative and held on to it all that night as the fires proliferated.

Bourgogne, lost in a labyrinth of burning streets, entered what he thought to be an ordinary house to discover that it was a palace stuffed with the most beautiful furniture he had ever seen. The habit of looting was strong among veterans of the Grand Army. In spite of his peril he stopped to open a chest and take away a pair of antique horse-pistols, inlaid with pearls and precious stones.

He and his party got back to their billet at two in the morning, bringing as prisoners four Russian policemen suspected of incendiarism. The danger of being trapped in a burning palace had not prevented the comrades he left behind from adding to their growing pile of valuables. Bourgogne later found them expensively robed as Kalmucks, Chinamen, Cossacks, Tartars and Persians! All the fires of hell would not prevent veterans of the Grand Army from dispersing to loot or reassembling to fight.

CHAPTER FOUR

'HOW STUPENDOUS A DECISION!'

Napoleon watching Moscow burn, September 1812

1

To men like Bourgogne, patrolling areas beyond the Kremlin walls, it was obvious that the continual outbreaks of fire were not a series of accidents, that there was indeed a large body of audacious and semi-organised fireraisers, mostly released criminals augmented, perhaps led, by Russian military police, who were systematically setting fire to their own capital in obedience to orders issued to them by Rostopchin, the Governor, not only as a diversion but also in the hope of creating confusion and making pillage that much easier to accomplish. In the Kremlin, isolated from much of what was happening in the suburbs, the Imperial staff continued to think of the fires as the work of careless soldiers bivouacking in private houses and possibly too drunk on wines and spirits to take ordinary precautions. On the 15th, the day after he had settled in, Napoleon reprimanded Marshal Mortier, the new Governor of the city, for his lack of supervision and then went to bed without a thought that he would awake to find the old Muscovite capital in the process of destruction.

Saint-Denis, one of Napoleon's valets, tells how the general awareness of what was happening beyond the Kremlin enclosures was brought home to the personnel of Imperial headquarters. With other valets he had gone to bed and was soon asleep, but shortly after midnight he woke up and was surprised to find the room as light as day. He looked out of the window and a single glance sufficed to convince him that the city was blazing at a dozen widely-separated points. Constant, Napoleon's chief valet, was at once awakened and asked to inform the Emperor and this Constant did, but even then Napoleon was not disposed to take the fire too seriously. He still thought of it as the work of careless looters, the kind of thing that had happened in every large city occupied by Imperial troops after an arduous campaign.

In the morning, however, he gave Mortier instructions to organise a fire-fighting corps and make strenuous efforts to check the spread of the flames. The marshal did his best and, to some extent, succeeded, at least keeping the fire away from the walled Kremlin where the Grand Army had parked its artillery and powder magazines. He could make little headway, however, in those sections of the city that were well alight, for the strong north wind carried showers of sparks from one wooden house to another.

Murat and Eugène arrived to urge Napoleon to evacuate the Kremlin and seek safer quarters. The Emperor refused although, by now, reports had half-convinced him that the destruction of the city was the result of a deliberate policy on the part of Rostopchin and perhaps Kutusoff, encamped thirty leagues to the east. Orders were issued to shoot any incendiaries caught in the act and these orders were immediately carried out, so that the Place de Gouvernement, where that part of the Guard not on duty in the Kremlin were still housed, was referred to as Place des Pendus on account of the number of Russians hanging from trees.

It was a vain act of savagery. What emerges from every eyewitness report of the burning of Moscow is the suicidal obstinacy of the thousand or so torch-bearers, who went about their work with an indifference to their own fate that amazed the veterans. All day throughout the 16th the fire continued to spread and the pleas of the men around Napoleon to shift quarters became desperate. Sparks, driven on a wind that had changed from north to west, now rained down on the Kremlin and a terrifying rumour passed from mouth to mouth that the citadel was mined. Then one of the turrets of the arsenal was seen to be alight and grenadiers, hurrying to check the blaze, caught a Russian military policeman who admitted that he was acting under orders by applying the torch. He was interviewed by Napoleon, taken down into the courtyard and bayoneted. His arrest, however, had at least made Napoleon think better of staying in the heart of a blazing city and he at once gave orders to pack the transport waggons and head for the Petrovsky Palace, a pretty château owned by the Tsar just outside the city limits.

It was one thing to give the order and another to execute it. By now the Kremlin area was an island in a sea of flames and De Ségur, who was attached to Imperial headquarters at the time, declares that every main exit was blocked by a wall of flame. Red-hot iron sheeting, with which all the better-class houses were roofed, crashed down into the littered streets and a volcano of sparks erupted where buildings collapsed. Huge pieces of furniture, including grand pianos, fell from upper stories. The entire area, he says, was now an inferno and to escape the Imperial party was obliged to use an alleyway that led to the Moskowa river and thence along a winding street where houses on each side were well alight.

Down this blazing arcade moved the Emperor, his staff, the Kremlin guard and their artillery, including a line of powder waggons. Miraculously there was no explosion and it says a good deal for Napoleon's nerve that one witness after another described his demeanour as 'calm and thoughtful'. En route he met a distraught Davout who, despite the crippling effects of his Borodino wound, had been searching for him in the blazing streets. Later the Imperial party were fortunate in finding some looters who knew the city streets and guided them to safety. In this way, almost step by step, the Headquarters group reached the safety of the Petrovsky Palace where the sections of the walls facing towards Moscow were too hot to touch.

In the meantime those units of the army still in the city simultaneously battled with the flames and pillaged. Overlooked by their officers, men like Mortier and Bessières, the Guard fire-picquets worked heroically, particularly around the Kremlin area, but once out of touch with authority, and led by their N.C.O.s, the veterans of the Grand Army concentrated on saving what could be saved of the riches so obligingly abandoned by their owners. The spoil, notwithstanding the vast number of valuables destroyed in the flames, was immense. Costly furs, items of jewellery, ingots from the Imperial mint, and all manner of plate and high-grade china, was stuffed into sacks or loaded on to the many little carriages that the spoilers found in the coach houses of all the larger houses. Sent out to forage for provisions Bourgogne was again lost in a maze of blazing streets, but he and his party made the most of the occasion. They found, beside portable valuables, plenty of flour, sugar, mustard and even eggs, and when they came upon three incendiaries at work they brained one with the carriage pole and harnessed the others to the foremost carriage, loaded down with booty. A second carriage, similarly loaded, was pulled by Guardsmen and the curious little procession then set off to find a way back to their billet.

It was not only extremely dangerous to traverse any of the main streets where houses were continually falling in and blocking the thoroughfare with blazing debris, it was also insufferably hot and men were half-blinded by a rain of ash. Bourgogne took the precaution of making the Russian hauliers travel at the head of the column and it was as well for him that he did, for a house collapsed on them and their cart and those following had to find a new way back to the more open Place where they were quartered. They left the second cart under guard and returned with volunteers an hour later. As to the first carriage and its two-legged horses, Bourgogne says, 'They were burned to a cinder and while we did not much regret the Russians the loss of our provisions distressed us very much, especially the loss of the eggs!' Campaigning under Napoleon could make a man as heartless as Lucifer.

Labaume, the officer attached to the staff of Prince

Eugène, was in the party accompanying the move to the Petrovsky Palace and being a man of greater sensibility he had sympathy to spare for the terrible plight of the 12,000 wounded, both French and Russian, lying in the blazing hospitals. He even saw some of them trying to crawl away and dying in the attempt, but what impressed him more was the nightmarish unreality of the scene as night fell but artificial daylight continued. Indiscriminate looting, he says, had resulted in many of the soldiers, officers and men, appearing in the garments they had taken from houses not yet destroyed by the fire. Soldiers moved about the new headquarters dressed like Cossacks, Bashkirs, Kalmucks and Chinamen and once the staff had settled in the Petrovsky Palace it resembled a gigantic fair or carnival more than the camp of the most celebrated army in the world. The surroundings of the palace were delightful, with English gardens, grottoes, avenues of acacia and linden trees and Chinese pavilions, but when rain fell, towards the end of a four-day stay, there was insufficient shelter for so numerous an assembly and the pretty gardens were soon churned into a morass. Business between looters of all ranks, says Labaume, was very brisk and every kind of article was sold or exchanged. There was an abundance of wines and spirits, saved from the cellars that had been spared by the flames, and there was also a glut of delicacies, such as pastries and confectionery of one sort or another, but bread was scarce and very little meat could be had.

Regarding the wholesale pillage, and its effect upon the army's discipline, Labaume goes on to say that men of the Imperial Guard even penetrated the vaults of the chapel of St. Michael where the Tsars were buried and forced open the Imperial coffins in the hope of finding valuables. Another observation of his would seem to prove the fact that Moscow was deliberately fired for at night, above the glow of the vast fire, he saw torches being thrown from the turrets of buildings not yet consumed. 'They looked,' he says, 'like meteors.' Marshal Berthier might have seen them too. Fascinated by the grandeur of the spectacle he mounted the Kremlin ramparts and was almost blown to his death by the fierce wind.

By September 20th, the day Napoleon returned to the Kremlin to find that it was not much damaged, more than four hundred incendiaries had been caught and executed, but there were many others still at large. What averted the complete destruction of the city was a downpour of rain, and when the engineers made a survey it was reported that of some 25,000 houses one-fifth remained standing. Contemplating the destruction Napoleon, now convinced that the burning had been deliberate, said, 'They did it themselves! How stupendous a decision!' It was as though he almost admired the ruthlessness of Rostopchin in carrying a defensive war to these terrible lengths.

The fire was out but the desolation remained. Acres of smouldering ruins, doused by the steady downpour, gave off an extremely offensive smell and Moscow did not appear a promising site for a winter billet. There were enough houses standing to shelter the Grand Army (now reduced to 108,000), and there was still plenty of drink in the cellars, but the prospect of inhabiting this charred ruin throughout the six months of a Russian winter was bleak and many of the veterans, totting up the cash value of their loot, began to think of retreat to Lithuania or at any rate Smolensk.

Yet no such order was given. Napoleon was still hoping for a favourable reply from the Tsar and it was very difficult to convince him that Alexander could afford to suffer a foreign army to occupy his capital and still remain ruler of Russia. He had already written two further letters, but he could not be sure that either of them had been delivered, for both were sent by the hand of a Russian, one by a mere captain who pleaded that he would not even be admitted to the presence of the Tsar. Napoleon brushed aside his protests. 'Approach him when he is out for a walk!' he said brusquely, illustrating how absolute power banishes commonsense.

The letter did, in fact, reach Alexander, but no answer was returned to Moscow. In a letter dated September 20th, when he had returned to the Kremlin, Napoleon deplored the scorched earth policy of Alexander's generals and of Rostopchin, pointing out that it had already reduced more than half-a-million Russian families to beggary and that he, for his part, was quite ready to go home if reasonable terms could be secured. After waiting throughout another interval Napoleon tried a direct approach to Kutusoff, who had now moved his main force south to a point near Tula where he hoped to remain astride French communications. This time Napoleon sent a Frenchman, General Lauriston, with secret orders to grasp at any sizeable straw. Lauriston saw the Old Fox in his camp but made no impression on him. Marbot, who was still with Oudinot's corps in the St. Petersburg area, says that Lauriston was fooled into granting a safe-conduct for a Russian despatch rider, purporting to carry a letter by Kutusoff urging the Tsar to make peace, but this does not seem likely. Kutusoff had no need to resort to stratagems of this kind. All he had to do now was to wait.

Pressures were indeed being exerted on Alexander to negotiate, mostly by members of the Imperial family, but he resisted them, reiterating that he would grow his beard and live on potatoes in Siberia rather than make terms before the last Frenchman had left Russian soil. This was probably his own inclination but his resolution was strengthened by the advice of Bernadotte, once a French marshal and now Crown Prince of Sweden, and also by a certain Baron von Stein, a member of the German aristocracy whom Napoleon had outlawed four years before.[1] Both these men knew Napoleon's character and Bernadotte especially could view the situation from the standpoint of a professional soldier. Both men hated Napoleon, Stein for the wrongs Napoleon had inflicted on Germany, Bernadotte because he had always been jealous of the Emperor's rise to power and now saw himself as a possible successor to the French throne. Their arguments prevailed over the waverers. Not a word was sent in reply to Napoleon's repeated appeals.

2

The Grand Army remained cantoned in Moscow for a period of thirty-nine days and once the fire had burned itself out the old campaigners made themselves tolerably comfortable. Here and there stray women were found and enrolled as laundresses, harlots or both. Bourgogne's company found themselves in an undamaged café equipped with billiard tables but there were no billiards enthusiasts among them. They took the tables to pieces and used the cloth to make cloaks. They also made punch every day in a large silver bowl and smoked Russian pipes filled with excellent Russian tobacco. Mortier and the cavalry general Milhaud organised a police force from French, German and Italian residents of Moscow who had stayed behind when Kutusoff's army moved out. The more experienced soldiers exchanged unwieldy loot for smaller items that could be stowed away in a knapsack and began to assemble supplies of food against the possibility of a retreat. Apart from this they were careless of the future. 'We sang, laughed, smoked, drank and amused ourselves,' says Bourgogne. They also went sightseeing, inspecting the pillaged tombs of the Tsars and the arsenal of the Kremlin, where they saw the great bell that had fallen from its tower and embedded itself in the earth. They watched working parties trying to remove the great cross of Ivan the Great from the highest tower of the cathedral. There was talk of it being carried to Paris as a trophy. They even organised a fancy dress ball, with Russian women dressed as French marquises.

Placidity, of a kind, returned to the Kremlin, where the Imperial headquarters had been re-established. Bored by such unwonted inactivity Napoleon arranged a theatrical entertainment, performed by a troupe of actors who had managed to evade the exodus just before the French marched in.

The virtual armistice, however, was soon broken by the Russians, who pounced on a detachment of cavalry, killing its colonel and inflicting a number of casualties. All this time Murat's horsemen had been active beyond Moscow and there was another sharp engagement when the squadrons of General Sebastiani, who had replaced the dead Montbrun as commander of the Second cavalry corps, were surprised and badly beaten at Druia. Marbot says that Sébastiani had no one to blame for this reverse but himself. Although a brave man he spent his time in slippers reading Italian poetry and had neglected to reconnoitre. The cavalry fought its way clear but were compelled to abandon the divisional artillery.

It was now clear that Kutusoff was going over to the offensive. Indeed, to a French emissary he had admitted as much, saying, 'The French campaign is over. It is time we started our own!' He then attacked Murat's cavalry screen all along the line and in the engagement the King of Naples was slightly wounded but it was not this engagement that resolved the last of Napoleon's doubts concerning the wisdom of maintaining the bluff and wintering in the capital. His mind was probably made up by a despatch from the west, reporting that his southernmost wing, where the Austrians were guarding his right flank, was in danger. Schwartzenberg, the Austrian commander, had allowed a reinforcement of ten thousand men to slip through and join his enemies. In spite of his marriage to Marie Louise Napoleon knew that he could not rely on Austria and a recent peace agreement between the Tsar and Turkey released an army of 40,000 Russians under Admiral Tchichagoff, who would soon be free to move up and oppose his crossing of the Dnieper and Beresina. Marshals St. Cyr and Macdonald still secured his northern flank but the south was crumbling and any withdrawal was likely to pose considerable difficulties. The senior officers in the Kremlin were under no illusions regarding their true position and the talk turned not only on retreat but on death itself. A huge flock of ravens wheeled croaking over the city and although the sun still shone—'the kind of October weather we get in France,' commented one officer —no one could fail to notice the autumnal chill of the late afternoons and early mornings. Perhaps it was this, or the first light fall of snow that soon disappeared, that made the commanders of the doomed army so gloomy and apprehensive, despite their presence here in the enemy capital with an army of 108,000 men around them. Saint-Denis, the Imperial valet, tells of a discussion he overheard between Napoleon, Prince Eugène, Berthier and Duroc one morning after somebody had raised the topic of the best kind of death. Napoleon said he would choose death by a cannon ball in action but added, 'I expect no such luck. I shall die in my bed, like a damned *coglione*!' It was an accurate prophecy, but his death was still nine years away. For Duroc, the popular Grand Marshal of the Palace and one of the Emperor's oldest friends, it was even more prophetic. Less than a year later he was killed by a cannon ball in Saxony whereas Berthier, who had only recently escaped death by a fall, was to die by crashing from a window, some said suicidally, during the Hundred Days.

By the second week of October it was clear that no answer would come from Alexander and the only reply to the embassies sent to Kutusoff were more probing attacks against French detachments east of the city. There was nothing for it but to pack up and go, perhaps to Smolensk, perhaps to Vilna, perhaps even as far as Kovno on the Niemen, but at all events out of this blackened, stinking ruin of a town, augmenting the strength of the army by making rendezvous with the corps of Oudinot, St. Cyr and Victor. The line of march was still open but it would not remain open long. Cossack marauders were becoming bolder, every day it was growing a little colder and soon the snow would convert the steppe into a trackless waste.

On October 19th the vanguard of the Grand Army began its five-hundred-mile march into the south-west, heading toward Kalouga and the promise of new, unspoiled country, with its prospects of provender for the horses and something more sustaining than vodka and sweetmeats for the men. This—the hope of food and perhaps warmer weather—was not, however, the only reason for a change of route. Another lay deeper in the recesses of the brain of a man aware, as was no other captain of that age, of the importance of psychological factors in the maintenance of morale. To march back along the devastated route to Borodino, Smolensk, Vitepsk and Vilna, would be an admission of defeat. The blackened towns and villages, and the shallow graves that marked the long inward journey would be the signposts of failure, not only to the veterans but to wavering allies, the Prussians, the Italians, the Austrians, perhaps even the steadfast Poles. To march south-west would create an illusion of a new advance, an expansion of conquest, and it was with this in mind that Napoleon led his 108,000 survivors along the road that pointed to the little town of Malo-Jaroslavitz towards which Kutusoff was already grouping his augmented columns.

3

Ten thousand men of the Young Guard were left behind under Mortier, with orders to wait three to four days, blow up the Kremlin, and follow on. The others, perhaps 95,000 strong excluding the thousands of camp-followers, left the ruined city in loose order. Anyone who watched their exit might have mistaken them for a vast horde of brigands that had attracted an equal number of pedlars, De Ségur describes them as a horde of Tartars returning from a successful expedition.

Typical of the load carried by an Imperial soldier on that first, unhurried stage of the retreat, was the contents of Bourgogne's knapsack. Stores of liquor and the large silver bowl in which his company had brewed punch dur-

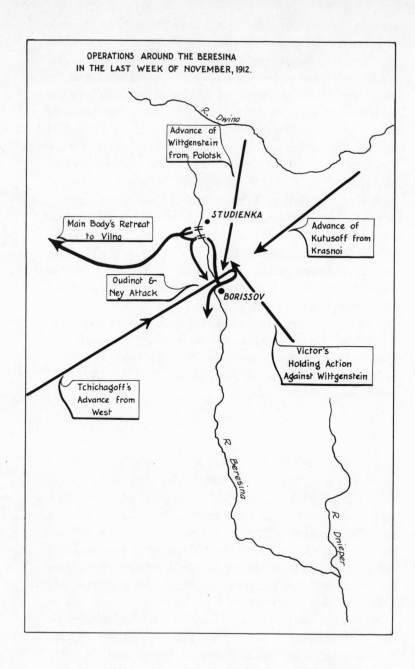

OPERATIONS AROUND THE BERESINA
IN THE LAST WEEK OF NOVEMBER, 1912.

R. Dwina

Advance of
Wittgenstein
from Polotsk

STUDIENKA

Main Body's Retreat
to Vilna

Advance of
Kutusoff from
Krasnoi

Oudinot &
Ney Attack

BORISSOV

Victor's
Holding Action
Against Wittgenstein

Tchichagoff's
Advance from
West

R. Beresina

R. Dnieper

90

ing their Moscow sojourn were carried on the cantinière's cart, but Bourgogne, an experienced campaigner, did not trust items of personal loot to wheeled transport, especially when the road was choked with carts and carriages of every description and, here and there, by wheelbarrows.

Finding his knapsack intolerably heavy he paused on the second day's march and made an inventory of what he had about him. His hoard consisted of a Chinese silk dress embroidered in gold and silver, several gold and silver ornaments, a piece of silver-gilt from the cross of Ivan the Great, a woman's cloak lined with green velvet, two silver pictures in relief (one of the Judgment of Paris and the other of Neptune drawn by sea-horses), several lockets and the spittoon of a Russian Prince, set with brilliants! Over his shirt he wore a yellow silk waistcoat, wadded inside, made from a woman's skirt, and above this a large cape, lined with ermine. In a pouch secured to his waist by a silver cord was a crucifix of gold and silver and a Chinese porcelain vase. All this, of course, in addition to his uniform, accoutrements, musket, bayonet, cartridge-case and sixteen cartridges. Seeking to lighten his load he threw away part of his uniform.

For all that Bourgogne showed more sagacity than many of his comrades, for at least he had had the good sense to leave room for some provisions. Tucked about his person in one place or another were several pounds of sugar, some rice, some biscuit and half a bottle of liqueur.

The pace of the march was necessarily slow. Even the most active infantrymen found it difficult to negotiate a road where vehicles and beasts moved wheel to wheel and nose to tail, their drivers quarrelling furiously over collisions and breakdowns. Several times men of the Guard had to wait in wayside woods before they could rejoin the line of march. It took them five days to reach a point within twenty-five miles of Kalouga and that was as far as many of them got along the new route for that same day, October 24th, the advance guard of the Fourth Corps under Prince Eugène, and numbering some 16,000 men, ran headlong into 70,000 Russians barring the way at Malo-Jaroslavitz.

The French had not expected resistance to harden so rapidly. General Delzons, commanding the van of Eugène's corps, bivouacked just short of the town, pushing forward a couple of battalions as scouts, but at first light the Russian general Dokhturov, supported by Platoff's Cossacks, came storming into the streets, the Cossacks uttering war cries like a tribe of Sioux. The French absorbed the shock successfully and Delzons, seconded by his brother, a colonel, rushed into action, disputing odds of at least ten to one. Hearing the thunder of the guns Eugène advanced at double-quick time and soon the two armies, now fighting four to one in favour of the Russians, were engaged in one of those terrible house-to-house combats that ensure a high rate of casualty on both sides.

Five times the Russians took the town and five times they were ejected at the point of the bayonet. The gallant Delzons and his brother were both killed and General Guilleminot took their places, barricading himself in the church and resisting all attacks until Eugène could send in reserves. After several hours' fighting the Russians drew off leaving 8,000 to 9,000 dead or seriously wounded. The French loss, which they could ill afford, amounted to 4,000.

Again it was another victory, but what did it serve? More and more Russians were massing in the wooded defiles and on the heights beyond the town and back along the Moscow road, at the little village of Gorodnia, Napoleon summoned a council of war consisting of Davout, Murat, Eugène and Bessières of the Guard.

He was in a gloomy indecisive mood. He knew, far better than any of them, that his sole hope of emerging from Russia with the minimum prestige must be to push on in this direction, but his military instinct warned him against another major battle in the wilderness. Come what may he had to get back and soon, before the heavy snow began to fall, before the last of his artillery and baggage horses died under the intolerable strain placed upon them.

That night, with Eugène's report of the battle before him, he seemed inclined to march on for Kalouga but before making a final decision he sent Bessières to reconnoitre.

It was a fatal choice. Bessières, the man whose caution had prevented the Guard from annihilating the defeated Russian army at Borodino seven weeks before, was no gambler. He returned with information that the French would have to fight their way step by step over the rising ground ahead.

Reluctantly Napoleon accepted his word and turned to his maps. He then gave the order to swing right and head for Mojaisk. It was another fatally wrong decision. At that moment Kutusoff, who did not want another full-scale battle at this stage, and had been greatly impressed by the spirit the French had shown at Malo-Jaroslavitz the day before, was pulling out all along the line. If the French had gone forward the only resistance they would have met would have been clouds of scampering Cossacks out on the flanks. They could have marched through them to safer territory, to the Kalouga magazines, above all into a longer and milder autumn.

The moment was not without high drama. That same day, October 25th, Napoleon came within a lance-length of capture. It is interesting to conjecture what might have happened here, on the Plain of Louja, if the average Cossack's political prescience had been as sharp as his nose for plunder.

Making a final reconaissance, surrounded by a staff of about fifty men, the Imperial scouting-party was suddenly enveloped in a mob of Russian horsemen who came flying over the plain uttering their wild cries of 'Hourra! Hourra!' There was no immediate help available and to turn one's back on these horsemen was inviting a lance thrust between the shoulder-blades. Napoleon took the only course possible, drawing a sword that had not been used in anger since the days of the second Italian campaign in 1797 and prepared to defend himself vigorously. Every member of the staff followed his example and the foremost

Cossacks were closely engaged, General Rapp losing his horse and getting yet another wound, his twenty-third. At that moment the Cossack leaders saw a convoy of waggons moving slowly across the plain and almost by instinct the attackers turned aside and made for the source of plunder. The Imperial group was hustled into a bank, slashing away at every Cossack within range. One officer, losing sword and cocked hat, flung himself on the nearest attacker, un-horsed him and took his lance. At that moment, attracted by the uproar which they had mistaken for cries of '*Vive l'Empereur!*' two squadrons of Chasseurs dashed up, to-gether with some mounted Grenadiers of the Guard. The Cossacks were overturned in all directions and a mounted Grenadier, mistaking the staff officer who had snatched the lance for a Cossack officer, ran him through the body. See-ing his error the unhappy man flung himself into the thickest of the fight in the hope of getting killed, but by now the wild horsemen were galloping back to their lines and the pursuit was called off. Napoleon's good humour was entirely restored by the lively brush. The staff officer who had been cut down by the Grenadier was given atten-tion and it is pleasant to record that he eventually reached France on a sledge, while thousands of his able bodied comrades perished.

.   .   .

On October 27th the main body took the road to Mojaisk, but now, with something like two hundred miles to go before reaching the imagined sanctuary of Smolensk, it was first necessary to reform and instil some kind of order into the raggletailed mob of infantry, dismounted cavalry and gunners who had no teams to drag their pieces. The army was formed into three divisions, Murat march-ing ahead, Eugène in the centre, Davout acting as rear-guard. Somehow the mass of non-combatants was absorbed into one or other of the three main bodies, but as they were mostly men and women unaccustomed to the rigours of long marches over bad roads they soon congregated in the rear, making it difficult for the precise Davout to maintain contact with Eugène. Napoleon himself marched long distances. In a letter to the disgraced Junot he said he preferred this mode of progression in order to combat the cold. When he was not marching he rode in a carriage, surrounded by that part of the Guard that had not lost cohesion and a sense of discipline. For already, although the weather was by no means unbearably cold, even the grognards were beginning to straggle and make their way along as best they could, turning aside and halting in little patches of woodland to cook the horseflesh which was their main, indeed almost their sole item of diet. It was deliberate policy on the part of Berthier to order what remained of the cavalry into the van for in this way every horse that died provided food for the famished footsloggers. On the 28th it began to freeze, but the snow held off for another twenty-four hours and Mortier came up with the main body, having left Moscow with his ten thousand on the 23rd.

Mortier had done his best to carry out his assignment, but he had failed to destroy the Kremlin, notwithstanding an explosion that units of the army away to the south-west had mistaken for an earthquake. Large quantities of gunpowder had been placed in the cellars, but the Marshal had had to take stern action to prevent the disintegration of his command, for 2,000 bottles of vodka were found there. To prevent the men drinking themselves insensible Mortier ordered every bottle to be smashed. A certain amount of damage was done to the Kremlin, but Russian troops began to pour into the city before the French moved out and one of their leaders, a general called Witzingerode, a German in Russian service was in too much of a hurry, for he rode into the Kremlin enclosure before the marshal had left. When he discovered his mistake he tried to bluff his way out again, saying that he had arrived under a flag of truce. Mortier was a jovial man (he was the one French marshal who never made an enemy) but there were limits to his amiability. Telling the general that it was not customary for a man of his rank to make calls upon the enemy under a flag of truce he placed him under guard and took him along to the point where he rejoined the main body. Count Witzingerode was doubly unfortunate. He happened to catch Napoleon in an extremely bad temper, was roundly abused as a scoundrel and threatened with a firing squad. He seems to have been a man of General Vandamme's temperament for all he replied, in response to the threats, was, 'As a Russian soldier I am always ready to meet a French bullet!' Napoleon growled, but there was no more talk of having the prisoner shot.

On the 29th snow began to fall and with nine degrees of frost the plight of less exalted prisoners was pitiful. The French ate horseflesh but the prisoners had nothing at all, and even at this stage of the retreat there were rumours of cannibalism. Bourgogne and other veterans half-believed them, for the guardsman tells of stopping to chat to a friend in a little wood on the outskirts of Viasma where he met a Portuguese N.C.O. attached to an escort charged with the security of 800 Russian captives. This man told Bourgogne that as one of them died he was cut up and cooked and eaten by the others, and the guardsman seems to have taken the story at face value, although he refused the Portuguese soldier's offer to go and see for himself.

4

It was now, with the first fall of snow and a sharp drop in temperature, that a spirit of *sauve qui peut* began to corrode the comradeship of the veterans. Every man who had anything to eat ate it in secret, nibbling a fragment of cake or a piece of sugar under cover of his cloak. Those who had flour or potatoes would not contribute to the bivouac kettle but moved off the road and built their own small fires in the woods. A man who had loaded himself with schnapps or potatoes was already regarded as the wealthiest man in the column. A bottle of brandy or a few packets of sugar or flour were worth more than their weight in gold.

It was not solely the cold, and the dawning certainty that the Grand Army was on the run, that undermined discipline. A severe shock was administered to all ranks by the act of traversing once again the charnel-house of Borodino, west of Mojaisk, which the main body passed on that first day of freezing temperatures.

Here, on a vast stretch of ground ploughed by roundshot and littered with military debris of every description, lay the unburied or half-buried bodies of 50,000 men and half as many horses. The spectacle was enough to melt the bowels of the toughest soldier in the army. None of the Russian dead and by no means all the French bodies had been interred on the field of battle, and even the minority laid in shallow graves had been washed clear of them by the heavy October rains. Heads, arms, legs and trunks lay among rusting casques, cuirasses, smashed gun-carriages and broken muskets. In every ravine, and especially under the Great Redoubt, were groups of bloated corpses, almost unrecognisable as men. At least one poor devil still lived with both his legs shattered. He had survived by eating horseflesh and drinking from a stream fouled by decomposing bodies of his comrades. He was carried along with the column, but it is unlikely that he survived the next few days.

The men of Napoleon were accustomed to carnage but the circumstances of this almost accidental return to the field of slaughter inclined the more thoughtful of them to reflect upon the fiction of glory, on the utter pointlessness of coming so far, and enduring so many exertions, to lie out here rotting in the wind and rain.

It would be a mistake, however, to assume that many Frenchmen in the retreating columns blamed the Emperor or, in fact, held him personally responsible for their past and present miseries. For eighteen years now his record had been one of almost unbroken success and most Frenchmen, deep in their hearts, believed implicitly in his "star" or his luck, and also that part of his general policy they could understand. They were children of the Revolution, the invincible enemies of inherited privilege represented by the Courts of Vienna, of Prussia and of St. Petersburg, and if the Revolution had changed course in the last few years they accepted, in the main, Napoleon's concept of a modern autocracy, wherein the dead wood of feudalism was cut away to clear the path for advancement by merit. Generations of children growing up throughout the long peace that was to follow Waterloo were to be taught that Napoleon was a bloodthirsty, power-corrupted bully, with no thought in his head beyond that of physical conquest, but in 1812 the men serving under him did not regard him in this light. A majority were not to do so even after his ultimate banishment to an Atlantic rock. His ideas reached a long way beyond those of the men who opposed his insistence on a spring-clean in the chancelories of the European powers. He was happier making law than making war and it was not wholly his fault that he found himself, time and again, challenged by the entrenched aristocracies of Russia, Britain, Austria, Prussia and the exiled Bourbons of France and Spain. A collision between these forces and the new ideas released by the French Revolution, would have occurred sooner or later, with or without a man of his administrative genius and demoniac energy, and if it had not been for him the growth of democratic government throughout Europe would have been much slower and probably just as expensive in blood. Perhaps very few of the men who trudged across the field of Borodino on the first stage of their return to Central Europe pondered these things, but survivors of that army were to reflect on them when Metternich and the restored Bourbons tried to put the clock back after the abdication of Fontainebleau.

Beyond Borodino was the convent of Kolotskoi where many of the wounded still lay in their filthy bandages. Napoleon paused long enough to gather up all who could be moved, emptying carts and carriages, including some of the Imperial transport waggons, in order that they could be given a chance to reach home. Few did; within days the

Marshal Ney

Marshal Oudinot

carters and sutlers had abandoned them by the roadside on one excuse or another, reloading the transport with loot that could now be gathered on the high road.

On the 30th the main body reached Viasma, nicknamed the "Ville au Schnapps" on account of the amount of brandy found there during the advance, but the weather grew steadily worse, a high wind driving the snow showers across the plain and temperatures dropping a point or two every few hours. More and more horses collapsed and were cut to pieces before they stiffened. Horse-blood broth became the staple diet, so that men marched with blood-smeared beards, dipping their fingers into a communal kettle as they plodded ever westward.

On October 31st the wind increased in violence, striking the columns like a scourge and causing men to reel and stagger as they stumbled over hillocks of dead overlaid with snow. And all the time, behind and on the left flank, trailed Kutusoff's equally wretched columns, in no condition, despite acclimatisation, to mount a major attack, Platoff's Cossacks were always in sight, but they never ventured to attack a compact body of men, concentrating on stragglers and laggards who remained behind to forage or warm themselves at fires of green wood, or perhaps cook a piece of horseflesh on the point of a sword or bayonet. Thousands were lost this way and of those taken prisoner few ever returned to the west.

On his approach to Viasma, on November 3rd, the Russian general Miloradovich made a determined effort to interpose between the straggling rearguard of Davout and the main body. He more or less succeeded, but Davout put up such a spirited resistance that the attack was held until Ney and Eugène could be detached and return to their colleague's assistance, driving the Russians from the road and re-establishing contact between the rearguard and the main body. Davout got away after abandoning twenty-five guns and several thousand prisoners. The following day the Guard marched over a lake that was frozen solid and the struggle towards Smolensk continued.

On November 5th the skies were blue-black with snow, promising a terrible storm and a further drop in temperature on the morrow. Flank guards of the French army were now beginning to come in and at Jarkovo a day or two before, units of the Imperial Guard had rejoined the column. At Dorogoboui, reached by the main body on the 4th, the veterans were made aware of the folly of not taking an alternative route at any cost, for here, and at almost every other town en route, the place was a burned-out shell affording no kind of shelter from the pitiless wind and snow showers. There remained, however, sufficient wood to make fires, and round them the men bivouacked in deep snow, sitting on their knapsacks and waiting for daylight in circumstances of acute misery.

Bourgogne, at this point, was the victim of another kind of scourge. Lying down to rest on some rush matting he soon found himself covered with vermin and had to strip himself naked in the snow and burn his breeches and one of his two shirts. The next morning handmills were distributed to the Guard, but as there was no corn to grind and not the slightest prospect of finding any, they were thrown aside, to add to the vast accumulation of other discarded equipment that marked the route.

That night one of the cantinières gave birth to a boy, attended by the regimental surgeon. The Colonel loaned her his horse and the following morning, mother and child, wrapped in sheepskin and the cloaks of two men who had died in the night, moved on.

On November 6th there was twenty-two degrees of frost. 'Our lips were frozen, our brains too,' says Bourgogne. 'There was a fearful wind and the snow fell in enormous flakes. We lost sight not only of the sky but of the men in front of us.'

At the village of Mickalevka a courier rode along the line anxiously enquiring for the Emperor. He bore despatches of the dangerous near-success of the dramatic Malet conspiracy in Paris, where an officer of that name attempted to take control of the capital by the simple expedient of spreading a rumour that Napoleon had been killed in action.[2] It was a factor that was to contribute to Napoleon's decision to hurry back at all costs, even if it meant abandoning the wreck of the army. In the meantime, however, he remained with that remnant of the Guard still marching behind their eagles.

After the rearguard action at Viasma Davout's First Corps was too weak to cover the retreat and from this point on Ney's Third Corps replaced it, the Marshal remaining as Commander of the rearguard all the way to the Niemen. It was here that the story of Ney's astonishing personal epic really begins. On taking station he had with him some 10,000 men, the majority of whom had not been as far as Moscow and were therefore comparatively fresh.

In the long saga of the First Empire there is no feat of arms to compare with that of Ney's rearguard action over a route of something like 400 miles, a march accomplished in fierce blizzards, in temperatures far below zero, with very little food, less shelter and under constant pressure from the Cossacks. The full story of the influence that this one man was able to exert over a few thousand desperate scarecrows will unfold as the retreat continues, but it is here, at Viasma, that it began. In the presence of the red-headed marshal, known throughout the army for his obstinate bravery and unshakeable faith in his own and his commander's invincibility, the rearguard plucked up courage and although swarms of Cossacks hung on the rear and flanks day and night not a single charge was pressed home. Forming square sometimes twenty times a day, Ney beat off all attacks, himself often handling a musket. His personal example instilled courage into every man who saw him and sometimes, when Cossacks approached within earshot, he would greet them with jeers and encourage them to come a little closer. Without his presence it is doubtful if half as many of the survivors ahead of the line of march would have reached Smolensk on the 14th of the month. Lacking his resolution, and the courage of the men he led, very few Frenchmen would have lived to recross the Niemen in mid-December.

5

It was on October 30th, the day after recrossing the field of Borodino, that the Emperor learned the full extent of dangers threatening the northern and southern flanks of his escape route. The news couriers brought him from the west would have caused most men in his situation to despair, for he was still some 200 miles from his nearest source of reinforcement and supply, but it had the opposite effect upon Napoleon. In the past he had been regarded as a master of the offensive. From now on, until he abdicated eighteen months later, his talents as a defensive general were to predominate.

From this date, the 30th, one begins to read into all eyewitness records of Napoleon's demeanour what Shakespeare might have called "a stiffening of sinews and a summoning of the blood," and the impressive thing about this rally on his part is that it was a direct contrast to an almost total collapse of morale among his men, particularly the more dashing of them, many of whom were to prove utterly useless in the face of disaster.

In successive stages of the retreat Murat's lack of moral fibre became obvious to all, but a loss of nerve was not apparent among most of the other marshals. Ney's magnificent example stands alone, a textbook performance for any leader facing adversity, but there were times when the behaviour of Napoleon himself was above reproach and the fidelity and astounding physical stamina of men like Davout, Mortier, Eugène and old Lefèbvre, are also worthy of commendation.

Communication with the flanks, and with garrisons strung along the main road between Moscow and the Niemen, was maintained during the retreat, despite the presence of so many partisans, and many extremely mobile groups of Cossacks, most of them more interested in plunder than following any overall strategy pursued by Kutusoff or his subordinate generals. Convoys had had some difficulty in getting through because they were cumbersome and slow-moving, but the matchless system of Imperial despatch-carrying met the challenge and head-quarters was in almost daily touch with outlying com-manders like Oudinot (convalescing at Vilna), St. Cyr, Vic-tor and even Macdonald, still commanding his half-mutin-ous Prussians as far away as Riga.

In this way, quite early in the retreat, Napoleon heard that the Russian General Wittgenstein, covering St. Petersburg after his rout by St. Cyr at Polotsk, had taken the offensive again and was now threatening the man who had defeated him. He heard also that the Russian Admiral Tchitchagoff, who should have been held in check by the Austrian Schwartzenberg in the south, had been allowed to advance still deeper into Russia and was now menacing the crossings of the Beresina above and below the town of Borissov. The ability of Tchitchagoff to exert such a threat pointed clearly at Austrian treachery, but there was little Napoleon could do about this now. He concentrated on re-inforcing the hard-pressed St. Cyr on the banks of the Dwina, despatching orders to Marshal Victor, then at Smolensk, to march to his assistance and prevent Wittgen-stein from making a junction with Tchitchagoff and menacing the line of retreat. Victor marched out and joined St. Cyr on November 6th, but in the meantime, as will be seen, The Owl was giving a very good account of himself.

This done, Napoleon pushed on with all speed for Smolensk where there should have been stores and food for 100,000 men for at least fifteen days. The shattered army made for the city like a desperate fox with the hounds less than a field away, and like many hunted foxes they were to find the haven they sought did not exist. Smolensk was, in fact, a well-stopped earth.

News of the appalling plight of the Grand Army had not run ahead. The French police (highly praised by the Russians on this account) had seen to that, so that the appearance of the first fugitives from Moscow struck the garrison troops dumb with dismay. Captain Roeder, the Hessian Lifeguard, was one of the first to make contact with the famished, frost-bitten, horde who came staggering out of the east. He had been sent forward to survey routes and billets as far as the ruined town of Dorogoboui, about half-way between Smolensk and Viasma, and it was at the latter town that he and his guardsmen were enrolled as body-guards to the Emperor. The King of Naples, he says, galloped in one end of the town and out of the other without a pause, but Roeder makes an interesting comment concerning the impact of defeat upon Napoleon himself. On guard outside the Imperial quarters that night he heard the Emperor at work until one a.m. At three-thirty in the morning he was again on foot and his voice, dictating orders for the immediate evacuation of the sick and wounded for Smolensk, was strong and clear.

The sight of the majority of the men marching with him, however, amazed soldiers who had been left behind along the route during the advance. Some of the Old Guard were still marching in formation but most of the other contingents had practically withered away and this in a matter of days. Most officers were on foot and many of them wore burned and ragged uniforms. In their eyes was the haunted look of men who had been pushed to the limit of their endurance, a look that a later generation was to associate with the trench veteran of the Western Front.

Every mile along the road to Smolensk conditions worsened and more men, among them some of the wounded who had made tremendous efforts to get this far in the hope of finding help at the depot, gave up the struggle and lay down in the snow to await death. Brutishness, at the end of a short day's march, knew no limits and old comrades fought one another for a piece of bread or a dribble of brandy. At some of the posting-houses, a regular feature of this highway, there were pitched battles for accommodation between men who realised that the choice between a night under a roof or in the open was the difference between life and death. Early arrivals packed themselves into these large, barn-like structures, officers, N.C.O.s and men, cavalry, artillery, infantry and camp-followers, until they were massed in a solid group and those nearest the doors and walls, or in the loft immediately under the roof, resisted the efforts of men outside to pull down the timbers for firewood with bayonet and musket-shot. A day's march short of Valoutina, where, during the advance, Ney's Corps had almost succeeded in trapping the Russians and Junot had let them slip away, a hideous tragedy occurred in a post-house. It resulted in the deaths of nearly 800 men.

Bourgogne, a latecomer, described a miniature battle between the privileged and the underprivileged, but during the night the latter group, Bourgogne among them, had their revenge, for the post-house caught fire and as the doors opened inwards nobody could get out. Bourgogne and his friends saved about half-a-dozen, including an officer, dragging them through a hole torn in the planking, but the greater part were roasted alive, or trampled to death in the surge towards the exits. Men gathered round the blaze unable or unwilling to help and others calmly foraged among the ashes for loot. The majority, however, stretched their hands to the warmth, saying, 'What a beautiful fire!' Bourgogne, himself a veteran with six years' active service behind him, admits that the scene sickened him and he made an early start to get away from it. On the road he met two infantrymen who told him that they had observed Croats dragging bodies from the fire, cutting them up and eating them. This is the second instance he gives of cannibalism during the retreat and hints occur in other records. Although unsubstantiated they are not beyond the bounds of possibility. On that 550-mile march in sub-zero temperatures almost any means of survival was employed.

It was near this spot that Bourgogne witnessed another tragedy, the burial of a fifteen-year-old girl, 'pretty even in death' who was handed out of a carriage by her mother and sister. They were one of several ex-patriot families who had decided to accompany the Grand Army back to France, together with a number of Russian girls who had formed attachments with the invaders. The lady and her surviving daughter died later in the retreat, as did all the Russian serfs who had followed the column out of Moscow in the hope of obtaining their freedom.

On the next day, November 9th, it was a little warmer and for the following five days temperatures continued to rise, so that in the end about 60,000 of the 108,000 who had set off from Moscow three weeks before staggered up to the gates of Smolensk and clamoured for admittance. The men of the garrison stared down at the rabble and refused to admit them, and one can readily appreciate their reluctance. What had this raging mob in common with Napoleon's Grand Army that had marched out of this same gate seventy-seven days before?

CHAPTER FIVE

'THE DEVIL'S OWN COUNTRY—HELL ALL THROUGH!'

Sergeant Bourgogne

1

FROM the beginning it had been a far-flung battle line and now, every day, it was becoming wider and more confused. In high summer it had been like a long, slightly shredded piece of elastic, pivoted on pro-French Warsaw and well-stocked German garrison towns, like Koenigsberg. From here it had stretched across the Niemen, through Vilna, through Glubokoe and Vitepsk, over the Dnieper to the towers of Smolensk, then east-north-east to Viasma, the ravines of Borodino and finally to Moscow. From mid-September until mid-October it had remained taut and strained, but since, when the withdrawal began, it had twisted into a tight loop enclosing Malo-Jaroslavitz, and afterwards had contracted a little every day. When this happened the western end of the long, taut line had begun to buckle under pinching pressures from above and below. As yet there was no severance, but the terrible possibility of such a thing happening was always present. Somehow the shredded ends of the retracting line must be plaited before tension could be eased and the pivots withdrawn and rebased. It was a task to which Napoleon addressed himself as soon as he entered Smolensk on November 9th. Among all that rabble he was like a sane man plotting his escape from a congress of lunatics.

The gates of Smolensk remained locked until the Guard arrived, marching in formation and still something of a rallying point. Close upon their heels came some fifty thousand derelicts who at once dispersed to every quarter of the ruined city. Frantic efforts to instil some kind of order into this mob were made by those among the officers who had kept their nerve and to a degree these efforts succeeded. On learning that no rations would be issued to stragglers a majority rejoined their units and awaited the life-saving issue of flour, biscuit, brandy and perhaps even a little meat from the carcasses of the thousand oxen said to be in the town. They might as well have continued their individual foraging. Only the Guard received a standard issue. For the others, including the hard-pressed rearguard arriving on the 13th, there was nothing, or next to nothing.

To understand how the carefully-planned system of staged magazines had broken down it is necessary to go back a few weeks and study what had been happening along the line of march since the main body had quitted Vilna on July 17th, Vitepsk on August 13th, Smolensk on August 25th.

Every town or large village along the route had been garrisoned and most of them, certainly Vilna and Smolensk, had been adequately provisioned. Great convoys of food, forage and ammunition had lumbered eastward at specifically timed intervals and all the time reinforcements had been drifting in from the German and Polish bases. And yet, for one reason or another, none of the big convoys had reached the main body during their thirty-nine-day stay in Moscow. Many had not penetrated as far as Viasma, the town beyond Smolensk, and of those that did the bulk of what they carried had been dissipated piecemeal, or disposed of fraudulently and in bulk.

To begin with, Cossacks and dispossessed peasants who formed into partisan bands had been very active north and south of the route ever since the French had crossed the Niemen and marched on Kovno, the first town to fall. Apart from the initial detachment of Oudinot's and Victor's Second and Ninth Corps to the north, and Schwartzenberg's Austrian Corps to the south, there had been no large-scale dispersals of personnel into the plains and forests above and below the road to Moscow. An early nineteenth-century army was incapable of such dispersion. It did not have the necessary mobility or the transport to enable it to advance on a broad front, as Von Moltke's legions advanced into France in 1914, or Hitler's armoured columns did in 1941 and 1942. In the main it was obliged to stick to the high road when there was one, and to the line of towns and posting-houses that stretched along the route between Kovno and Moscow. Such flank parties as did venture ten to twenty miles north or south of the line consisted of squadrons of light cavalry, perhaps a hundred to two hundred troopers in search of forage and stray cattle.

Several large convoys had been caught and plundered by the Cossacks and by partisans, operating under such leaders as Davydov, Orlov and Denisov, the kind of men Tolstoy depicted in *War and Peace*, but more stores had been lost through peculation. The thousand oxen the troops expected to find in Smolensk were not available because they had been sold to local Jews, who had resold them to the Russian army! Many of the Jews had remained behind when the Russians left their homes in advance of the French, and in all the markets along the route trade was brisk between civilians and soldiers with loot to sell. The columns were also at the mercy of army commissaries, who had leeched upon the French divisions even in the days of the early triumphs in Italy, but Napoleon could not complain on this account. His own brothers, Joseph and Lucien, had both made large personal fortunes in this particular field.

Despite maurauders and swindlers, however, there would still have remained sufficient food in the depots to supply the greatly reduced contingents who dragged themselves into Smolensk between November 9th and 13th, had it not been for the fact that for something like four months every centre had had to support the passage, east and west, of numbers of reinforcements, wounded, sick and prisoners, who passed to and fro along the route in disorderly droves. These men—and they could be numbered in tens of thousands—had arrived in every town with a sharp appetite and at that time there had seemed plenty of provisions to spare. There would have been enough even now if the famished horde who rushed into the city after the Guard had been less demoralised, or content to await their turn. They were far too desperate to show patience, however, and when stores were distributed they fell upon the supplies with such frenzy that a great deal of it was trampled into the snow. Then they dispersed again, to seek what could be found or bartered for in the suburbs.

No kind of preparation had been made to guard against anything but an orderly retreat. In early autumn Captain Roeder, the Hessian, had been sent on a mission from Smolensk to Dorogoboui, to prepare for such a contingency. He had orders to survey the villages north and south of the route, prospecting for supplies of food and for billets. He carried out his mission with efficiency and under very trying conditions, for his German troops were quarrelsome, nervous of attacks by Cossacks and partisans and, above all, stricken with dysentery from which a number died, but no use seems to have been made of Roeder's carefully-compiled report and in any case it was already too late. The shattered columns were now within a few days' march and as early as October 7th (odd in view of the fact that on that date no firm resolve had been made to quit Moscow) convoys had received orders to turn back and head for Smolensk.

Out on the flanks Roeder found plenty of provender and a population that was by no means hostile so long as they were protected from pillagers and Portuguese rapists. Riding along with him on this occasion was the Colonel-General of Dragoons, Baraquay d'Hilliers, who had been governor of Smolensk and was now taking over an active command. It was a short-lived appointment. The Colonel walked into an ambush with two thousand men and was made prisoner before the main body was across the Beresina.

Roeder also found evidence of savagery on the road that was reminiscent of the kind of thing that was happening in

Spain and had, in fact, been common practice in the Peninsula for the past four years. He came across a Russian prisoner who had been shot by his escort because he could march no further, and tells us that about the same time a batch of thirty prisoners had been shot by order of the Governor of Viasma. The French had not made war in this way until they had crossed the Pyrenees in 1808.

The Hessian captain was one of those who was almost overwhelmed by the tide of fugitives. During the period when he was attached to the Young Guard and acting as bodyguard to the Emperor, he went to great pains to compile notes of the strength of various regiments then being regrouped at Smolensk. On November 12th, three days after Napoleon had reached the city, Roeder's own regiment had been reduced to eight sergeants, one drummer and forty-nine men. He lists forty-five guardsmen as missing, thirty-one absent and sick and a further ten and two N.C.O.s present but too sick to march. Among Davout's First Corps, so heavily involved in the rearguard action at Viasma, the wastage had been much worse. The 111th Regiment had lost twenty officers and 449 men, the 15th Light and the 33rd of the Line had dwindled from 4,500 to 450! The Old Guard had lost three in four, the Young Guard nine out of ten!

On his return to Smolensk Roeder billeted himself and the remnants of his company in a single house, but they were soon ejected by the veterans of the Old Guard. It was, as he says, a case of 'look to yourself!' Knowing that the French would soon be called upon to evacuate Smolensk, Roeder, an old campaigner, made his preparations. He loaned his horse to the artillery and acquired a pony that would be far more serviceable on icebound roads. On November 15th, the day after Napoleon quitted the city, the Hessians marched out to take their chances with the remnant of the Grand Army on the long road to the Niemen.

They marched in comparatively good order for much had been achieved during the five-day stay in the city. The indecisive mood of Malo-Jaroslavitz had gone and Napoleon, like the hard-pressed Richard III at Bosworth, was himself again. He gave his orders clearly and concisely. He looked impassive as he sat over his maps with the impeccably dressed Berthier at his elbow. The advice of men like Davout, Eugène and, when he arrived, Michel Ney, was sought but not necessarily taken. He made his own dispositions from what facts were available. It was, as he said, Egypt all over again, and, in defiance of all odds and predictions, he had returned safely from Egypt. Then he had had no fleet. Today he could be said to lack an army, or so most Russians and neutrals would have said, forgetting that what he did have, the rump that had somehow survived the snow, blizzards and starvation rations of the last twelve days, was an élite led by the most experienced captains in the world. Davout, the Iron Marshal, was still present, a man who had once fought the Prussian army to a standstill with a single corps. Eugène and his Italians were still to be reckoned with and maintained some sort of order. The hard core of the Old and Young Guard still carried their eagles and marched shoulder to shoulder under Bessières and Mortier. But above all Michel Ney was holding the rear against every attempt by Kutusoff to drive it in upon the main body.

The old fox of the North did not try very hard. 'Let winter do the job,' he told an impatient subordinate, 'I don't want to arrive at the frontier heading a rabble!' He followed at a discreet distance, moving east and south of the Grand Army, but the Cossack Hetman Platoff kept up his harrying tactics. It was death or captivity to any laggard in the French rearguard.

Messages went westward out of Smolensk to Marshal Victor, telling him at all costs to co-operate with St. Cyr, hold the Russian armies of Wittgenstein and Tchitchagoff apart and keep the crossing of the Beresina open. The task of reorganisation and regrouping inside the town had been achieved, the survivors being divided into three main bodies under the Emperor, Eugène and Davout, with

Mortier marching in the rear of Davout and Ney last of all, with his reinforced rearguard. The day before the first columns marched out the Guards' band played under headquarters windows, striking up *'Ou peut-on être mieux su'au sein de sa famille'*. Napoleon, hearing the tune, came out on to the balcony and ordered them to play something more stirring. They broke off and struck up *'Veillons au salut de l'Empereur!'* The Old Guard would be the last men in the world to admit that the Empire was falling to pieces.

News of the near-success of the Malet conspiracy was digested in Smolensk and its message to the Emperor was clear. Here was a nonentity who had forged a document, taken command of 1,200 National Guardsmen, fooled any number of officials, including a prefect, released a spy from prison and had only been checked in his bid to take over the capital by the alertness of two officers who demanded better credentials. It said very little for the fidelity and intelligence of the people at home. 'What about my son?' Napoleon demanded, of a glum and silent council of war. 'Did no one think of him?' Daru, one of his intimates, muttered that it was essential the Emperor should be seen in Paris alive and healthy without delay and secretly Napoleon agreed with him. He gave orders that the retreat should continue in the morning, one day's march separating each division.

Men had struggled towards Smolensk believing it to be a storehouse of plenty. When the truth was discovered a majority of stragglers, still coming in in ones and twos, gave way to despair. One commodity only was in good supply and that was vodka. Hundreds of men drank themselves insensible and were found dead when N.C.O.s searched the houses in the morning. Some of these desperate men died without the solace of the bottle for snow had covered the entrances of burned-out houses and careless walkers fell headlong into deep cellars. 'Their bodies,' says Bourgogne, 'were dragged out the next day, not for burial, but for the sake of their clothes.' Bourgogne himself was among the more fortunate. Being with the Guard he received an ounce of biscuit and a little rye flour mixed with straw and with this miserly issue he made a pudding. It was as heavy as lead. In the comparative shelter of the skeleton town, however, the claims of comradeship began to reassert themselves and Bourgogne spent a night searching for his oldest friend, a sergeant-vélite called Grangier. He knew he was somewhere in the city, having gone ahead at Viasma as escort to a baggage waggon belonging to Bessières. So Bourgogne went back to the guardroom of the gate by which he had entered and found it full of sick and wounded, among them an old Chasseur with nearly all his toes frozen and his beard and moustache filled with icicles. Given brandy the old fellow roused himself. 'The right sort never die!' he commented, anticipating a song men were to sing as they marched along the Menin Road more than a century later.

Bourgogne's adventures during his five-day stay in Smolensk were perhaps typical of the experiences of the able-bodied survivors of the march from Moscow. It was essential to his morale to link up with a few old comrades and he searched for them desperately, risking his life on the snow-covered ramparts in almost pitch darkness and a howling north wind. Every now and again weariness and despair would engulf him and he would sit on a shattered gun-carriage, reflecting that he would be lucky indeed to see the end of this campaign. But always he would get up and move on, and when he measured his length over a dead dragoon and his cry of pain advertised the presence of another survivor crouching in the darkness, he found sufficient strength to continue his search.

In the meantime, however, he had had two remarkable encounters, one with a band of deserters and another, as he then thought, with the next world. Falling down a snow-slide into a cellar he found himself in the presence of a gang of French, German and Italian thugs who had left their regiments and decided to extract a profit from the disaster. Each day, starting very early, they had moved ahead of the army, and later concealed themselves until exhausted survivors were asleep. Then they crept out and made off with officers' portmanteaux. The French army had long been plagued with these soldier-brigands. Even at the camp at Boulogne, in 1805, an organisation known as "The Minions of the Moon" pilfered millions of francs' worth of personal property from the troops. Their presence and purpose here disgusted a man of Bourgogne's temperament and he left them at the first opportunity, marking their lair with a cross in the snow in the hope of being able to bring them to justice in the morning.

Later on, still rambling about the ramparts in the dark, he heard the unlikely sound of thunderous organ chords and assumed that his mind was playing tricks with him and that his end was near. His curiosity, however, was that much greater than his fear, and he poked about until he found the source, a group of bandsmen, drunk on brandy, who were practising on the organ of a half-ruined church close by. In the church he found warmth, comfort and a little rice, for the men were from his regiment, but to reach them he first had to scale the churchyard wall and grope his way across a yard piled with two hundred corpses lightly covered with snow. The hospitals were using the churchyard as a burial assembly point but the ground was far too hard to be turned.

Inside the church a kind of carnival of death was going on. The brandy had been discovered in the crypt, together with some fur-lined Rabbis' caps. As the organ thundered out some more ambulance men arrived with another load of bodies and were so unwise as to lead their emaciated horse into the church and go to sleep. In the morning the horse was gone; the guardsmen had eaten it.

Furious at losing their sole means of transportation to and from the hospitals the ambulance men departed, throwing the bodies they had brought during the night in the church porch. The guardsmen went on eating, even when one of their number broke his leg in a fall from the organ loft. There had been a ladder there the night before but someone had taken it away and chopped it up for firewood.

Bourgogne eventually found his friend Grangier and his patience was well rewarded. Grangier had a piece of beef and some bread. It was twenty-three days since Bourgogne had eaten anything but horseflesh and thin soup.

2

The wreck of the Grand Army was now on the point of marching to effect a junction with its outlying corps, under the leadership of Oudinot, the grenadier, St. Cyr, the enigmatic Owl, and the self-important Victor, whom the army knew as *"Le Beau Soleil"* on account of his rosy complexion. They were an odd, unmanageable trio, but upon their resolution rested the sole hope of the main body making its way home. To follow what occurred at this stage of the retreat it is again necessary to go back in time a few weeks, and trace what had been happening out on the northern flank, towards St. Petersburg.

Oudinot's early skirmishing in this area had been successful in keeping Wittgenstein's northern army at bay, but during the late summer there had been some bloody fighting in the river country round the town of Polotsk, and the French cavalry in particular had distinguished itself. Major Marbot, soon to be a Colonel, is our main authority for the engagements in this area, and he tells of headlong charges against Russian artillery and the steady maintenance of the offensive against Russian cavalry.

In this area the Polish population were friendly and the French received a good deal of help from the resident aristocracy, so that Wittgenstein could do little but cover St. Petersburg and maintain a succession of probing attacks against the entrenched camp at Polotsk, on the Dwina.

Here in late August, it will be recalled, the brilliant strategist St. Cyr had won a notable victory and been awarded his baton. The rank and file, Marbot says, admired St. Cyr's unquestioned ability without being able to like him and they received the news that Oudinot was returning to them with mixed feelings.

Oudinot, a brave, loyal but bull-headed man, had received no specific orders from headquarters to reassume command, but did so on learning that St. Cyr had in his turn been wounded. The brewer's son had been convalescing at Vilna where his wife, the devoted Maréchele, had joined him and here they enjoyed a few weeks' social life, visiting other officers and going for country rides, although they too suffered from a general shortage caused by the invasion. The women were animated by a patriotic spirit and were quite ready to sell shawls, pearls, plate and diamonds in order that their husbands could keep their regiments up to strength. 'All,' says the pious Duchess of Reggio (Oudinot, like all the marshals, had been made a duke during the flood-tide of the Empire), 'all was successively swallowed up in the vortex of war from which those noble hearts and vivid imaginations refused to draw anything but hope!'

The October weather was deceptively mild and every day Oudinot and his wife would ride out and explore the neighbourhood. She did not admire the flat, featureless country around the outskirts but the town itself, containing thirty-six convents, presented an impressive array of domes and steeples.

Stationed at Vilna during this period was Maret, Duke of Bassano and Minister of Foreign Affairs, to whom Napoleon wrote frequently, so that anxiety concerning the situation of the Grand Army began to increase during early autumn and Oudinot's wife, preoccupied as she was with parties and picnics, read as much in the faces of some of her diplomat guests. 'On the 29th or 30th of October,' she records, 'I noticed such a going to and fro; the Marshal, in a low voice, gave so many different orders to his officers; his people too moved about to such an extent that I had a presentiment of departure and all my doubts were dissipated when I saw him arranging his war-charts and telling Pils (the valet) to put them in his boxes.'

What had determined Oudinot to rejoin the army before his wound was properly healed had been news that St. Cyr, his replacement, had become a casualty and also that, under extreme pressure from Wittgenstein, he had been obliged to evacuate Polotsk, the pivot upon which the northern flank of the Grand Army rested.

The Second and the Ninth Corps were now the only organised French troops in Russia. Apart from the threat of Wittgenstein in the north, and the positive advances of Tchitchagoff's army in the south, they had to contend with the possible desertion of Macdonald's Germans in the west so that their position was becoming, if not as desperate as that of the main body, then at least extremely dangerous.

St. Cyr acted with his usual coolness. His infantry were concentrated in the town of Polotsk and several more bridges were constructed to keep open his retreat across the Dwina. Repulsed on October 17th, Wittgenstein, a very obstinate adversary, attacked again the following day and after suffering considerable loss managed to break into the entrenched camp. Seven times he was driven out by Legrand and Marion and when the marshal was wounded he continued to direct operations. In the end the Russians drew off into the forests but French relief was tempered by news that another Russian army group under General Steingel was moving up the left bank of the river to turn St. Cyr's position and sandwich the hard-pressed Second Corps between Wittgenstein's 50,000 and Steingel's 14,000. St. Cyr's Corps, at this time, did not muster more than 15,000 men, but they were good fighting material, mostly French and loyal Croats. St. Cyr engaged Steingel's advance guard and beat them back, the Russian Commander losing his nerve and digging in, but the French position was now so perilous that it was essential Polotsk should be evacuated and an effort made to reach the crawling head of the main French army to the south-east. The evacuation was carried out very efficiently, aided by a thick fog, and St. Cyr drew off, escaping the jaws of the trap. The town was set alight, however, and a fierce rearguard action fought in the light of the flames. Like so many other Russian towns Polotsk was destroyed.

The northern wing might yet have been secured had it not been for that blight of Napoleonic armies, a built-in reluctance on the part of the marshals to co-operate with each other and waive rights of seniority. There was no hope whatever of this in a clash of personalities between St. Cyr and Victor. Victor, created a marshal after Friedland in 1807, was the senior of the two, and St. Cyr, who would almost certainly have remained in command despite his wound, refused to serve under him. Saying he could campaign no longer he handed over command to General Legrand and rode away, heading straight for France. The troops regretted his departure. 'All that St. Cyr needed to make him a consummate commander was a smaller share of egotism and the knowledge how to attach men and officers to him by attending to their wants,' comments Marbot, adding, 'But no man is faultless!'

Soon after this Marbot had a curious experience concerning which he often laughed in retrospect. Sent out on patrol with 700 troopers he advanced into a thick, low-lying mist and was amazed to see, in the dyke country around Ghorodie, thousands of watch-fires in the hills, signifying the presence of a large Russian army. He estimated that they represented the presence of at least 50,000 men and was making ready to cut his way out when a "watch-fire" settled on the cloak of one of his men. It was a will-'o-the-wisp as large as an egg, caused by a slight frost following a day of autumn sunshine.

In the meantime Oudinot, who never liked to miss a fight, was hurrying up from Vilna, so eager to reassume command of his old corps that he rode across country practically alone and was almost made prisoner by Russian dragoons. His escape is one more indication of the courage and ingenuity demonstrated by senior officers in this campaign.

Finding himself cut off and surrounded he retreated to a stone hut in the forest and barricaded himself inside with one aide-de-camp and a dozen French stragglers on their way to rejoin their regiments. Close by, at Zapole, Marbot noticed the arrival in camp of two peasants and one of them he at once recognised as Captain De Bourgoing, one of Oudinot's aides. The captain told him that he had been sent on in advance in disguise and had passed a body of enemy dragoons en route. Taking him for a Russian they let him pass. He urged Marbot to ride out and meet the marshal who was almost certainly in trouble, for as De Bourgoing hurried forward he had heard the sound of firing.

Marbot rushed off with his regiment and bursting into a clearing was a witness to the remarkable siege of a French marshal and thirteen men by a strong body of cavalry. During his brisk resistance the former grenadier had received yet another wound.

News that Oudinot had arrived disgusted Marshal Victor. He had been glad enough to see the back of St. Cyr, but he remembered that Oudinot, created a marshal two years after Victor, was none the less the real commander of the Second Corps, and therefore technically in charge of operations up here. Disdaining to serve under a junior marshal he marched away, taking his men with him. Oudinot, not caring a damn, established his headquarters near Lukulen. Marbot was to remember this little town with affection. It was here, after twelve years of almost unbroken active service and many wounds, that he at last received confirmation of his colonelcy.

Napoleon had written his Minister of Foreign Affairs from Dubrovna, west of Smolensk, stressing anxiety about his avenue of retreat. His language was testy: 'I hear that the enemy has entered Minsk,' he said. 'Where then was Prince Schwartzenberg? I know not!' The men in closer touch with diplomatic intrigues knew well enough; Schwartzenberg was now a proven traitor, and nothing could be expected from him but further acts of treachery. Minsk, well south of the line of retreat and some fifty miles west of the Beresina, was taken on the 16th, three days after the main French army left Smolensk, and it looked very much as if the two jaws of the Russian bear-trap were about to close. If they did, if Wittgenstein and Tchitcha-goff succeeded in effecting a junction, then all was indeed lost. News would soon be broadcast that the Emperor of France, along with some of the most celebrated of his marshals, were prisoners in Russian hands. In the hope that this would be achieved one Russian general went so far as to issue a description of Napoleon to his men.

Orders now arrived at Oudinot's headquarters to march as fast as possible on Borissov, a town north-east of Minsk and actually sited on the Beresina, but although he set off at once and hurried there by forced marches, he was too late. The Polish general defending the vital crossing-place, finding himself surrounded and greatly outnumbered, crossed over to the left bank and headed for Orcha, with-out waiting for Oudinot to come to his aid. He managed to rejoin the marshal and together they marched back to find town, bridge and fortress in Tchitchagoff's hands. The bear-trap, it would seem, had all but closed and the strug-gling remnant of the Grand Army was cut off.

3

The road from Smolensk to the wide curve of the Dnieper at Orcha, where the great river sweeps south on its winding course to the Black Sea, runs through a gully some four hundred feet deep near the town of Krasnoi. The pass is called the gully of Losmina and is a short way west of the scene of the Russian rearguard action outside Krasnoi during the summer advance. It was at this point, on steep ground, that Kutusoff made his first serious attempt to seal the fate of the retreating army, to end at a blow the long-drawn-out agony of the toiling columns in their crawl towards the Niemen and safety.

Kutusoff's patience or caution, whichever it was, had surprised and irritated some of his subordinate com-manders. On the evidence of their eyes, as well as that of reports coming in every day from the Cossacks in close touch with the French, it seemed to them that the time for a decisive blow had not only arrived but already been lost at Viasma, Dorogoboui and even Smolensk, where the enemy had been in no sort of position to sustain a determined assault. Yet, disregarding the fierce fight at Malo-Jaroslavitz, there had been no major clash between the two armies since Borodino. The attempt to detach Davout's rearguard on November 3rd had been a half-hearted affair, easily checked by the appearance of Ney and Eugène with reinforcements. There had been sporadic fights every day of the retreat, sometimes involving a few thousand men, sometimes a few hundred, but usually a running battle between forty or fifty resolute French and perhaps a couple of hundred Cossacks, who occasionally rode within pistol range but almost never came close enough to use their long lances.

This was not due to lack of resolution on their part but to sound military precept and love of booty. Why should they risk casualties charging a formation under men like Davout or Ney, when there was so much easier game to be flushed from the fir copses, or from around the fires in the ruined villages? Helpless men were to be found here every morning and often during a midday halt, soldiers who could no longer fire their muskets because their fingers and thumbs were frostbitten, who could no longer march because they had lost all their toes. There were plenty of dead too, some of them still carrying plunder in money-belts and in the lining of their greatcoats. There were even waggons abandoned for lack of horses or the loss of a wheel, and most of these, besides containing dying wounded, held Moscow booty carefully wrapped in sheepskins.

Most of the heavier loot had been abandoned, trophies such as the great cross of Ivan and the Gothic armour taken from the Kremlin arsenal. A good deal of it had been thrown in a pond at Semlevo, west of Viasma, but there were still plenty of private fortunes to be found along the road and the Cossack preferred to hunt for them rather than to fight, although he was always ready to defend what he found.

Napoleon's five-day halt at Smolensk gave Kutusoff an opportunity to place himself in strength aslant the route. It also gave the more impetuous of his lieutenants an opportunity to persuade the Generalissimo that here was a magnificent chance to capture Napoleon, the King of Naples, the Viceroy of Italy, together with Marshals Davout, Mortier, Bessières, Berthier, Duroc and Lefèbvre in a single swoop. They were not so sure about Ney and his rearguard. They were probably too far behind and could be gathered up later, when the war was virtually over, and the illustrious French prisoners were already on their way to St. Petersburg. There were still the two corps of Oudinot and Victor to be reckoned with but what could 40,000 men achieve against three Russian armies bearing down on them from the east, north and south?

Kutusoff's hesitation to engage the remnant of the Grand Army in a decisive action was understandable, to him at all events. Every general in Europe at that time stood in awe of Napoleon as a strategist, and Kutusoff had never forgotten his enemy's brilliantly co-ordinated movements that led to the smashing of the Austro-Russian centre at Austerlitz, or the terrible drubbing Bennigsen had received at Friedland, eighteen months later. Napoleon's name was synonymous with victory. In a dozen major battles, some of them fielding armies of over a hundred thousand men on either side, he had settled the issue in a few hours. In only two exceptions, at Eylau, in 1807, and at Essling-Aspern on the Danube in 1809, had he been fought to a standstill, but on the first of these occasions he had slept on the battlefield, and the second had been followed by the shattering victory of Wagram. His reputation as a manipulator of divisions and as an artillerist was unique, not only when measured against living soldiers but when compared to that of every celebrated soldier in history. He had beaten so many generals so many times and in so many different circumstances that every commander opposing him went into action with the prospect of a hurried withdrawal in mind. This did not make for resolute decisions on their part. Commenting on this Sir Walter Scott compares the Russian general to a Greenland fisherman who is careful not to approach a dying whale.

There were other factors, not all of them frivolous, that made Kutusoff hesitate. His own men were not immune to cold and hunger and the Russian commissariat ws as antiquated as most departments in the armies of the Czar. The Russians had been marching south of the Grand Army but still near enough to their route to pay the penalty of crossing a pillaged, depopulated country. There was also the delaying factor of loot that had already slowed the pace of Platoff's Cossacks. An army largely composed of starving peasants, finding itself moving along roads strewn with objects of great value, is not likely to hurry its step.

The primary factor in the old fox's caution, however, was neither Napoleon's genius, his own shortage of supplies, nor the gold and silver ikons and crucifixes that could be found in so many abandoned knapsacks. It was his own conviction that there was no necessity to fight a pitched battle, for the Grand Army was melting away before his eyes and if things continued as they were it seemed likely that hardly a Frenchman would survive to recross the Niemen into the Duchy of Warsaw, or Eastern Prussia. Being a Russian he was not much concerned with conserving Russian lives, but it must have seemed to him stupid to waste men and gunpowder confronting an enemy who was already as good as beaten and virtually incapable of defending himself.

Approaching Krasnoi, however, he came round to the decision that a serious attempt to end the war at a blow might be made and was prevailed upon to send General Miloradovich ahead to dispute the passage. Marching on lines parallel to the French Kutusoff had with him about ninety thousand effectives, the Russian guns being dragged on sledges, with special tackle for getting them across ravines such as the deep depression at Krasnoi. Everything pointed to a major clash, but even now nothing on the scale of Borodino resulted. The battles that followed were confused affairs, spread over a period of three days, from November 15th until the 17th.

Leaving Smolensk with the first column, consisting largely of what remained of the Old and Young Guard, plus a body of about two hundred horse (largely composed of officers and given the name of the "Doomed" or "Sacred Squadron") Napoleon marched on foot, with a much deflated Murat at his side and the other marshals of the leading division—Berthier, Bessières, Duroc and Lefèbvre—in close attendance. He carried a birch staff and wore a long greatcoat. On his head was a red velvet hood, covered with a cap of marten's fur. When they told him that Miloradovich lay ahead he did not seem much concerned, not even when the first of the balls fired from the guns sited on the heights began to fall on the column. 'Bullets have been flying round our legs these twenty years,' he said, and prepared, if necessary, to lead the attack in person.

Bourgogne, who was now present with the van and reunited with his regiment, the Fusiliers-Grenadiers, estimates the strength of the Russian advance guard at about 25,000, and his is one of the few detailed accounts of the very confused fighting during the next seventy-two hours. The first to see the enemy and conclude a battle was impending, were the stragglers ahead of the line of march and these at once turned back and rejoined the main body. One hopes that, among this group, were some of the early starters Bourgogne had encountered in the cellar at Smolensk, men who had pushed on ahead in the hope of concealing themselves in anticipation of the night's foray among portmanteaux and saddlebags.

The Grenadiers and Chasseurs formed into close columns around the Emperor and at once advanced but there was no head-on clash after all. Miloradovich's men fled and left the road open, but took up position on the heights, whence they plied the column with a continuous rain of small-calibre balls. The French, however, had not abandoned the whole of their immense artillery train, and guns were immediately brought into action to reply, among them a few pieces of General Longchamps' brigade. This checked the cannonade somewhat and after two hours Krasnoi was occupied, Bourgogne's regiment, with the Fusiliers-Chasseurs, encamping behind the town.

Napoleon now had to decide whether to push on alone or delay his march in order to give time for the rearward divisions to join him. To his credit he chose the latter alternative and it was this decision that led to a good deal more fighting, much of it hand-to-hand encounters.

All the time Kutusoff's main body was moving closer on a parallel line whereas Miloradovich, having decided that the French were by no means as helpless and demoralised as he had supposed, fell back slightly to rejoin his chief. This movement brought him into sharp collision with the following French division led by Eugène, that had quitted Smolensk on the afternoon of the 15th. Another sharp encounter resulted and it is doubtful whether Eugène would have been able to continue his march had it not been for a determined night sally on the part of the French, who had cleared the road and bivouacked. Bourgogne has vivid memories of this night encounter in which he took an active part.

Having received orders from General Roguet to rejoin his regiment and attack, he says, 'To tell the truth I was very much disgusted at this order. I do not mean I was afraid of fighting but I grudged the time lost for sleep terribly!'

He got no sleep that night. At two a.m. the French attacked in three columns, the Fusiliers-Grenadiers and the Fusiliers-Chasseurs in the centre, with two companies of skirmishers on the right and left. The cold was intense and the difficulty of advancing by night over soft snow very great. In half-an-hour, however, they ran headlong into the Russians, who opened up a murderous fire from small-arms and artillery firing grape. The infantry were supported by some heavy cavalry, cuirassiers in white uniforms with black cuirasses. Despite this formidable opposition the Guard went straight in and a terrible hand-to-hand combat was fought in the light of blazing villages.

Overrun by the speed and determination of the French attack a party of several hundred Russians adopted the well-known stratagem of stretching themselves in the snow in the hope that the Guardsmen would assume they were dead. The leading files were deceived, but as soon as the Russians rose and began to fire they were overwhelmed by a reserve battalion coming up from the rear. Not a man survived. One of the first men killed in this night encounter was Bourgogne's comrade Béloque, whom he had met on the ramparts at Smolensk when they had both listened to the thunder of the church organ.

In the blazing village beyond the Russian position the battle raged from house to house. The butchery here must have been frightful for it impressed even Bourgogne. In the thick of the fighting the Guardsman saw his colonel, the oldest in France whose battle experience went back to the engagement under the Pyramids. He also saw Adjutant-Major Roustan cutting his way out of a bayonet fight with a sword. A sizeable party of Russians offered to surrender, but although Adjutant-Major Roustan ordered the French to stop firing some of them refused and the Russians died when the building in which they were barricaded caught fire.

Having lost all sense of direction in the ebb and flow of the battle and the glare of the blazing villages the Fusiliers-Chasseurs stayed where they were and remained on the battlefield throughout the 16th and 17th, when another bloody engagement took place.

.   .   .

Eugène's division, isolated between Krasnoi and Smolensk, was battling its way towards the leading division almost yard by yard and against impossible odds.

Cheated of the big catch Miloradovich strained every nerve to drag something into the net, attacking the Fourth Corps almost from the hour it emerged from Smolensk. Yet once again the Russian commander underestimated the staying power of the French, and the tenacious courage of Napoleon's stepson.

Other people had made this mistake about Eugène, supposing that the ties of loyalty to the Emperor had been weakened by the divorce of Josephine and that cynicism had replaced the respect and admiration he had entertained for the man who had married his mother when Eugène was a boy of fifteen.[1] They were wrong, then and later. Eugène was still Napoleon's man and was to remain so, long after the myth of his invincibility had been exploded. His loyalty was never in question, not for a moment, and when a fortnight later the King of Naples turned his back on the demoralised French army it was Eugène Beauharnais, the son of a man who had died under the guillotine, who replaced him and returned to France with a reputation second only to that of Michel Ney.

Eugène was thirty-one years of age when he faced this particular challenge and had already seen as much active service as any of the men he led across the snow towards Krasnoi. At seventeen, when he was acting as aide-de-camp to General Bonaparte in Egypt, he had been obliged to witness his stepfather's involvement with Pauline Fourès, an officer's wife and ride beside her carriage when the grenadiers greeted the blonde adventuress with ironic shouts of 'Vive Cléopatre!' Later, when his mother's tomfoolery brought her within an inch of divorce, he had added his pleas to hers and those of his sister Hortense, and had won Josephine a nine-year respite.[2] Since then, grave, silent and attentive to duty, he had served in a dozen campaigns, proving by far the most intelligent puppet ruler Napoleon had established in a conquered capital. As Viceroy of Italy he had shown administrative ability equal to his ability in the field, and his devotion to France, to the Empire, and to Napoleon personally, had withstood the shock of the Imperial divorce. Napoleon had no better servant, unless it was Davout, and now these two were within a day's march of one another, each making his way through an angry, cheated, watchful enemy, each quietly determined to rejoin the vanguard of the Grand Army even if they did so alone and on foot.

Eugène lost very heavily during the running fight, but every attempt on the part of the Russians to block his path failed. When a position had to be stormed it was stormed. When the way seemed open but a murderous shower of balls fell on the column from gun-sites on the flanks, the men of the Fourth Corps marched on, carrying their wounded and keeping formation. Even so Eugène was lucky. By the end of the second day his strength was reduced to less than half and ahead was another entrenched wedge of Russians waiting for daybreak to renew the battle. The Viceroy knew that his remnant could not survive a frontal attack and decided to gamble all on a night march around the periphery of the enemy's position. It meant marching across knee-keep snow in the darkness but it was his only chance. The ruse succeeded by a perilously narrow margin.

Watchfires were replenished and left burning to deceive Russian outposts, but one alert sentry, hearing the prolonged squelch of men struggling through snow-drifts, shouted a challenge. Eugène's Polish orderly saved all that remained of the Corps. Approaching the sentry he said, in faultless Russian, 'Quiet, you fool! We are a detached group out on a secret expedition!' The sentry was satisfied. Eugène and his survivors skirted the position, rejoined the road and met the Emperor beyond Krasnoi. They mustered 4,000 men, perhaps two-fifths of the number that had left Smolensk on the afternoon of the 15th.

Two more divisions still remained to cut their way through; Davout's reorganised First Corps, and Ney with his reconstituted rearguard of almost 10,000. Beyond the ravine, with the dead of three days' fighting already buried under drifting snow, Napoleon waited with superhuman patience. Every second counted. He had no hard news from Oudinot and Victor regarding the safety of the crossings of the Dnieper or the Beresina. At any hour Wittgenstein and Tchitchagoff might unite, perhaps had already united and occupied Borissov on the Beresina. Every discharge of hovering Russian artillery reduced the chances of survival, of bringing even the wreck of his battalions home to France. Yet he waited and his faith in Davout was justified. On the afternoon of the 17th the marshal's division was seen marching across open ground surrounded by swarms of Cossacks. They marched in square, calmly and almost silently, as though the troops of horsemen hanging on their flanks had been swarms of flies able to pester but not equipped to sting. Kutusoff made another attempt, abandoning Davout's men and detaching cavalry ahead of the route to take up another intercepting position on the main road. He was just too late. A battalion of the Old Guard was already there and the Russian cavalry drew off, not caring to come within bayonet range of these iron men. The three divisions closed up, Napoleon's, technically commanded by Murat, Eugène's and Davout's. Together they advanced, scattering the last of Kutusoff's troops, the leaders marching with arms linked. There could be no question of waiting another day for Ney. Ney and his 10,000 were given up for lost.

They did not get off without more casualties. Thoroughly alive now to the prospect of his prey escaping, of forcing the passage of two rivers and withdrawing into the Duchy of Warsaw, Kutusoff and Miloradovich made another great effort, hanging on the rear of the marching battalions like packs of wolves and bombarding them with grapeshot. Veterans who had survived every hazard of the march died at Krasnoi, for only the walking wounded could be taken along and Bourgogne reports that the cries of the abandoned were pitiful, for most of them were stripped and left to die within sight of their comrades. The French passed a ravine choked with dead oxen, carcasses that might have sustained them as far as the Niemen but were now frozen stiff. They had died from want of fodder. That night the sergeant was again fortunate in a chance encounter. He met a friend who was marching with a Hungarian cantinière and they gave him a little oatmeal broth and some horseflesh. It was two days since he had eaten.

And yet, despite all trials, the spirit of the Grand Army was not yet broken. Once again they had succeeded in cutting a path through vastly superior numbers and infinitely greater fire-power than they were able to bring upon the enemy. Very few guns were left. Even the gallant Longchamps, whose salvoes had saved the rearguard in the last stage of the battle, was forced to abandon his pieces for want of horses to draw them. The rear of the main body was now covered by Roeder's Hessians.

An example of the fortitude and ingenuity displayed by some of the veterans can be found in the story of Dragoon Mellé, a man from Condé and one of Bourgogne's old comrades. That same night he appeared at the miserable bivouac on his horse Cadet, a mount that had carried him through the Prussian and Polish campaigns, across Spain, throughout all the bloody Danube fighting of 1809, down into Spain again with Masséna, and across Europe once more to Moscow. Mellé was leading a Russian prisoner. To provide for his horse he had just made one of several night raids on the Russian camp and come away with fodder and, as he said, 'a witness'. His theory was if he looked after the horse Cadet would get him home and this proved to be the case. Mellé did get home but Cadet was killed in one of the great cavalry charges at Waterloo, thirty months later. At a subsequent stage in the retreat Bourgogne saw the dragoon breaking the ice of a pond in order that Cadet could get water. 'With a dozen men like these,' Ney was to say some miles further on, 'I don't give a damn for all the Cossacks in Europe!'

Accomplishing the almost suicidal task of covering the rear, Captain Roeder actually marched back along the Smolensk road towards the enemy. In one engagement

with the Russian cavalry his regiment (apparently augmented) lost ten officers and 119 men. Roeder's feet were
dangerously swollen and his hands frostbitten, but he went
on fighting and retreating, living upon what he could find
in the pockets of the dead, including those of his own cook
who, killed by a cannon ball, provided enough coffee for
six cups at the next bivouac. For extra warmth the Captain
wrapped himself in the tatters of a blood-stained fur coat
that had been cut and slashed by projectiles.

But the last word on this stage of the retreat rests with
the plodding Bourgogne and it has a wryness that perhaps
explains why this man, who fought in every part of
Europe, did not consider any other campaign worthy of recording when he was a prisoner of war a year later. 'I could
never discover,' he says, 'what these peasants lived on. Our
men would come back sometimes bringing bits of bread as
black as coal and filled with long pieces of straw and grains
of barley, so terribly hard that no teeth could bite into
them; and besides, our lips were all split and cracked by
frost. During all this miserable campaign I never saw a
man bring so much as a cow or a sheep with him. What
these savages live on no one can tell. They have no beasts,
that is certain, or we should have seen some. It is the devil's
own country, for it is a hell all through.'

CHAPTER SIX

'IF NECESSARY I MARCH ALONE!'

Ney at Krasnoi, November 1812

1

SOLDIERS are only civilians in uniform and even a strong military tradition, a high code of honour or the ingrained habit of discipline does not necessarily make them more courageous or even hardier than civilians with a cause. Yet the military history of a people often seems to prove the opposite and the pitiless record of war across the centuries is so often relieved by brilliant flashes of personal achievement that they have the effect of diverting the eye from the misery that humanity has suffered, and still suffers, under the scourge of war.

Such a flash is provided by Leonidas, holding the pass of Thermopylae against the Persians; by the Spartan's namesake, Leonidas Polk,[1] last of the warrior-bishops, who fell in the American Civil War; by the dogged endurance of French, British and German trench veterans on the Western Front, between 1914-18; and, to approach more closely to our own time, the miraculous rescue of the British Army at Dunkirk and the achievements of Churchill's "few" in the air-battles of the same summer.

Such a flash, illuminating the entire catastrophe of the Retreat from Moscow, is the courage of Michel Ney and his band of starving cripples, between November 16th and 20th, 1812.

.   .   .

Quitting the bloody fields and ravines around Krasnoi on the 17th, Napoleon and the closed-up divisions of Eugène and Davout had resigned themselves to the loss of the most popular subordinate commander in the Grand Army. He was now at least two days' march behind and since the morning of the 16th nothing had been heard of him. Between him and what was left of the army were approximately 80,000 Russians, well served with artillery and flanked by both heavy and light cavalry. It had cost the three leading divisions half their effective strength to force a passage beyond Krasnoi. What hope could there be for Ney and his contingent of upwards of 10,000 men, most of them wounded or frostbitten and all of them at the point of starvation?

Napoleon had waited as long as he dared and longer than it was safe to wait. When he set out again for the Dnieper crossing at Orcha he despaired of ever seeing Ney again and his certainty in this respect was shared by Berthier, Murat and all the other Marshals. Unjustly Davout was blamed for abandoning Ney to his fate. Davout's own escape had been a miracle and no blame at all can be attached to him for making his own way towards the van, without detaching a body of men to await the rearguard. He could not have afforded to sacrifice a single file for this purpose and even if he had they would have been cut down or driven away as prisoners long before they made contact with Ney's advanced guard.

So the main body struck out for the elbow of the Dnieper, expecting to hear, by one means or another, that Ney, recently created Prince of the Moskowa in recognition of his heroic work at the Great Redoubt, was a prisoner in the hands of Kutusoff and on his way as a trophy to the Tsar at St. Petersburg. That this did not happen is entirely due to Ney himself.

He was a strange, unpredictable man, admittedly hot-tempered and jealous, perhaps to the point of pedantry, of his honour. He had made enemies during his rise from hussar to marshal of France, for he often said and did things his essentially generous nature regretted within the hour. Nobody, however, doubted his integrity or his personal courage. What amazed Europe when it heard of his achievements during these next four days was his incredible physical hardihood and the hypnotic effect he exerted over the minds of the men he led. There were a very large number of brave officers in the Napoleonic armies but not one of them could have extricated himself from the situation in which Ney found himself on the night of November 16th, much less led the survivors of the rearguard to safety.[2]

Ney was attacked in Smolensk before he set out in pursuit of Davout's division. Cossacks stormed into the suburbs and large bodies of Russian troops were already closing in on the only road to Krasnoi. Ney first made it his business to collect and encourage every straggler, every man capable of walking a step and when he had mustered them he set out to force his way through any opposition awaiting him beyond the city gates. About 6,000 wounded had to be left behind.

He was immediately engaged and the opposition hardened every hour. Frustrated in their successive assaults upon Napoleon, Eugène and Davout, the Russians were determined to make certain of at least one illustrious prisoner, Orders went out to stop Ney at all costs and when Russian cavalry came within range of the miserable procession it must have seemed to them that it could be overwhelmed by a single determined attack. The reputation of its commander, however, was very high in the Russian camp and thrice thwarted Miloradovich was taking no chances. He fortified the vacated areas around Krasnoi and confined his offensive to probing flank attacks until Ney should march into a death-trap where the road ahead was blocked by infantry and every piece of rising ground was sited with cannon.

Ney reached this impregnable barrier on the second day of his march and at once attacked, notwithstanding a message that reached him from Davout, urging him to break off contact and march round the Russian flank if that was possible.

The attack failed as it was bound to do, although Ney's

leading assault column penetrated the first line and captured two Russian guns. Their own artillery was now reduced to six pieces but these were soon put out of action by the thunderous Russian cannonade. Ney attacked again and then again, leading his men in person with the same desperate courage he had shown in the assault on the redoubt at Borodino and on many other fields in the past. It was useless. His men withered away under the accurate gunnery of the Russian artillerymen who were firing 200 guns from fixed sites. As the short winter's day drew to a close Ney realised that penetration of the Russian position, even if achieved, would be pointless. It would cost him the life of every man in the rearguard.

In the early evening Miloradovich, a generous man and one who made no attempt to hide his admiration of French gallantry, sent an officer under a flag of truce. He offered Ney surrender with the honours of war. The message was couched in almost apologetic terms. Ney refused to entertain such a proposal and returned the same answer to two other staff officers who arrived later. Nineteenth-century historians, made aware of Ney's obstinacy by De Ségur's account published after the fall of the Empire, have made a great deal of this incident, putting words into Ney's mouth that are reminiscent of Roland or Sir Walter Manny in a more chivalrous age. He is alleged to have said, 'A marshal of France never surrenders!' and it is just possible that he made some such remark. It is far more likely, however, that he replied in less exalted terms, saying, as someone present at the parley declares, 'No surrender! My sword will get me out of this!'

Marbot, who was operating with Oudinot far to the west at this time, tells another story of the negotiations. He says that Ney was so incensed by the demand for surrender that he refused to acknowledge the flag of truce but declared the envoy a spy and threatened to kill him if he did not guide them to the Dnieper. It does not sound very probable. Such an action would be uncharacteristic of Ney, who was a strict observer of the etiquette of war.

Before the truce parties had retired the Russian artillery opened up again. The French position seemed utterly hopeless.

And so it would have been if anyone but Michel Ney had been in command. Even a man of Davout's iron nerve would probably have surrendered, given honourable terms and a promise to care for his sick and wounded. But Ney was incapable of admitting himself beaten; he had old-fashioned notions of a soldier's duty, particularly a soldier charged with the command of a rearguard. He could not and would not bring himself to the point of surrender not even to save the lives of the helpless wretches crouching over their bivouac fires, knowing that the first light would mean a choice of death or years of captivity in this wilderness.

The hills continued to erupt like volcanoes. The rearguard had now shrunk to about 1,500 effectives and 2,000 to 3,000 wounded. Ney summoned his staff, half-a-dozen desperate men in burned, tattered uniforms. Icicles hung on their beards. Not one among them had eaten a square meal for a month.

'We march back towards Smolensk!' Ney said, briefly.

They were too astonished to protest. They stood round him in the punishing wind and reading into their silence a rejection of this monstrous proposal Ney added, 'If necessary I march alone!'

They knew this was not a gesture. They were not dealing with Murat, who led charges with a gold-tipped wand, or Victor, who would bluster and then commit them to some hopeless manoeuvre. This was Ney, always to be found out with the skirmishers' line, the man who, as one horse was shot under him, would bellow for another and press home the attack. They knew that if his example failed to inspire them he would indeed set off, a solitary figure in a cocked hat, towards the city they had just left. They made ready to obey the order.

The bivouac fires were built up, the troops got under arms. With the minimum of fuss and noise the little column turned its back on the enemy and took the debris-cluttered road to Smolensk. They were heading straight back into hell but what was the alternative with a man like Ney in command?

2

They did not march very far on familiar ground. Out of sight and sound of the Russian outposts they took a new track, north of the main road, and when someone asked where they were heading Ney said, 'To the Dnieper. We must put the river between us and the enemy!' They had thought him mad and here was confirmation. The Emperor was known to be heading for Orcha, on the wide bend of the river, but at Orcha, that lay well beyond Krasnoi, there were bridges and the nearest Russian army, discounting Kutusoff's, was much further west in the area of the Beresina, or away to the north, in the vicinity of Polotsk. There was no bridge in this direction save that at Smolensk and that had been in enemy hands when they left the city.

'How do you intend crossing?' someone asked at length.

'On the ice!' Ney said. He could be a talkative man and sometimes in the past he had talked too much, but since leaving Moscow he had become very taciturn. It is recorded by those near him during the march out of Russia that he spoke very little and only then to encourage failing men with exhortations or to jeer at the encircling Cossacks.

'Suppose,' he was asked, 'the river is not frozen?'

It was a pertinent question. Ever since the rearguard's arrival in Smolensk on the 13th the temperature had been much higher than during the early stages of the retreat.

'It will be frozen,' Ney said.

But first the Dnieper had to be found. They were marching in almost total darkness, by guesswork it might be said, but a signpost was there for those with sense enough to follow it. They broke the ice on a stream and noted which way the current flowed.

'This stream will lead us to the Dnieper,' said Ney, and they marched on, the few waggons loaded with wounded creaking along in the rear. In this way, long before daylight, they reached the big river and here they found their first crumb of comfort. They encountered a lame peasant, the only person they met during the march, and the man told them that although, as Ney's aide had suspected, the river was not frozen hard, there was a sharp bend where floating ice had piled up during the colder weather of the previous week and here, if care was exercised, the river could be crossed.

Ney was desperate but he was not to be hurried. He ordered three hours' rest before the crossing was attempted and then, wrapping himself in his cloak, lay down and slept on the bank. 'Like a child,' comments someone who saw him sleeping.

It was still dark when the crossing began. The men went over in single file, sometimes stepping from floe to floe, the stronger assisting the weaker. One man, an officer called Brigueville, found himself on a floating piece of ice and in danger of being carried downstream. He was personally saved by the marshal. The waggons, together with baggage and all but the walking wounded, were abandoned. It was a terrible decision to make but there was no hope of getting an injured man across and the passage of wheeled transport was out of the question.

Once across the rearguard began to perform a wide, semi-circular march towards Orcha that lay more than fifty miles downstream of Smolensk. The ground over which they passed was partly open, partly wooded and wherever possible Ney stuck to the woods. Cossacks who had followed their tracks to the river pursued them at a distance. Other parties of Cossacks, commanded by the famous Platoff, were known to be on this side of the Dnieper and before long the French came within sight of their main camp. They marched on as if it had not been there and no attack was made, probably because Platoff had no accurate information regarding their strength but according to one authority because he was sleeping off a debauch and nobody dared awaken him. Whatever the reason they got past unchallenged and continued marching on Orcha, beating off any attempts made upon their rearward files. The Cossacks snapped up a few stragglers or dying men but that was all.

It was not until they were almost within sight of Orcha that they had to face a determined attack by Platoff's men. Cossacks were now closing in on the column in ever increasing numbers. Whenever possible Ney sought the cover of woods but once or twice, caught in the open, he formed square and continued marching. They had no artillery and powder for the muskets was running short. In another day they would have had nothing but their bayonets.

But now they were within reach of help and a Polish officer, Pechebendowski, mounted on one of the few horses that had crossed the river, forged ahead, bringing the incredible news that Marshal Ney had fought his way through but needed immediate assistance. 'The news,' says Caulaincourt, 'was received at headquarters like that of a famous victory!' Not since sighting the gilded domes of Moscow from Mont du Salut in early September had the Grand Army received such a boost in morale. The news was relayed from billet to billet. Ney had got through. Ney was almost within range and needed help. Exhausted men, snatching a few hours' rest before starting on the next leg of the endless journey, jumped up and buckled on their cartridge belts. Napoleon was overjoyed. The day before, counting Ney lost, he had said, 'I have millions in gold in the Tuileries. I would give it all to save him!' It was not gold that Ney needed at that moment but instant succour and he got it from Eugène and Mortier, who rushed out to meet him. 'It was a national event,' continues Caulaincourt, 'for it seemed to us now that the French were invincible!'

The rearguard, 900 strong, marched in. Sheer will-power and complete confidence in the man who led them had enabled them to achieve the impossible. The mere presence of Ney had brought them to Orcha.[8]

CHAPTER SEVEN

'HE IS SHORT, PALE, HAS A THICK NECK AND BLACK HAIR...'

Russian 'wanted' description of Napoleon

1

GENERAL TCHICHAGOFF, conqueror of Minsk, was an optimist. He believed good news when he heard any and usually acted upon it. They had told him that Schwartzenberg, the Austrian, would not oppose him and so it proved. Schwartzenberg let him pass and he had captured Minsk and Minsk was only about two days' march south of the line of retreat.

Word now reached him that the Grand Army was a disorderly rabble and Tchichagoff saw no reason why either old Kutusoff, his second-in-command Miloradovich or the stubborn Wittgenstein operating in the north, should pass into Russian history as the man who had captured the great Napoleon and all his marshals in the month of November 1812. His own army was in good heart. It had, beside plenty of effectives, a great number of guns and an immense train of store waggons, loaded with everything the troops could want from smoked fish down to new boots. There seemed to Tchichagoff no profit in hanging about Minsk waiting for Kutusoff to herd the enemy towards him, or to co-operate, to any great extent, with Wittgenstein, now reinforced by General Steingel. He made up his mind to advance on the Beresina with all speed and gain a famous and final victory. He was so certain that he would catch Napoleon that he issued yet another police description of the man in case the ignorant peasants under his command should fail to recognise the prisoner when he was brought to bay. The description was headed, "*The*

Author of All Europe's Miseries"; and read, "He is short, pale, has a short neck and black hair." This detail attended to, the Russian general put his army in motion.

It was a bold but not particularly rash decision. All that month reports had been coming in describing the disintegration of the Grand Army, of its immense losses in men and material, of its abandonment, near Krasnoi, of Imperial treasure and its few remaining guns, of its thousands of dismounted troopers struggling towards the frontier in heavy riding boots, wholly unsuitable for long marches over snow and ice.

On the other hand the Russians were gaining in strength every day. They were now fielding three armies, each superior in numbers and equipment to the shrinking French columns. Kutusoff, cautious though he was, had more than enough weight to push the Imperial army out of Russia without assistance, and Wittgenstein, having expelled the Second Corps from Polotsk and joined forces with Steingel, could now place himself across the route if the French veered north-west to avoid the oncoming Tchichagoff.

The key to the whole situation was the Beresina, which ran south in this area to join the Dnieper. It was not much of an obstacle to an army as experienced as Napoleon's, and would have barely delayed them had they been equipped with pontoons of the kind used in the crossing of the Danube three years before. Tchichagoff, however, very much doubted if the Grand Army had dragged its bridging equipment thus far and his guess was quite accurate. The pontoons had been destroyed at Orcha, for Napoleon meant to cross the Beresina at Borissov and Borissov had a good bridge and a fort, both held by the Pole, Dombrowski.

Tchichagoff's plan was to storm Borissov, capture the bridge and effectively block any further progress by Napoleon. As far as it went the plan was excellent and had, indeed, the approval of the Tsar and his advisers at St. Petersburg. Orders had already gone out to Kutusoff to

maintain pressure on the French rear, others to Wittgenstein and Steingel to hurry south from the Polotsk area
and make a junction with Tchichagoff's army of the
Danube. There was no further need to take Schwartzenberg's Austrians into account. Schwartzenberg could be re-
lied upon to give the French no help at all.

To guard against this convergence on the part of the
Russian armies Napoleon had, in this area, about 20,000
men, made up of Oudinot's reduced corps, now numbering
about 8,000 and Victor's Ninth Corps, numbering about
12,000. Both corps were in good heart, however, and
Oudinot was strong in cavalry. His colonels had used the
lull in fighting between the two battles of Polotsk to bring
in the remounts and sweep the country for supplies of
fodder and oxen. Marbot, the best authority on the fighting on the northern flank of the Grand Army, is a good
example of the type of officer the marshal had about him.
Anticipating the severe Russian winter he had ordered
every trooper in the 23rd Chasseurs to equip himself with a
sheepskin coat. During the hot weather the men grumbled
at the unnecessary bulk of these jerkins but they had cause
to be grateful to their commander in the next few weeks,
Marbot's regiment was the only one to emerge from the
campaign with a full muster roll. In addition to taking
great pains to see his men were well fed and adequately
clothed against the cold, he had sent all his dismounted
men back to Warsaw where there were plenty of horses
awaiting riders. This party not only augmented the regiment when the retreat was over, it proved an invaluable
reinforcement for the German campaign in the following
spring.

.   .   .

In the third week of November Tchichagoff launched
his eastward attack and at first everything went splendidly
for him. Dombrowski, facing overwhelming strength at
Borissov, abandoned the town and fell back towards Orcha,
hoping to rejoin the van of the Grand Army. Had he

waited another day or so Oudinot would have come to his assistance and when he met the marshal on the march Oudinot was furious to learn that Borissov was now in Russian hands. Realising that the town and bridge were vital to the French he at once despatched a regiment of cuirassiers to ride ahead and reconnoitre, at the same time hurrying his march with the intention of throwing Tchichagoff back to the western bank. To their astonishment the cuirassiers ran headlong into the Russian vanguard under General Lambert. The battle for the crossing was joined.

It was soon clear what had occurred. Tchichagoff, in his anxiety to win his place in history, had stormed beyond Borissov, determined to challenge the Grand Army without awaiting support from the north and east. In his eagerness to force a decision he made the worst mistake a general could make. Not only did he allow his vanguard to advance far beyond the town, placing a river, spanned by a single bridge, between itself and supporting infantry, he went on to make things a great deal worse by permitting his baggage train to cross in advance of the main body.

The Russian general paid a heavy price for his folly. Oudinot's cuirassiers bore down on the advance guard and routed it in five minutes. The survivors wheeled and galloped for the shelter of the fort but en route they ran into the baggage train and the mêlée resulting put the entire column at the mercy of the French. The heavy cavalry of Oudinot, their big horses blown by the charge, reined in to let the 23rd and 24th Chasseurs through and soon the leading contingents of Tchichagoff's army were tumbling back across the bridge in the greatest disorder, harried by Colonels Marbot and Castex, commanding the best equipped and best disciplined light horsemen in the Grand Army at that time.

The chasseurs did not turn aside to pillage the baggage train but rode right on to the bridge, desperately anxious to secure it and ensure the safety of the army. Tchichagoff, no less eager to keep control of the crossing and put himself out of range of this surprisingly aggressive rabble of fugitives, gave orders for the bridge to be fired. Russian infantrymen succeeded in setting it alight while the chasseurs, pressing home their attack, dismounted and peppered them with carbine fire.

Had the French infantrymen been given time to come up in support the bridge would have remained intact and in Oudinot's hands and the history of the campaign would have taken a turn in favour of Napoleon but the advance of the cavalry had been so rapid that the nearest grenadiers were still three leagues back along the road. Marbot's men did their best, and even succeeded in extinguishing the fire before it got a hold, but a column of Russian infantrymen counter-attacked and drove them back to the eastern bank where, having no bayonets, they could make no headway until reinforcements arrived. Ten minutes later the bridge was in flames and the exit of the Grand Army was blocked. Oudinot held the town but Tchichagoff's army was now massed just across the river. There being no means of crossing, the engagement ended. With despair in his heart Oudinot sent a despatch-rider towards Orcha to inform Napoleon of the news.

Neither the marshal nor his subordinate commanders were under any illusion of what the loss of the bridge entailed, but the troopers who had taken part in the fight found some consolation in the immense train of waggons the Russians had abandoned in their flight. Marbot puts the number of wheeled carts at 1,500 but this is probably an exaggeration. It was, however, a most fortunate capture for it was found that the waggons contained an immense variety of stores. There were furs, boots, hams, pies, meat, cheese, wines, biscuit, rice and many other provisions. In addition there were all the horses harnessed to the train. Most of them were in splendid condition and could be used as remounts for the worn-out horses of the cavalry.

Oudinot had been a grenadier himself, He knew the disorder that would almost certainly prevail in his corps if the troops were given permission to help themselves. Within minutes discipline would break down and quarrels would flare up. Accordingly he staked off the line of waggons and placed them under guard, issuing instructions that under no circumstances whatever were articles other than clothing and food to be taken out and shared among the men. Then, knowing that Victor was guarding his right flank against a descent by Wittgenstein, he sat down to await the arrival of the Moscow fugitives.

2

On November 18th Napoleon had written to Maret, his Foreign Minister, from the village of Dubrovna, and his letter was an unusually frank appraisal of the main body's situation and prospects.

Commenting on the loss of Minsk, two days before, and asking (as well he might) after the whereabouts of Schwartzenberg, he went on to admit that the army was in very poor shape after its long, fighting withdrawal from Moscow. Sixteen degrees of frost, he said, had accounted for 30,000 men and 300 pieces of artillery, together with their ammunition caissons, had been burned. 'In consequence of the cold the number of men left behind has greatly increased. The Cossacks have taken advantage of our absolute lack of cavalry and artillery to harrass us and cut our communications, so that I am somewhat uneasy about Marshal Ney ... apart from that, a few days' rest and good food will set us on our feet ... we cannot get an ammunition waggon or a gun up the smallest ravine without losing twelve to fifteen horses and wasting twelve to fifteen hours, whereas they (the enemy) with their skates and their specially made contrivances, move it more quickly than if there was no ice.' He went on to instruct Maret to send news of Paris and see what artillery could be got together at Kovno and Vilna.

Two days after writing this letter he was relieved of his main anxiety, the possible capture of Ney, so that the following day, the 21st, he left Orcha and headed directly for Borissov, knowing nothing of what had occurred there after the advance of Tchichagoff. He did not, at that time, know of the whereabouts of Victor's Ninth Corps but assumed it was carrying out his last orders to keep the northern flank open, so that he could cross the Beresina and march on Vilna.

.   .   .

For the survivors of Krasnoi the march to the Beresina via Orcha was another terrible experience. The journey occupied most of them exactly a week, but in spite of the fact that Orcha, three days' march from Krasnoi and four from the Beresina, was able to supply a certain amount of food, the plight of the men was a good deal worse than it had been during the bitter weather preceding their arrival in Smolensk. Temperatures were relatively mild, at least for the first part of the march, but the half-thaw made the roads treacherous and Captain Roeder, still marching with the rearguard, complains of deep slush that impeded their progress every step of the way.

The climate, and the terrible exertions he had undergone since reuniting with the main body, were beginning to tell on Roeder. He had a bad cough and a bout of dysentery. There was practically nothing to eat and, although snow had ceased to fall and the day temperatures were relatively mild, the nights were bitterly cold and the scattered bivouacs cheerless.

Even so he was luckier than most. He was able to buy three platefuls of groats from one of his troopers for the sum of three francs and, in addition to the coffee he had taken from his dead cook, he found some sugar in the pockets of a dead French officer beside the road. Nothing better illustrates the plight to which these men were reduced than Roeder's casual rifling of a dead man's kit. In happier circumstances he had been a proud, rather pedantic officer, but a march under these conditions proved a great leveller. All the way from Smolensk to Vilna he was as self-centred and mendacious as a conscript. He made soup and drank coffee whenever he could and when he was marching along in the slush he sucked pieces of sugar, only occasionally sparing a little for less fortunate comrades. Even then he regretted his generosity. 'I was more liberal than I should have been,' he comments glumly.

There was no opposition to the crossing of the Dnieper (many of the French called this river by its old name, the Borysthenes) where the bridge was intact, although coated with ice. Roeder's pony slipped and fell and had it been less intelligent an animal he would have been thrown under the wheels of passing waggons. He struggled into the town in pitiable condition, relieved to find that small amounts of flour and brandy were being distributed from the magazines previously established there. The spirit issue did not do the starving men much good. Some of them, drinking on empty stomachs, became so drunk that they were unable to carry away the flour.

With the miraculous arrival of Ney on the 20th, the main body pushed on for the Beresina, moving out on the 21st. The next four days of marching were sheer hell to officers and men alike, for the weather worsened and the north wind got up, driving showers of sleet and snow upon the trailing column. Sometimes the brief storms were so fierce that they could not see where they were going and walked in involuntary circles.

Roeder's long-suffering pony, seeking a drink at a water-hole, fell in and was drowned, and Roeder himself was thrown into the freezing water. He got out, however, and trudged on, still suffering terribly from dysentery.

At the village of Losznetza Napoleon received the bad news from Borissov, taken by Tchichagoff on the 21st. He had no means of knowing, as yet, that Oudinot had retaken the town within forty-eight hours and captured enough stores to fortify the survivors for the next stage of the march. The Emperor's nerve proved equal to the strain. Commenting grimly, 'We seem to do nothing but make mistakes,' he at once ordered all his papers to be burned, together with some of the eagles, standards which some regiments had carried since that far-off day in 1796, when the young Napoleon had led them to victory at Castiglione and opened the gates of Milan. Then the army marched on, hoping for another miracle like the reappearance of Ney.

The road now lay through immense forests and more open sections of highway lined with giant birch trees. In this part of Russia birches grow to a great height and their branches provided firewood when there were insufficient broken carts and ruined houses along the route. Hearing gunfire the advance guard concluded Wittgenstein's army must have made its way south and joined up with the army of Tchichagoff, but a scouting party, sent on in advance, returned with cheering news. The gunfire had been Marshal Victor's, still checking the southerly advance of the northern Russian army, and soon the two groups intermingled, Victor's men staring with amazement at the emaciated wrecks who had tramped all the way from Moscow.

.   .   .

For another account of this section of the retreat we turn to Bourgogne, who was a straggler most of the time and only survived this week because he had far more than his share of luck and stamina. He too comments on the thaw but says the nights were almost unendurably cold. He withstood them because, a long way further back, he had found a bearskin which he now turned with the fur inside but the effort of getting along in the teeth of the wind taxed his strength to the utmost. To survive successive nights on the march one had to be pitiless, At one point, where men ahead, Italians and Germans, had taken shelter in a church, Bourgogne joined a party of French who threw them out and took their places. In the morning most of the men ejected were lying dead in the snow. At Orcha Bourgogne had a chance of assessing the cost of the retreat so far. The Guard, he says, arrived in the town 7,000 to

8,000 strong. When it had set out for Moscow in late June it had mustered 35,000 and it had taken no part in the bloody battle of Borodino.

He pushed on the following day, with the Emperor and the Doomed Squadron marching well ahead. On the 22nd, at Toloczin, he met a woman whom he had encountered in the thieves' cellar at Smolensk and travelled with her for a time. He also met his friend Grangier, but in the confusion he soon lost contact with both. The terrible sights he witnessed were beginning to sap his morale and the loss of old comrades in the Krasnoi engagements affected him as similar losses had never done in the past. He still witnessed, however, instances of loyalty and comradeship that were able to touch him. A day's march out of Orcha a sledge passed him carrying a wounded officer escorted by four of his men, probably all he had left. The men were staking their own survival on the prospect of bringing their helpless commander to safety. Despite their appalling plight men of the Guard, and even less dedicated troops, could still demonstrate their loyalty to Napoleon. When news of the loss of the bridge at Borissov reached the vanguard, and the Emperor made a personal address to the troops assuring them of his determination to fight their way to the frontier, Bourgogne says: 'It was a splendid moment and for a time made us forget our miseries!' Marshal Mortier also made a wayside appeal and both speakers were cheered.

Bourgogne was not the only man whose spirit was sometimes braced by adversity. Among the crowd of officers at one halting place was old Marshal Lefèbvre, whose campaigning went back to pre-Revolution days, when he had been a hussar in the Bourbon army. As long ago as 1791 he had commanded the escort conducting Louis XVI and his family back to Paris after their abortive attempt to escape over the frontier. At the time of the Russian campaign he was fifty-six years of age, an old man to be sleeping out in twenty-two degrees of frost and living on horseflesh and sips of Danzic gin. Yet Lefèbvre had not lost his courage and was not to lose it later on. At a halting place on the road between Orcha and the Beresina Bourgogne heard him urging stragglers to close up and march as a body, saying, in his strong Alsatian accent, 'Stay together! Better large battalions than a pack of brigands or cowards!' A few days later, at the crossing of the Beresina, Marbot heard him making the same appeal to a rabble of stragglers awaiting their turn to cross.

By now, however, even the toughest of the veterans were beginning to wonder whether there was much chance of escape from this devil's country. Bourgogne's experiences between November 22nd and 25th, the time it took him to march from Toloczin to the river, are typical of those of most stragglers but with this difference; not one in a hundred of the men who underwent them survived to tell the tale. Bourgogne's survival is a saga in miniature.

On the evening of the 22nd he found himself, as darkness fell, walking almost alone, with men collapsing in front and behind, and no comrades at hand to sustain and encourage him. Soon a terrible sleepiness, the certain fore-runner of death, overtook him and he constantly fell, sometimes because of sheer exhaustion, at other times when he stumbled over a corpse or a piece of debris. Men too weak to rise tried to grab at his legs and when he turned aside to see if he could help one of them the poor wretch received his offer with howls of insane laughter. The impact of this and similar encounters made the sergeant burst into tears and the tears, he says, brought a curious relief so that he again found strength to go on.

He tried to hack a piece of flesh from a dead horse but it was frozen hard and he had not sufficient strength to do it, even though he used a hatchet. He did, however, salvage some pieces of frozen horse blood which he sucked and then stored carefully in his knapsack. Thus far had a veteran of the Guard been reduced in just over a month— from hoarding gold to pieces of ice.

At length he made up his mind to spend the night in an

abandoned waggon. The cantinière to whom it belonged was stretched dead beside the vehicle and the horses were dead between the shafts. Inside was another dead man and a soldier with an amputated leg, who cried out for water. Bourgogne placed a fragment of frozen blood between his lips but the man was beyond human aid; he died in Bourgogne's presence. At this same spot the guardsman slipped from the shafts and fell among a pile of bodies, his face touching a dead man's hand, the thumb penetrating his mouth. The isolation and the hopelessness of his plight, reacted upon him in a curious way. At first he was horrified but a moment later he was in a transport of rage, cursing the sky, the wind, the army, Russia and everything about him and trampling and kicking the bodies at his feet.

When he became calmer he pushed on, although it was now almost pitch dark and seven in the evening. He rolled forty feet down a slope and landed beside a ditched waggon of the Imperial Guard and, providentially, on the almost extinct remains of a fire. With a wisp of his shirt and tiny fragments of wood he relighted the fire. Finding horsemeat at hand he cooked a piece and prepared to spend the night with his feet to the fire and his back to the waggon. But his adventures that night were by no means over. A wounded Cossack crawled up to him, horribly slashed about the face and with a musket ball in his belly. Then a huge white figure emerged from the waggon and Bourgogne, his nerves at breaking point, took it for a ghost. It was not a ghost but an old comrade called Picart, who had marched well in advance of the army all the way from Moscow while escorting a convoy of Imperial waggons. The ghostly impression he had created was caused by a long white cavalry cloak.

The two men were delighted to see one another and Picart described how the escort had fought a pitched battle with 600 Cossacks that day and succeeded in killing many and driving the others off, only to have their wrecked waggon pillaged by French stragglers. There had been several bottles of brandy in the waggon but in the struggle for their possession, as so often, the bottles had been broken and the wine spilled. Bourgogne, who had suffered a great deal more than his comrade, asked to see the spot where the brandy had been wasted and when it was pointed out to him gathered up handfuls of brandied snow. Picart had some biscuit so they made a meal, using a discarded breast-plate as a soup tureen.

As soon as it was light they looked to their arms and set off, hoping to rejoin their regiments. On the outskirts of a wood, however, they saw Cossacks attacking a group of French stragglers and were able to bring down two and see others fall into a hole in the ice covering a lake.[1] They were pursued but managed to ambush the Cossacks, eventually killing one and capturing his horse which was carrying a French cuirassier's portmanteau. On stripping the Cossack they found he had two French uniforms underneath his own, but, what was more important, a bottle of excellent gin. They made a bivouac and cooked soup made of oatmeal, horseflesh and seasoned with salt which Picart had tied in his handkerchief. 'It was,' says Bourgogne, 'the best meal I have ever had in my life.' For the remainder of his life he was to remember it as such.

They then continued their journey, riding back to back on the Cossack pony so that they could observe the road in both directions. In this way they avoided running into a convoy of two hundred French prisoners who were being herded back along the road to Orcha. Most of the poor wretches were already half-dead although a Russian officer showed them some kindness and used his whip on peasants who tried to strip the wounded. It was while lying concealed and waiting for the convoy to pass that Bourgogne and Picart heard a Russian tell a French officer that Napoleon and all his staff were prisoners.

Later on, half inclined to believe this might be true, they tried to help a straggler whose nose had all but disappeared and whose fingers had dropped off, leaving only the thumbs. The man died at their bivouac fire. They avoided a patrol of Russian cuirassiers and calculated their chances of rejoining what was left of the army on the banks of the Beresina. Picart, who feared the worst, said he had forty gold Napoleons and seven Russian gold pieces in his knapsack. He would willingly have given them all to be reunited with his regiment.

Their luck persisted. In a grey canvas bag he had picked up Bourgogne found some tobacco and Picart, a smoker, was consoled by his pipe. Later that evening they were shown great kindness by a family of Poles and given shelter in a cottage where the unaccustomed heat almost suffocated Bourgogne. The Polish women washed and anointed their feet. It was twelve days since Bourgogne had had his boots off.

Here they had leisure to examine the contents of the portmanteau they had captured. They found nine silk handkerchieves, four of which they gave to the Poles, three pairs of officer's epaulettes, three silver watches, seven crosses of honour, two silver spoons, two dozen Hussars' gilt buttons, two boxes of razors, six 100-rouble banknotes, and a pair of linen trousers stained with blood. It was a good haul. The Cossack they had killed in the wood must have been very active during the retreat.

During the night wolves howled outside the door and Picart, who seems to have been an imperturbable soldier, drove them off with a torch and a lance.[2] In the morning they paid a local Jew to guide them to the Beresina but the weather became so bad that they got into terrible difficulties, often losing their way. At length, however, they heard gunfire and the sound greatly encouraged them, for it told them that the Emperor and main body were still free and not far away. Through a terrible snowstorm they moved on and at last, on the morning of the 25th, they crossed the line of march of the main body east of Borissov.

This time it was Bourgogne who was shocked by the appearance of the men who had conquered Europe. A few generals were still on horseback but the majority were walking, including the survivors of the Doomed Squadron that had almost melted away in three days. Officers and men shuffled along on frozen feet, wrapped in rags or bits of sheepskin and then, just ahead of the Imperial party, came what was left of the cavalry of the Guard. The Emperor himself followed, marching with the help of his birch staff. On his right was the King of Naples, shorn of the last of his finery, and on his left Prince Eugène. Behind these three came Marshal Berthier, Chief of Staff, Marshals Ney, Mortier, Lefèbvre and General Grouchy, together with a number of other generals whose divisions had been annihilated. Seven to eight hundred officers and men followed and after them the remnant of the Imperial Guard, still in formation.

Sergeant Picart, who had not seen the main body for weeks, gazed at this bedraggled procession in amazement. To a man who had followed the eagles since youth it must have seemed like a parody of the Grand Army. He rejoined the wreck of his regiment and Bourgogne marched with them for a time, less from his need of comradeship than in order to make certain of his share of the Cossack pony they had captured.

The total strength of the main body at this point was approximately 30,000 men. Over 70,000, irrespective of camp-followers, had perished or had been made prisoners since the army had evacuated Moscow thirty-eight days before, but even this reckoning does not take into account the bodies of men, amounting to several thousands, who had rejoined the column at garrisons en route. The true figure of the losses up to November 25th, the day they reached the river, would probably be nearer to 90,000.

There were still a few pieces of artillery under General Negré and at last Bourgogne recognised men of his own regiment, the Fusiliers-Chasseurs. Everyone was astonished to see him, having given him up for dead since the 22nd. That same night the army straggled into Borissov. To the optimistic the main part of their ordeal was over. A few marches beyond the unbridged river lay the road to Vilna and beyond that Kovno and the Niemen, with a promise of reinforcements, food and warm billets. But an ordeal worse than that they had already survived lay directly ahead. Not one in five of the men who had covered the distance from Moscow to Borissov was to live to see France again.

CHAPTER EIGHT

'THE ARMY IS NOT FOR EXHIBITION PURPOSES AT THE MOMENT'

Napoleon at Zavinski, November 1812

1

NAPOLEON'S contemporaries, and after them generations of historians, have been misled in regarding the river Beresina as a major obstacle to the remnant of the Grand Army. They have been encouraged to do so because the losses incurred in fording this stream were appallingly high, higher indeed, than over any previous or subsequent stage of the retreat if one reckons in terms of time and distance. The facts, however, are otherwise. The Beresina was not a serious obstacle to any army, even an army as wildly disorganised as Napoleon's when it reached the banks on November 25th. Colonel Marbot, who had a better opportunity than most to assess the problem it presented, speaks of it in almost contemptuous terms. 'It was no wider,' he says, 'than the Rue Royale opposite the Ministry of Marine,' and although he was obviously referring to the stream itself, and ignoring the marshy approaches on each side, he is right in assuming that the disaster that occurred here was due to bad staff work rather than the nature of the hazard and the presence in the immediate vicinity of two Russian armies.

The Beresina claimed over 30,000 victims in a matter of forty-eight hours largely because something had gone from the leadership of the French officer class. Heroes were still to be found, a few unconquerables like Ney, Oudinot, Eblé and Lefèbvre, but in the main the virus of defeat had spread from the ranks to the top echelons of the army. We hear of men like Murat pottering about the crossing saying

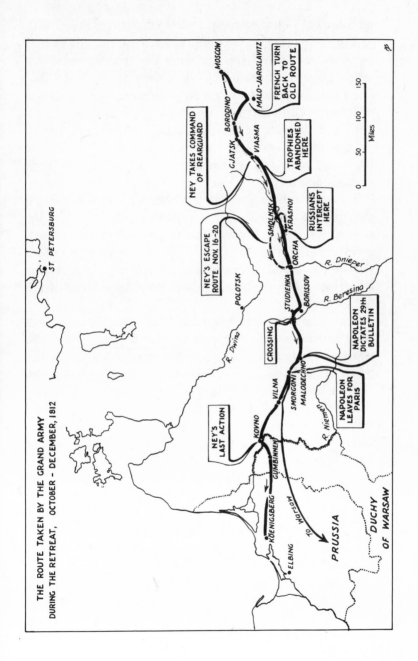

THE ROUTE TAKEN BY THE GRAND ARMY
DURING THE RETREAT, OCTOBER – DECEMBER, 1812

ST PETERSBURG

MOSCOW
MALO-JAROSLAVITZ
BORODINO
GJATSK
VIASMA
SMOLNSK
KRASNOI
ORCHA
STUDIENKA
BORISSOV
POLOTSK
R. Dwina
R. Dnieper
R. Beresina
VILNA
SMORGONI
MALODECHNO
KOVNO
R. Niemen
GUMBINNEN
KOENIGSBERG
Warsaw
ELBING
To
PRUSSIA
DUCHY
OF WARSAW

FRENCH TURN
BACK TO
OLD ROUTE

TROPHIES
ABANDONED
HERE

RUSSIANS
INTERCEPT
HERE

NEY TAKES COMMAND
OF REARGUARD

NEY'S ESCAPE
ROUTE NOV 16-20

CROSSING

NAPOLEON
DICTATES 29th
BULLETIN

NAPOLEON
LEAVES FOR
PARIS

NEY'S
LAST ACTION

Miles
0 50 100 150

nothing and doing nothing, and of officers concerned with saving their personal baggage rather than men. That having been said credit for achieving the crossing must certainly go to Napoleon himself, always at his best when faced with a difficult strategical problem. His exploitation of Russian gullibility on this occasion was faultless. Without it, or the care he took to ensure that his orders were carried out in detail, not a single man would have reached the right bank and set his face towards Vilna, the next rallying point.

It has never been finally established who actually located the ford at Studienka as a practical substitute for the burned bridge at Borissov. It was probably the French cavalryman Corbineau, whose brigade was attached to Oudinot's Second Corps and was operating in this area several days before the main body completed their march from Orcha.

Corbineau is said to have stumbled upon it by accident after watching some peasants ford at a place where the water was only three and a half feet deep. That was on the 22nd, three days before Napoleon arrived, and the cavalry at once tested the practicality of the passage by swimming their horses across. The milder spell of weather that had followed a spate of violent snowstorms was certainly welcomed by the shoeless, frostbitten men trudging westward from Krasnoi, but lower temperatures would have helped them now, for the entire army could have passed over the ice. As it was the river was still flowing and not a great deal of ice was floating downstream. There was no prospect of reaching the right bank as Ney's men had crossed the Dnieper on the night of the 16th–17th. Corbineau informed Oudinot who at once told Napoleon of the existence of the ford. The Emperor made his dispositions in a matter of hours; they were reminiscent of a younger man who had bundled the Austrian armies out of Italy in the closing years of the old century.

Studienka was only a few miles above Borissov and Napoleon told Oudinot, 'You shall be my locksmith and open the passage for me!' He then despatched the marshal's cavalry upstream, at the same time taking three steps to ensure that the watchful Tchichagoff, just across the river, was successfully hoodwinked.

First he despatched a body of three hundred infantrymen and a large number of stragglers downstream, with instructions to collect materials for a bridge below Borissov. Then he enrolled the services of a party of Jewish guides to lead him to the first practical downstream crossing, knowing that at least one of their number would make it his business to inform the waiting Russian general of French intentions. Finally he ordered men to start work on repairing the burned-out bridge at Borissov and take care that they went about the business with ostentation.

The triple hoax succeeded far better than he could have hoped. Tchichagoff was completely fooled and at once began shifting his men south, leaving only a few Cossacks and two guns to watch Studienka. The rest of his army was concentrated opposite and below Borissov, where there seemed to be great activity among the French on the opposite bank.

Kutusoff was now some way behind. He had suffered a severe check at Krasnoi and some say he had less than 30,000 effectives at his disposal. Nothing was to be feared from him at the moment, but Wittgenstein's reinforced army, moving down from the north, was getting uncomfortably close, so Marshal Victor's relatively fresh Ninth Corps was sent to block his advance and later, after the French had crossed, to act as rearguard. Oudinot was told to attack Tchichagoff's army the moment he had crossed over and hold him in check until ordered ranks, the stragglers and such waggons and guns as remained, had passed from the left to right bank. Once across (and with the intention of bypassing the captured town of Minsk) Napoleon intended to march north-west for Vilna.

At first everything went according to plan. Oudinot's advance guard swam the river, each trooper taking an infantryman behind him. First across was General Jacqueminot and the Polish cavalryman, Count Predzieski. After this forlorn hope went 400 infantrymen, ferried over on two improvised rafts. The few Cossacks guarding the crossing fled after firing their guns and Oudinot issued strict orders that no reply was to be made to their volleys for fear Tchichagoff's rearguard, still crowding downstream, took alarm and retraced their steps.

In the meantime, from first light on the 26th, General Eblé's pontonniers worked like madmen to build two bridges, one a light structure for the infantry, the other a more solid causeway for the artillery and wheeled transport. Very few French waggons had got this far along the route but the French were now using some of the vehicles captured by the charge of Oudinot's cuirassiers and chasseurs on the 23rd, the day Borissov had been retaken.

The bridges were built on trestles resting on piles driven into the mud and for timber the engineers used beams from adjoining buildings and felled trees. In order to make the structure sound they were obliged to work for periods of seven hours in water reaching to their shoulders but they stuck to their task and sacrificed their lives for the rest of the army. It is recorded by several men who were present that not a single pontonnier survived the next few days when the weather once again became unbearably cold.

Napoleon and his staff, escorted by the closed-up ranks of the Old and Young Guard, arrived at the ford on the 26th and the Emperor established his headquarters at a flour mill on the left bank. With the object of encouraging the poor devils at work in the freezing marshes he constantly showed himself and personally distributed wine to the half-frozen men at work on the piles. He also made a point of congratulating the cavalry of the Second Corps on their general turnout and morale. Marbot proudly records that he was praised for the splendid appearance of his 500 chasseurs, comprising the 23rd regiment. The other colonels in the corps could only field 200 troopers.

It was while waiting for the bridges to be completed that

Prince Joachim (Murat, King of the Two Sicilies)

Eugène de Beauharnais (Viceroy of Italy, Prince of Venice)

an impromptu council of war was held by the Imperial party. Several leaders, including Murat, urged Napoleon to abandon the army and make a quick dash for Paris. To his credit he refused. He was to accompany the march for another week and leave it when it was within easy reach of Vilna.

By two p.m. on the 26th the first bridge was finished and three hours later the heavier structure was ready to bear the weight of horses and guns. Without a moment's delay Oudinot's men followed their advance guard and the battle rolled away downstream as the marshal furiously attacked the bewildered Tchichagoff. Gunfire was also heard from the east, where Victor was engaging the advance guard of Wittgenstein.

The French army was now operating in three separate but interrelated spheres. On the right, or western bank of the river, Oudinot was hotly engaged with Tchichagoff, now alive to the fact that something significant was happening upstream. To the east Victor was fending off Wittgenstein and between these two flank battles the main body was crossing and reassembling on the further bank. Tchichagoff's army was centred on the town of Stakavo and was about 30,000 strong. To hold it in check Oudinot had no more than about 8,000, being his original 6,000 reinforced by driblets sent over by Napoleon. His men, outnumbered by nearly four to one, behaved splendidly; in the annals of the Grand Army there is no better example of aggression under circumstances of extreme difficulty.

As soon as he realised that the French were established in force on the right bank the Russian general attacked with everything he had and succeeded in routing the Polish Legion of the Vistula. The French at once counterattacked in a wood of huge firs, where the ground was still sufficiently open for cavalry to operate. Russian artillery, firing high, severed heavy branches that crashed down on men and horses. Here General Coudras was killed, and the heroic Legrand, who had played such an important part in covering the retreat at Krasnoi, dangerously wounded. Oudinot, himself right up in the firing line, saw that the counter-attack must be pressed forward at all costs and sent an aide to order the 7th Cuirassiers to charge. At that moment the marshal, hardly recovered from the wound he received at Polotsk in the summer, was shot out of the saddle and only saved from being dragged along by his horse by the prompt action of a member of the staff who caught his bridle. A bullet, fired from below, had entered Oudinot's body at an angle of forty-five degrees and those who saw him fall assumed him to be mortally wounded. He was carried away, unable to speak but still conscious. Ney at once took his place.[1]

In the meantime the attack of the cuirassiers under Colonel Dubois had proved brilliantly successful. It succeeded in cutting the Russian column in two, routing six squares of infantry, and driving the enemy back as far as Stakavo.

As successor to Oudinot Ney performed another legendary feat, advancing sword in hand at the head of a column ploughed by artillery. It is recorded of him here that he improved the occasion by reminding a colleague of Trappist fatalism, saying that Trappists stand on the edge of their own graves repeating one to the other, "One must die, brother!" The officer took his point. "One must die, brother!" he said and Ney, setting himself and his column in motion, repeated the phrase. Renewed attacks by the Russians failed to break through the thin screen of gallant men interposing between them and the bridges. All that day Ney continued to keep the crossing beyond Russian artillery range.

2

While this desperate fight was going on troops and transport were passing over to the right bank in increasing numbers.

Bourgogne, who reached the Studienka ford on the 26th,

164

saw the pontonniers at work and watched Oudinot's advance guard swim across, infantrymen riding behind the cuirassiers and chasseurs, followed by Legrand's division who marched over the first bridge to be completed. Captain Roeder, with the Hessian Lifeguards and the remnant of the Prince's Own, arrived later the same day but neither of these men was as concerned with the army's achievement as with their personal sufferings. Roeder was in a pitiful state, although he had ridden from Borissov in his Colonel's chaise. His hands and feet were badly swollen, he still had dysentery, and he was suffering from an agonising pain in his right breast. Unable to keep watch on his personal belongings, he had been the victim of several thefts. Someone stole his overcoat—a very serious matter in these circumstances—and also a jar of honey that he was treasuring. He still retained, however, the ill-used fur coat that had been ripped by a cannon-ball, but complains that, owing to the rents and to the condition of his frostbitten hands, it was very difficult to put on or take off!

Bourgogne was also very low in spirit and dreaming of potatoes, bread and butter *à la flamande* and beer. His friends, however, were still taking good care of him. One brought him a bowl of broth and another a sheet of waterproofing taken from one of the waggons but he seems to have come very close to the point of resignation. Waiting orders to cross the river during the comparative lull of the 27th, he watched everything that was going on and remembered it in such detail that, months later, as a prisoner of war in Germany, he was able to set it all down in chronological order. He saw the Emperor and a thousand men of what was still called the Third Corps cross to the right bank, but still no orders were given for the Fusiliers-Chasseurs to follow.

The low ground around the bridgehead on the eastern bank had now become a vast camping-place, covered with troops and stragglers of almost every European nation and with the arrival of milder weather the sense of urgency seems to have deserted them. For the most part they sat about warming themselves at huge fires and grilling horse-steaks. One can hardly blame them. They had marched hundreds of miles in freezing temperatures and here at least there was plenty of wood and horseflesh available. The thunder of artillery on both banks where Ney and Victor were holding off two Russian armies seems not to have concerned them. It might have been the echo of a far-off war in which they had ceased to take any active part.

Bourgogne's instinct of self-preservation, however, soon routed his fever and depression. Hearing that the Emperor had spent the preceding night in a flour mill he at once asked a man to point it out and lost no time in going there, poking about between the floorboards with the point of his sword until he had found treasure in the form of two pounds of flour. It was mixed with dirt and splinters of wood but no less welcome on that account. He sought out a bandsman who possessed a cooking pot and together they made cakes, sharing them equally. Bourgogne shared his half with the men who had helped him over the last stretch of road from the point where he rejoined his regiment after his adventures as a straggler.

He was very moved by some of the scenes he saw that day. The women, he says, seemed able to bear their privations much better than the men. He saw a cantinière supporting the head of a dying veteran, the father of her children, two of whom had died further back along the road. This couple, he said, had lost everything except a beautiful girl about fifteen, who stood looking down on the scene. The fate of the woman and child continued to interest him and later on he tried to discover if they survived, but was unsuccessful. Then the same instinct to ensure his own survival again intervened to save him from almost certain death. Waking up about seven p.m., and seeing no one on the bridge except a few of the pontonniers stationed there to keep it in repair, he quietly crossed over to the right bank. It was as well he did. Within minutes he met one of his men who told him that the regiment had crossed while he was sleeping and were now in the second line of the corps battling to keep the obstinate Tchichagoff at bay. Deciding that it was better to die in action than perish of cold and hunger he at once set off to rejoin his comrades, already being shelled by the enemy. A sick corporal whom he overtook and led to a fire was killed at his side and Bourgogne envied him.

Marbot, who had been on the right bank since the previous day, also comments on the curious lassitude that prevailed among the thousands of stragglers still encamped on the left bank, and goes so far as to say that a little chivvying on the part of an organised body of troops could have averted the terrible tragedy that followed. Having mislaid a baggage horse carrying the regimental paychest and account books, he rode back to the bridgeheads on the night of the 27th and was amazed to find both bridges deserted, the left bank chequered with fires and bivouacs, and nobody at all taking this splendid opportunity to cross. It was the first chance he had of examining the survivors of the Moscow army and like all the men in the detached corps he was appalled by their physical condition and lack of discipline.

Realising that it would not be long before there was a stampede for the bridges and also that they would soon be targets for Wittgenstein's artillery, he collected some troopers and, partly by persuasion partly by force, succeeded in driving some 2,000 to 3,000 over to the right bank. He estimates the crowd of *rôtisseurs* (army slang for a stray separated from his regiment) at approximately 50,000 but this figure, even if close to the mark, must have included vast numbers of civilians and possibly droves of Russian prisoners, concerning whom nobody troubled themselves any longer.

Downstream, at Borissov, Victor had broken off his running fight with Wittgenstein and was preparing to march for the crossing. He had under his command at this time about 8,000 men but he left 2,000 infantry, 300 cavalry and three guns under General Partouneaux to cover his withdrawal. Late on the 28th he came up with the mob still encamped on his side of the river but with Partouneaux in the rear there seemed no particular urgency, for news reached him that the Emperor and the Guard had crossed the previous night and that Ney was still blocking Tchichagoff's desperate push for the village of Zavinski, beyond the ford on the right bank.

It was now, however, that a freakish error deprived the French of their rearguard. Marching up-river from Borissov General Partouneaux made a fatal mistake at a crossroads, marching right-handed instead of left-handed along the bank. Why he did so is a mystery. He was an experienced officer, charged with a heavy responsibility, and ought not to have followed the path of a few light-infantrymen marching ahead and thus failed to keep the river on his left. He and most of his 2,000 marched straight into the advance guard of Wittgenstein's army and were instantly engulfed. He fought valiantly and the division was reduced to a few hundred men before it laid down its arms. Only the last battalion, a few hundred men commanded by a more alert officer, took the left fork and rejoined Victor opposite Studienka. The error left the hard-pressed Ninth Corps wide open to attack by overwhelming numbers.

The scene was now set for the most terrible episode in the long retreat. As soon as Wittgenstein's cannon balls began to fall among them the huge mob of unattached men and camp-followers who had been camping on the left bank for upwards of two days began a wild stampede for the bridges. Victor had arrived on the bank about nine p.m. but the panic began an hour or so before and the confusion around the approaches to the bridges, when the first of the Ninth Corps arrived, defied description. Men, women and children, teamsters still in possession of their waggons, and cantinières who had managed to bring their carts this far or had acquired replacements en route, made a concerted attempt to reach one of the two causeways that offered a chance of escaping from the oncoming Russians. By eight-thirty the bridges themselves were choked with fugitives and beginning to break down under the strain, and the approaches became cluttered with interlocked vehicles and plunging beasts, every driver shouting threats and abuse at the top of his voice in an attempt to force a passage through the press. A witness describes it as a scene from Dante's *Inferno,* and when Russian cannon began to play on the bridge and approaches the wedge of men and vehicles was churned into an inextricable mass. Waggon after waggon rolled or slid into the shallows and on the bridgeways themselves bodies piled up to form a barrier over which the most active clawed their way to safety. When the artillery bridge collapsed under the impossible strain placed upon it there was a frenzied scramble for the remaining causeway but even those who succeeded in crossing became hopelessly involved in another mêleé where the ground had not been shaved away and the right bank was steep and slippery. Some teamsters, seeing that it was impossible to make headway drove their vehicles into the water, but few of these were able to ascend the further bank.

It was here that Bourgogne witnessed scenes that remained in his memory until the day he died. The most poignant of them concerned a corporal in his own company, one of three soldier brothers called Gros-Jean, who gave Bourgogne his knapsack and after fighting his way free of the hell on the bridge actually went back to rescue his brother. Spellbound by the scope of the tragedy he was witnessing Bourgogne kept Gros-Jean in view for a long time, watching him fall on his face as he tried to fight against the mainstream of fugitives. He tried to pull himself up by the leg of a cuirassier and the cuirassier, steadying himself, grabbed a third man, so that all three rolled together into the water. Even then the corporal saved himself by climbing to a support against which he found a horse and climbed on its back, imploring aid from those above. Some engineers threw him a rope and he was dragged to the further bank. Later Bourgogne heard that he succeeded in finding his brother who had already crossed but was in a dying condition. Gros-Jean did not survive the next stage of the retreat and neither did a third brother who was a lancer. When he returned to France Bourgogne called upon their parents and left them with a spark of hope, saying that he believed they had been made prisoners.

Personal tragedies like this occurred by the thousand during that terrible night and the panic on the sole remaining bridge mounted even higher when Victor's Ninth Corps, marching in formation, were obliged to cut their way through the press in order to rejoin the main body. Two senior officers stood their ground during these frightful scenes. One was Marshal Lefèbvre, who remained on the bank trying to control the panic until he was forced across the river by the tide of fugitives, and one other elderly officer, General Eblé, who had superintended the building of the bridges. To these two men go some of the laurels that Ney, Eugène and Oudinot carried out of Russia in the winter of 1812. Eblé was still on the left bank when daylight revealed the fearful extent of the tragedy, but by that time the Russians were within musket range, so he ordered all remaining waggons and then the bridge itself to be fired. The few thousand stragglers who had preferred capture to the risks of crossing were made prisoners that same day.

The full cost of this frightful and largely unnecessary stampede was not known until the following spring when the Beresina ice melted and a total of 32,000 bodies were lifted from the area around Studienka and burned on the banks. Of this total probably three-fifths were noncombatants, among them a large number of women and children.

Roeder's life was saved by the devotion of his Sergeant-Major who saw him trying to cross on a wretched pony that lacked a bridle and had one stirrup two spans too long. Fighting his way towards the captain he gained control of the animal and led it to the further bank. In the subsequent, and, for Roeder, the final stage of the retreat,

Sergeant-Major Vogel's courage and loyalty brought the Hessian Lifeguard to safety in Vilna where he was taken prisoner and well treated.

3

'My sergeant-major makes himself of indescribable service to me,' says Captain Roeder in his diary, recording what was to be for him the last stage of his ordeal, the hundred odd miles from the Beresina to Vilna. Fortunate he was to have such a faithful friend, for even the loose marching order that had prevailed after Smolensk now disappeared as the army degenerated into a mob of ruthless, half-insane individualists, concerned only with their own chances of reaching the next garrison town where there was a prospect of rest, shelter and, above all, food.

The temperature began to drop almost as soon as the main body turned its back on the river. Twenty-two degrees of frost were recorded on the 29th and the thermometer continued to fall. Flesh and blood were unable to withstand a march under such conditions and there was still no prospect of anything to eat but half-frozen horse-flesh, washed down by melted snow.

From Zavinski, on November 29th, Napoleon sent off another despatch to Maret, his Minister of Foreign Affairs, still awaiting him in Vilna. In this letter, comparatively frank but still making a brave attempt to distort the situation, he announced that he was marching on the town of Vilekia, just east of the Niemen, and asked Maret to do what he could to check the condition of existing bridges and have materials on hand to make new ones. Confessing himself 'completely in the dark' regarding affairs outside Russia, he described the recent encounters with Tchichagoff and Wittgenstein on the banks of the Beresina, stating that the former had been drubbed and the latter checked but admitting the loss of General Partouneaux's rear-guard.[2] He also claimed 6,000 prisoners but does not add that there was no prospect at all of feeding them, or that

they melted away in the forests as their escorts concentrated on their own immediate problems. *'The army,'* he
said *'is strong in numbers but terribly disorganised. It
would take a fortnight to reconstitute the regiments and
where is a fortnight to come from? We shall soon be at
Vilna; shall we be able to hold out there? Yes, if we can do
so for a week; but if we are attacked during the first week
it is doubtful whether we could stay there. Food, food,
food! Without it there is no limit to the horrors this un-
disciplined mass of men may bring upon the town. Perhaps
the army will not rally until it is behind the Niemen.
Things being in this pass I think it may be necessary for
France, the Empire, and even the army that I should be in
Paris. Give me your advice.'*

One has no difficulty in reading into this hotchpotch of
half-truths the fact that Napoleon had now faced up to the
prospect of the total destruction of the Grand Army but he
had not lost faith in the future, even the immediate future,
for he took care to prime Maret on the importance of concealing as much as possible from observers who might
hasten to spread the news of the disaster among wavering
neutrals and former allies in the west. He concludes: *'I am
particularly anxious that there should be no foreign agents
in Vilna. The army is not for exhibition purposes at the
moment.'*

This last is, perhaps, the most truthful sentence in the
despatch. It warned those awaiting in Vilna to prepare for
the worst but it was still an understatement. Ten days'
march in terrible weather conditions lay between the
wreck of the army and possible (but by no means certain)
succour at Vilna. For many, for a majority of those who
had struggled this far, it was to prove a fatal stretch.

Also anxiously awaiting news at Vilna was Oudinot's
wife, the Duchess of Reggio, who had received word of her
husband's fresh wound caused by the upward-curving
bullet in the fight with Tchichagoff on the 26th. She had
every reason to be anxious. Oudinot's wound was a
dangerous one and only his astonishing fitness and re-

silience prevented it from being mortal. Hurried from the field he was seen by a surgeon who probed to a depth of six to seven inches for the bullet but without finding it. They gave him a napkin to bite on while this agonising examination was carried out and when there seemed no hope of extraction the veteran was patched up and sent by carriage to Vilna. Hearing that the marshal had been wounded Napoleon at once sent his son, Victor Oudinot, to escort his father. Having made sure the marshal had a good chance of recovery the young man rode forward to relieve the anxiety of his stepmother. The Duchess records that Victor, seeing the remains of her breakfast on the table when he entered the room, 'fell on it like a wolf!' The mere sight of cooked food at that particular time had this effect upon any man serving with the Grand Army.

Oudinot did not reach safety without another narrow escape. Again he was surprised by a band of Cossacks and fought them off, pistols in hand, until help arrived. He eventually reached Vilna where he made light of his injuries. His sickroom was always full of friends enquiring after his health and the fate of the army. Fragments of shirt, vest and uniform emerged from his wound from time to time but Oudinot carried that Russian bullet about with him for the remainder of his life, proof of one wound among thirty-four. His wife, learning of the part her husband had played in saving the Emperor and describing what had taken place between her husband's recapture of Borissov to the moment he was shot from his saddle, wrote, proudly, 'It is your father, my children, who saved what returned from Russia.' Disregarding for a moment Ney's magnificent contribution this was the simple truth. Oudinot has never received full credit for his gallantry during this campaign.

.　　.　　.

The retreat continued. On the 30th Napoleon reached Plechnitzi, on the 1st Slaiki, on the 3rd Malodechno, but the ranks of the French were thinning more rapidly than at any time during the long march. Roeder still dragged himself along, supported by his faithful Sergeant-Major Vogel, and when his pony was stolen on the 29th he was extremely lucky to find another by the roadside. All the time the weather got worse. The number of stragglers increased as men broke their ranks to search for food and fell prey to roving Cossacks, still hovering along both flanks. Prisoners were abandoned by the hundred and again there are sinister rumours of cannibalism, this time recorded by Sir Robert Wilson, British attaché serving with the Russian army.[3] Wilson says that he actually saw stragglers eating human flesh round a bivouac fire, but Marbot indignantly denies this, declaring that there were so many dead horses on this section of the route that the statement is nonsense.

And yet, even in these straits, the men in personal contact with the Emperor preserved their loyalty and their affection for him. Guardsmen like Picart might growl 'Conscript!' when contemplating the ruin of the army, but Picart would have been among the first of those who surrendered a portion of their firewood when staff-officers appeared at their bivouacs asking for fuel for the Emperor's camp fire. The only signs of incipient mutiny among the few thousand starving scarecrows marching in close touch with headquarters was the cry of some of Eugène's Italians—'*Maestra, non abbiamo di che mangere!*' ('Your Majesty, we have nothing to eat!') Labaume, still marching with the Viceroy of Italy, heard this despairing cry as the Emperor moved among the survivors of the Fourth Corps, but no eye-witness mentions an instance of disloyalty among men who had every right to feel they had been sacrificed to inept direction. In fact, as history was to prove, the esprit de corps of the Grand Army was virtually indestructible. It not only survived the horrors of the Russian campaign, it was to survive Leipsic and the Abdication, respectively eleven months and sixteen months later; and after that it was to survive Waterloo.

.　　　.　　　.

Sergeant Bourgogne, nearing the end of his tether, abandoned his precious bearskin soon after setting out for Vilna. Successive wettings and a sharp drop in temperature had left it as stiff as a board. Its final service was to cover a dying man in the snow and its sacrifice half-convinced the sergeant that he would never complete the last stage of the journey. At one point he actually did abandon hope, sitting in the snow to await the sleep of death, but was roused by a conscientious officer who kicked him and pulled his hair. He joined another group of guardsmen who, to his surprise, seemed relatively happy now the Beresina was behind them. 'They embraced and congratulated themselves,' records Bourgogne, 'as though it was the Rhine they had crossed! They even felt sorry for those we had left behind!' They felt sorry for him too and urged him to walk ahead, in case he slept in the snow again. Pre-eminently a man of good sense, he took their advice.

The cold now became far more intense—twenty-nine degrees of frost on December 3rd—but food seems to have been a little more plentiful than it had been back along the road. Advance troops met a convoy from Vilna, and some of the footsore cavalrymen found remounts. Marbot, wounded in the knee on the banks of the Beresina, travelled side-saddle in the midst of his regiment. 'And where?' he asks, 'would I have been better off?' At least, with so many of his loyal comrades around him, he did not have to forage far and wide for food, as did Bourgogne and the remaining score or so of the Fusiliers-Chasseurs.

The temperature now dropped to thirty below and the wind, says another survivor, 'had a cutting edge that drove through flesh, muscle and bone.' Marbot, his injured leg propped across the pommel of his saddle, suffered terribly from the cold but seems to have had no doubts that he and his regiment would survive as a unit. He saw the remnant of the Old Guard marching in a compact body round its eagles and counted them. Discounting stragglers they now numbered about 300. Labédoyère, a staff officer who was later shot for his part in the Hundred Days, computes that between the Beresina and Smorgoni, reached on December 4th, the army had lost 6,000 killed and 15,000 prisoners. The very last of the trophies dragged all the way from Moscow for display in Paris were abandoned on this stretch of road. At Malodechno, reached on the third, some attempt at reorganisation was made but there was little left to organise. Where possible the sick and wounded were sent on ahead and Ney remained, as before, the sole screen between the fleeing column and the Cossacks.

It was at Malodechno that a bitter quarrel flared up between Nay and Victor, commander of the Ninth Corps, who had covered the army's passage of the Beresina and had therefore been the last to cross. This quarrel, from which Victor emerges as a selfish scoundrel, set the seal upon Ney's heroism, for it ended in his occupation of the post of honour to the very last moments of the retreat.

Ney, and the 900 or so men left of the famous Third Corps, had now been acting as rearguard all the way from Smolensk. Indeed, he actually took command of the rearguard before reaching that city, when he had turned about and extricated Davout from the engagement west of Viasma. He had therefore every right to be relieved. Of his original command only a few dozen men were left, but he had been reinforced at Smolensk, and again after rejoining the army at Orcha. During the right-bank fighting against Tchichagoff while the army had been crossing the Beresina he had replaced Oudinot as commander of the Second Corps and now his shrinking command was made up of Frenchmen, Bavarians and Swiss, soldiers who had drifted into the orbit of his magnetic personality and had remained to die with him or continue to defy the Cossacks as far as the Niemen. One "regiment" consisted of four men, but they still carried their eagle.

Realising that he could not hope to ward off attacks with so few men in so poor a condition, Ney asked that Victor, with his relatively strong command, should fall back and take his place. Victor, whose personal courage like that of all the other marshals was beyond dispute, was none the less determined to bring what he could of his corps out of this wilderness of snow and ice. Declining the honour he and his men slipped away during the night.

Ney rode after him and tried to get him to change his mind but failed. Then he cursed Victor to his face and turned back to take up station with his devoted followers at the tail of the miserable procession. Veterans who witnessed or heard about this dispute at Malodechno were not surprised by Marshal Victor's subsequent behaviour when the Empire had fallen and the Bourbons employed him to hunt down old comrades who had served under Napoleon during the Hundred Days.[4]

On December 4th, when the column was approaching Smorgoni, the weather grew even worse. Bourgogne describes it as the most terrible day of the retreat, with heavy snow, a further drop in temperature, and a wind that drove the hardiest men half-crazy as they battled along a road signposted with corpses. Still the Guard did not lose formation but moved, according to one Russian observer, 'like a 100-gun ship amidst a fleet of fishing boats'. Bourgogne not only lost his place in the ranks but lost direction. Together with a small party of his friends, he found himself miles off the Vilna road.

When night fell the group made some miserable shelters and tried to rest but the wind got up again and the shelters were blown away. The sergeant spent the night sitting on the knapsack of Gros-Jean, the man who had recrossed the Beresina to look for his brother. He had already turned this out to see if it contained anything of value and had found some oatmeal mixed with rye, tied up in a handkerchief. It was probably this find, together with some miserable provisions he had been able to buy the previous day, that enabled him to sustain the rigours of the night. Encountering a man who had some potatoes Burgogne asked where he had found them and on searching the house found three more. Later on, near the spot where Oudinot had risen from his stretcher to fire his pistols at attacking Cossacks, he struck a bargain with a Jewess, exchanging some lace for a bottle of vile gin and a small oval-shaped cheese. He shared the gin with his sergeant-major and another guardsman and all three became tipsy, prancing along the icebound road and falling headlong into a deep ditch from which they were extricated by a party of Westphalians.

The punctilious Captain Roeder was still being watched over by Sergeant-Major Vogel but his moral standards had slipped another notch or two since his successful crossing of the river and he recalls, with a touch of shame, that he had now become a thief. 'Vogel and I stole some bread and a copper saucepan,' he records, adding in extenuation, 'Overmastering need! We had to do as all the rest!'

At Smorgoni, some forty miles short of Vilna, there was a change in command. Early on the morning of the 5th Napoleon, accompanied by only one other sledge and a few companions, finally decided to head direct for Paris. What little cohesion that remained departed with him. From now on, save in the heart of a single man, there was no other purpose beyond that of individual survival. To everybody except Michel Ney the Grand Army had ceased to exist.

CHAPTER NINE

'I AM GOING FOR 300,000 MEN!'

Napoleon at Smorgoni, December 1812

1

NAPOLEON had resisted the persuasions of Murat and others to leave the army while it was waiting to cross the Beresina. Nevertheless, the wisdom of doing so, of making a lone dash across Europe for the nerve centre of affairs, lingered on in his mind, resolving itself into a firm decision by November 30th, three days after he and the Guard were well advanced on the road to Vilna.

The decision was actually made at Malodechno, where he began to dictate the famous 29th Bulletin, informing Paris of the magnitude of the disaster. On the night of the 4th, at Smorgoni, he sent for the Governor of Lithuania and ordered him to prepare three sleighs and teams for what was to prove an almost record-breaking winter journey from the frontier of Russia to the Tuileries, a fortnight of almost incessant travelling. During that fortnight there was hardly a moment when the Emperor was not talkative and General Caulaincourt's recollections of their conversations provide what is perhaps posterity's most revealing insight into the mind of this extraordinary man.

The Bulletin which preceded him was very frank. It made no attempt to hide the truth of the army's almost complete disintegration but threw the entire blame for the disaster upon the weather, as though snow in Russia was a most unusual phenomenon in late November and early December.

.   .   .

It is interesting to conjecture why the 29th Bulletin was so frank. None of its predecessors had been, but this does not brand Napoleon as an habitual liar, or not more of one than any head of state. The commanders of the armies in the field in the early nineteenth century were no more addicted to truth than their successors in the First and Second World Wars. Ludendorff and Haig minimised their losses and magnified those of the enemy during every assault between First Ypres, in 1914, and the storming of the Hindenburg Line, in 1918. In the Second World War Goebbels out-lied Baron Munchausen in his propaganda broadcasts and so, to some extent, did the British authorities, reporting on the Battle of Britain, in 1940.

This would imply that Napoleon had some specific purpose in mind when he dictated the famous Bulletin and what that purpose was we can only guess, for it never emerged from his interminable sleigh monologue with Caulaincourt or, indeed, in self-justifications dictated during his six years' captivity on St. Helena. He was possibly encouraged in his determination to hold back little or nothing by an awareness of what was now at stake, finding it essential to stimulate a backs-to-the-wall attitude among the French, and the allies upon whom he thought he could rely. He was under no illusion now that the great gamble had failed, that for the moment he had no reserve counters to recoup his losses. Winter, that rapacious croupier, had scooped the pool, and his opponent, Tsar Alexander, had access to fresh supplies of manpower that would more than cover the frightful losses he too had sustained since June 24th.

Napoleon's first need was to stabilise his throne, to show himself as not merely alive and well, but as a reigning monarch with his faculties unimpaired. It was only by doing this, and doing it with the utmost speed, that he could hope to re-establish confidence in Western Europe. His second need, just as urgent, was to raise another army and his success in this respect, during the early spring of 1813, was possibly the greatest of his many administrative achievements.

On December 5th, when his sleigh slid out of Smorgoni, he had about him some 9,000 effectives. On May 1st, when he went over to the offensive in Saxony, the Grand Army mustered 320,000 men. It was a miracle of improvisation and perhaps owes something to the shock produced by the 29th Bulletin.

A great deal of pious nonsense has been written condemning his dash for Paris as a betrayal of his men, an act of cowardice for which a lesser man might have faced a firing squad. This somewhat pompous stand, favoured by a majority of historians down to this day, is even less justified than the once fashionable pronouncement that Napoleon Bonaparte was a bloodthirsty wrecker who gratuitously plunged the Continent into a welter of slaughter from motives of personal greed and ambition.

In the light of what later generations have suffered at the hands of pre-First World War diplomats, their harvest at Versailles, and a gang of German psychopaths exercising military power on a scale undreamed of in the early nineteenth century, Napoleon's impact upon his own generation was not only less harsh but certainly more wholesome if a man is to be measured by the standards of his time. This is not an attempt to whitewash his reputation as soldier or administrator, although in both rôles he emerges greatly superior to the mediocrities who defeated and replaced him. A cursory inspection of what in fact he did achieve in a variety of fields will convince any student of this. He was, from first to last, a man with an idea, and that idea was in direct conflict with those who then occupied the seats of privilege from Pekin to Lisbon. Like any head of state of his period Napoleon was prepared, whenever necessary, to use an army as a means of enforcing a policy, but one has only to read his letter to Francis of Austria, dictated from the field of Marengo in 1800, to understand that he regarded the bludgeon of war as a clumsy and often ineffectual instrument.[1] He was no more tyrannical or egocentric than the Tsar, the Emperor of Austria, or the British autocrats who poured so much money into Europe to ferment new wars. He was far less so than the Spanish Bourbons, or the Prussian autocrats he overthrew in 1806.

At least Napoleon did not order private soldiers 800 lashes for stealing food when no rations had been issued for a two-hundred-mile march in mountainous country, and this kind of thing was common practice in the British Army. In addition, as the British soldier Napier points out, the French conscript who fought under the eagles shared in the glory of a victory which is more than can be said of cane-driven peasants who marched behind Blucher, Kutusoff and the Austrian Archdukes. If he was prodigal with men's lives then he was usually within range of the guns when they began to roar and had, moreover, examined the ground over which they were to fight. This is far more than can be said of Douglas Haig, who sent three hundred thousand men to die at Passchendaele without considering whether it was possible for the hardiest infantryman to advance ten steps without sinking to the armpits in slime.

The charge of desertion from Smorgoni is absurd. If he was to survive, if the Empire was to survive, then it was imperative that he should return to Paris without a moment's delay. The staff knew this and did not question his going. At the Council of War summoned on the night of the 4th, Ney, Davout, Lefèbvre, Murat and Eugène concurred with his decision. As to the men who had struggled to within forty miles of Vilna, they neither knew nor cared who was in command of the army. To the Picarts, the Marbots, the Bourgognes and the Roeders, a crust of bread and a mouthful of brandy was of far greater significance to them at that moment of time than the whereabouts of the pale man speeding across Europe in a sleigh.

2

He took with him his Polish interpreter Wonsowicz, Caulaincourt, who had been ambassador to Moscow and a close companion throughout the campaign, Duroc, his Grand Marshal of the Palace and close personal friend, the cavalryman Lefèbvre-Desnouettes and his veteran aide-de-

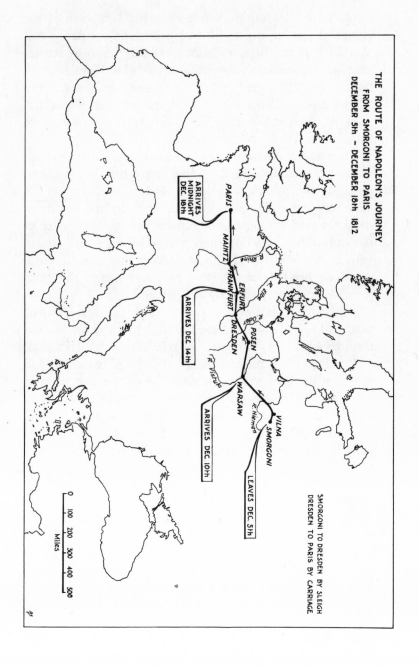

THE ROUTE OF NAPOLEON'S JOURNEY
FROM SMORGONI TO PARIS
DECEMBER 5th – DECEMBER 18th 1812

ARRIVES
MIDNIGHT
DEC 18th

PARIS

MAINTZ

R. Rhine

ERFURT

FRANKFURT

ARRIVES DEC 14th

DRESDEN

R. Elbe

POSEN

R. Oder

R. Vistula

WARSAW

ARRIVES DEC 10th

R. Nieman

VILNA

SMORGONI

LEAVES DEC 5th

SMORGONI TO DRESDEN BY SLEIGH
DRESDEN TO PARIS BY CARRIAGE

0
100
200
300
400
500

Miles

camp, General Mouton, whose dramatic recapture of the village of Essling during the 1809 Danube campaign had won for him the title of Count of Lobau.[2] Also in attendance were Napoleon's favourite Mameluke, Roustam and three valets. The party set off in three sleighs, one being alloted to the Emperor and Caulaincourt. For the initial stage of the journey they had a small cavalry escort of Frenchmen, Poles and Neapolitans.

They had a narrow escape almost at once. At the village of Youpranoui a Cossack raiding party had just finished pillaging the houses in advance of the French. They remounted and rode off exactly an hour before the three sleighs passed through, thus missing the greatest prize of the campaign. At Vilna there was a brief stop to confer with Maret, Minister of Foreign Affairs, and then the little cavalcade headed straight for the Niemen and the comparative safety of the Duchy of Warsaw.

The journey, however, was beset with hazards. News of what had occurred east of the Beresina had already filtered through to the storm centres of rebellion in East Prussia, and various plots, most of them harebrained, were afoot to intercept the Emperor, assassinate him on the spot, or hold him prisoner until the arrival of Kutusoff's main army gave Prussia sufficient moral support to join the new coalition. Ex-marshal of France Crown Prince Bernadotte, who had already come to terms with Russia and England, was soon to launch his Swedes against his comrades and there was now little doubt that Austria could not be trusted, although Swartzenberg still retained command of the Thirteenth Corps. Marshal Macdonald, with his Prussian Tenth Corps, could give no protection. Doubtful of the loyalty of some of his men he was already retiring towards Koenigsberg.[3] Reynier's Seventh Corps was dispersed all over Poland. Speed and secrecy were essential to the fugitives. The sleighs headed for safer ground and as they left the wilderness behind doubt and rumour advanced to meet them.

At the other end of Europe a climax was not far away.

King Joseph, maintaining a tenuous hold on parts of Spain, now had old Marshal Jourdan as his chief adviser and three other marshals, Marmont (badly wounded at Salamanca in July), Soult and Suchet, nominally under his direction. The marshals, however, ignored every royal decree from Madrid, continuing to rule as virtual dictators in the areas where they had sufficient men to keep the partisans at bay. There were still something like 200,000 French troops in Spain but they were scattered in widely separated provinces and were often unable to communicate with one another. Wellington, taking advantage of the large-scale withdrawals Napoleon had made when recruiting his army of invasion in early summer, was now pursuing a cautious offensive and the French could do little to halt his progress. Soult withdrew from Andalusia and after Salamanca the entire French army passed over to the defensive. It seemed possible, indeed likely, that within six months a British army would be hammering at the back door of France, while an enormous confrontation of Russians, Prussians, Swedes and possibly Austrians, moved on the Rhine from the east.[4] There was so much to do and so little time in which to do it. The three sleighs rushed on across a snow-bound Poland, travelling day and night without escort. On December 10th, five days after leaving Smorgoni, they thudded into Warsaw.

·   ·   ·

Acting as French Ambassador here was a curious character known as the Abbé de Pradt. His place in history rests upon a single encounter. He was the first man of affairs to see and converse with Napoleon on the latter's re-entry into French-dominated Europe. The Abbé was a writer of talent and a detailed account of his interview on the night of the 10th has come down to us almost verbatim. It offers a remarkably clear insight into the state of Napoleon's mind during the initial stage of his breakneck journey across Europe.

The Abbé had just received a despatch from Maret,

warning him of the impending descent of the diplomatic corps from Vilna, when a cloaked, hooded and fur-booted figure was ushered into his presence. It was his old friend Caulaincourt, but the Abbé was so thunderstruck by his appearance that he not only failed to recognise him but momentarily took him for a phantom. Caulaincourt, stiff with cold from the five-day sleigh ride, told him that his presence was required at the Hotel d'Angleterre, where the Emperor was waiting.

'Why doesn't he stay at the palace?' demanded the astonished ambassador.

'He doesn't want to be recognised!' said Caulaincourt briefly.

The Abbé considered this. Slowly it began to occur to him that the world had now turned a political somersault, that the man whom he was accustomed to regard as king of kings was now awaiting him, cold, hungry and almost alone, in a wretched hotel room, and this surely implied that the Grand Army had vanished like a puff of smoke. When he tentatively touched on this subject Caulaincourt blandly confirmed his fears. 'All gone!' he said, and cast his eyes upward.

The Abbé hurried over to the hotel where he saw the carriage mounted on a sleigh in which the Emperor and Caulaincourt had travelled from Smorgoni. Two other sleighs stood nearby, the transport of Generals Lefèbvre-Desnouettes and Mouton, the Mameluke Roustam and the valets. 'This,' he reflected, 'is all that remains of so much pomp and splendour!' It was a sobering thought.

The interview that followed had the same nightmarish unreality. Napoleon was sitting in a small, icily cold parlour, warming himself at a fire of green wood over which a slatternly Polish maidservant crouched puffing and blowing in an effort to transform smoke into flame. The last time the Abbé had seen Napoleon was at Dresden, just before the great surge into Russia but then he had been surrounded by a covey of obsequious kings and dukes. The contrast was almost too great to be accepted. Pacing the room, still in his hood and furred leather boots, the Emperor enquired after the state of Poland. The Abbé could give him no encouraging news. Only that morning two battalions of new recruits had flung away their arms during a brief engagement on the Bourg, and four hundred horses had been lost through want of care on the part of the same soldiers. Russians were marching on Zamosk. The finances of the Duchy of Warsaw were ruined. News of the battle of the Beresina had reached Warsaw via Maret and the Abbé asked Caulaincourt what had happened to the 6,000 prisoners mentioned in the bulletin. 'We had something better to do than look after them!' was the reply. Napoleon asked what the Poles wanted and was told that if they could not have their independence they would prefer to become Prussians. His reply to this struck the Abbé as totally irrelevant. 'Raise 10,000 Polish Cossacks,' he said. 'They only need a lance and a horse. That will stop the Russians!' The Abbé said nothing. He was thinking that a declaration of Polish independence in June might have sealed the eastern frontier of the Empire for a generation. Now it was too late to contemplate such measures.

Imperial irrelevance of this kind occurred again and again throughout this extraordinary interview. It was as though Napoleon was conducting it with the surface of his mind, using the Abbé as a kind of sounding board for the various lines of propaganda he meant to pursue the moment he was within reach of a Paris printing-press. Count Stanislas Potocki and the Finance Minister were summoned, the Abbé having named them as the two most influential members of the Council. Every now and again Napoleon laughed, his intolerable nervous pressures demanding some kind of hysterical relief. 'From the sublime to the ridiculous is only a step!' he said over and over again and when the officials, hoping to steer the conversation back to more formal channels, congratulated him on his escape from so many dangers, he exclaimed, 'Dangers! Not the slightest! Unrest is my lifeblood! The more plagues the more I flourish! Only do-nothing kings grow fat in palaces; I fatten on horseback and in camp!' And then, once more, he repeated the phrase that had taken his fancy; 'From the sublime to the ridiculous is but a step!'

He apparently mistook the acute embarrassment of the officials for terror, but when he accused them of fear they said they knew nothing but rumour of what had occurred in Russia. Napoleon then launched into a tirade directed more against fate than human failings on his part, or the part of the army. 'I've always beaten the Russians!' he said emphatically. 'They daren't face us! They are not the men of Eylau and Friedland. They'll be held at Vilna. I am going for 300,000 men ... I'll fight them on the Oder, and in six months I'll be back on the Niemen!⁵ I weigh more on my throne than at the head of my army. All this is nothing. It's an accident. It's due to the climate. The enemy had no hand in it. I've beaten him everywhere...'

The monologue went on and on, jerky, incisive, sometimes not even making sense. 'I've seen a lot worse. I was beaten at Marengo until six in the evening. Next day I was master of Italy. At Essling I was master of Austria ... I can't stop the Danube rising sixteen feet in a night ... but for that the Austrian monarchy was finished. The same in Russia. I can't stop it freezing!'

He then said goodbye six times but nobody left, so he went on rambling. 'Our Norman horses can't stand more than nine degrees of frost. The same with the men ... it may be said I stayed in Moscow too long. Possibly. But it was fine. Winter came earlier than usual...'

It would be easy to assume from this jumble of vainglory and half-truth that Napoleon's wits had succumbed to the horrors and fatigues of the retreat and perhaps the Abbé, and others listening to this jerky recital in the parlour of a drab Warsaw inn, thought so at the time. But events proved otherwise. What Napoleon needed at that moment was what he got—a respectful, submissive audience and the desperate need for this was to continue throughout the length of his journey back to Paris. He was, in fact, engaged in the task of reassuring himself. That much is indicated by his flashbacks to other moments of peril like Marengo, the closest finish of all Napoleonic battles, and Essling, where the Danube current had swept away his bridge of boats and isolated part of his army. He had emerged successfully from these hazards and he would do so again. That was what he was trying to tell himself. It required the mind of a genius to succeed in the attempt.

'My health,' he said on leaving, 'was never better. If I had the devil I should thrive on it!' and with that parting shot he dismissed them, climbed in his sleigh and drove off. Passing through the gate of the courtyard a severe jolt almost overturned the vehicle.

3

They traversed Silesia, taking their chances in a country where revolt had been simmering a long time, where every belt of forest might conceal a Prussian ambush. Caulaincourt, his travelling companion, was acutely aware of the danger but Napoleon did not seem to take it very seriously. He reminded his friend of a remark of Charles XII of Sweden who, warned of similar dangers on the same ground, had said that the Berliners were discussing today what they would do if they had captured him yesterday. At the same time he was prepared to put up a fight if stopped and said, jestingly, that the Prussians would probably hand him over to the English. 'Can you imagine, Caulaincourt,' he said, 'how you would look in an iron cage in the Tower of London?' And when Caulaincourt said he would not complain if he was sharing his fate with the Emperor, added, 'It's not a question of complaining but something that may happen at any moment—and the figure you would make in that cage, shut up like a wretched Negro being exposed to the flies after coating him with honey!'

The macabre spectacle he conjured up amused him. He laughed for a quarter of an hour.

Yet not all his comments were frivolous. He talked of his early life in Corsica, of his schooldays at Brienne, of his love affairs with women like the Polish Countess Walewska, whose home they passed and where he suggested making a stop but was persuaded to drive on. He admitted to a yearning for peace and what he would do if he ever achieved it. 'Every year we'll spend months travelling about the country,' he said, jovially. 'I shall go by easy stages on my own horses. I shall see what the cottages of fair France are like inside. I want to inspect the departments that are short of communications, to make canals and roads, to help trade, to encourage industry. There's a vast amount to be done in France, departments that are still virgin ground.'

The endless journey continued, to Posen, to Dresden, across Saxony and into Thuringia to Erfurt. Dresden was reached on the 14th and here he met his most faithful ally, the old King of Saxony, who had a sincere liking for him as a man rather than an Emperor. He paused to write letters to the King of Prussia and Francis of Austria, his Imperial father-in-law, and then, exchanging the sleighs for the King of Saxony's carriages, the tiny fragment of the Grand Army swept on towards Frankfurt and Mainz. Still the Emperor talked, of his childhood, his friends, his policies and his bedroom conquests. Especially the latter, holding nothing back. It was as though Caulaincourt was his psychoanalyst, a willing receptacle for the sludge of the best brain in Europe.

Hearing that he was near at hand Brother Jerome, King of Westphalia, wrote offering to join him in Paris. Napoleon ignored the letter until he had time to answer it in Paris, on December 29th. Then, in a brief note, he told the young man who had bungled the first stage of the campaign that he would be more useful in his tinsel kingdom of Westphalia, putting the fortress of Magdeburg in a state of defence against the invasion that would come out of the east in the spring.

.   .   .

At fifteen minutes to midnight, on December 18th, the

fugitives drew up outside the Tuileries and were challenged and almost fired upon by the Palace guard. The 29th Bulletin had preceded them by forty-eight hours. News of the disaster was on the streets of Paris. Nobody, not even the Empress, recognised the gaunt, pale, unshaven figure who came stamping into the royal apartments in his fur-encased boots. In the doors of the gallery opening on to the garden they met the porter in his shirt, holding a guttering candle. The man was so uncertain of his visitors that he summoned his wife, who only recognised Caulaincourt after she had thrust the candle under his nose.

Her hesitation was understandable. Caulaincourt had a fortnight's growth of beard and a costume sufficiently outlandish to promote the gravest doubts as to his intention, particularly after the recent Malet scare. The porter then sent for a footman, just to make sure.

The Empress had been on the point of retiring to bed but Caulaincourt summoned two women attendants and asked them to inform Her Majesty that the Emperor had arrived. Then Napoleon appeared from the background and the little coterie of minions stared at him as though he had returned from the dead. Impatient with this reception the Emperor walked past them into the Empress's bedroom, saying, 'Goodnight, Caulaincourt. You need rest yourself!' It was a curious ending to an odyssey that had begun amidst scenes of splendour at Dresden six months before.

CHAPTER TEN

'SOLDIERS WITHOUT CHIEFS, CHIEFS WITHOUT A COMMAND'

La Maréchale Oudinot, at Vilna, November 1812

1

CLOSE on the track of the Emperor as he glided westward towards the Niemen, travelled another party of fugitives, packed into two carriages and riding out of Vilna with an escort of twenty cuirassiers.

Three days in bed had sufficed to restore Marshal Oudinot to a state of health enabling him to make a carriage journey across the snow to Kovno, Warsaw and beyond. He was accompanied by his adoring wife, her uncle, the marshal's coachman and maître d'hôtel, and three wounded officers of the Fourth Corps. They had evacuated Vilna, notwithstanding the marshal's unhealed wound, on the advice of Maret, Minister of Foreign Affairs, and despite grumbling protests by the marshal himself, who, from his sickbed, begged them to hold the city as an outpost against the westward surge of Wittgenstein and Platoff, now so close as to be almost mingling with the French column.

Good food did much to restore the wounded commander of the Fourth Corps. At the age of forty-four he had now received two serious wounds in four months. Between recovering from the first and receiving the second he had led his corps into action on numerous occasions. The fact that within three days of arriving in Vilna on a stretcher he was able to attempt a long journey across Eastern Europe in the depths of winter says a great deal for his singularly robust constitution.

The Maréchale, overjoyed at being united with her

husband again, fussed about his bedside, tempting him with succulent dishes procured from heaven knows where, and all the marshal's officers who came in to see him partook of the invalid's grapes with relish. They were astonished and delighted, records the Maréchale, by the sight of food, candles and clean table linen. Oudinot ate his share. 'Is it not a dream,' his wife records him as saying, 'to find a well-supplied table again?'

It was a short-lived dream. Within forty-eight hours of his arrival advanced units of the rabble army came drifting into the town and looting began on such a scale that there was no hope at all of putting the city in a state of defence. In vain Oudinot protested against further retreat. His wife, seconded by General Pajol and the Minister of Foreign Affairs, packed him into the first two coaches and the party set off for the west. The Maréchale records that their escort of cuirassiers, although well mounted and wrapped in huge white mantles, dropped away one by one. Looking back on the last pair she saw their moustaches full of icicles. Not one of them was present at the first bivouac. Despite this, and the paralysing cold, the party reached safety, most of them suffering miserably from dysentery, exacerbated by the good food they had eaten at Vilna.

Back along the road from Smorgoni humbler men struggled forward in temperatures that had now dropped to twenty-seven, twenty-nine and finally thirty degrees of frost. Colonel Marbot, with the remains of his 23rd Chasseurs, were among the best disciplined of them, rescued perhaps by their colonel's insistence on every trooper supplying himself with a thick sheepskin coat back in the summer, but also, Marbot says, by the fact that the harvest had been gathered in during the five months since the Grand Army had passed this way and stores of grain could be found by expert foragers in villages each side of the route.

Men who had not acclimatised themselves to the low temperatures and miserable diet suffered far more than the hardy remnant who had marched all the way from Moscow. Twelve thousand conscripts came out from Vilna to meet the army. Within four days—the thermometer standing at twenty-nine and a half degrees of frost—almost all had died; another party of Neapolitans, belonging to Murat's bodyguard and left behind at Vilna during the advance, died to a man after a single night in the open. Not only casualties but desertions multiplied, especially among the Germans and Italians. These sometimes left the line of march and hid in villages, awaiting the arrival of Russian units to surrender. 'Saving themselves by a means repugnant to the French!' declares the patriotic Marbot.

Nobody could understand why Kutusoff did not hurry forward and capture or exterminate every man of the raggle-tailed column. They were there for the taking, practically helpless at this stage of the march, but the old fox of the North still dawdled and the survivors had only Platoff's Cossacks to contend with. Marbot explains the Russian delay by saying that Kutusoff's men were less able to stand the intense cold than were the French, partly because they spent their winters in houses heated by stoves with all draughts excluded by heavy shutters. This may or may not be so; the fact is that the Russian advance guard rarely came within musket-range of the rearguard, still led by the indomitable Ney. Only the Cossacks hung upon the flanks and when they caught a straggler they usually contented themselves with stripping him and abandoning him to the frost. To take prisoners would mean turning their backs on the prospect of more loot and there was still a great deal to be gathered along the road, including most of the Imperial treasure. These Cossacks sometimes brought up one of their light guns on a sledge and fired into the crawling column, but their artillery practice was poor and they did little harm. Every time a mounted body of French rode across the snow towards them they scattered and disappeared. In this way Marbot and his men reached Vilna on December 9th, stopping every now and again to free the bits of their horses from icicles formed by breath. 'Vapour,'

Marshal Ney leading the rearguard

In the Museum of Versailles: engraved by Henry Wolf

says Marbot, 'hung in a cloud around our heads and when it condensed it fell back with a rattle like grains of millet.'

Joachim Murat, King of Naples, proved a contemptible failure as commander of the broken army. It was a task for which he was ill-equipped and it seems strange that Napoleon, who knew his brother-in-law's weaknesses so well, did not take them into account and appoint either Ney or his stepson Eugène Beauharnais when he left for the West. The Gascon innkeeper's son had performed prodigies of valour (and, in the view of Davout and Ney, crass stupidities) during the long advance, but there was no opportunity here for displays of dash and circus riding. What was needed to hold these men together was an iron will and a fanatical devotion to the demands of the military code. Murat, brave as he was, had never exhibited these qualities in eight years as a marshal and four as a king. He made no decisions and issued few orders. Even the remnant of the Imperial Guard resented him as Commander-in-Chief. For too many years now their privilege, jealously guarded, had been to protect the person of the Head of State.

Bourgogne struggled into Smorgoni on the 6th, the day after Napoleon had left, and when he heard the news he came to the conclusion that Napoleon had made a sensible decision. Such protests as there were, he tells us, came from well-dressed officers of allied units riding out from Vilna. He dismissed their complaints as the propaganda of paid English agents. At Smorgoni the sergeant had a small slice of luck, spending the night in a house where there was a stove. For company he had a young officer who could go no farther and for his supper he was able to buy some onions and nuts from the householder, a Jew. 'We were charged too much,' he says, 'but the shelter was worth it.' In the morning he left very quietly, in order not to disturb the dying man and that same day he fell in with the remnant of the Guard and marched with them.

The resolution shown at Krasnoi, the occasional camaraderie of the Beresina crossing had all but disappeared. Little knots of survivors, sometimes numbering no more than eight or nine men, now formed themselves into closely knit units, willing but not eager to help one another but extending no aid to others and driving them off if they attempted to join the group. Brutal squabbles over the source of firewood occurred at every halting place. Sometimes private soldiers would fall upon a half-ruined house or barn sheltering officers and rip it to pieces in order to feed their bivouac fires. Discipline was gone. Every unit of the army was mixed together in one ravening, jostling mob.

Just beyond Youpranoui, where he spent the night of the 7th in a huddle of his comrades, Bourgogne helped to set fire to a house in order to warm himself. On the 8th they were lucky again, and caught a stray horse but nobody had an axe or a knife to dismember it so they killed it and caught its blood in a saucepan. Before it was lukewarm they had to move on to avoid Cossacks. That same night, his last before reaching Vilna, the sergeant passed through a village that had for him a bitter memory. It was the halting place where, during the advance, he had lost what he calls his "trophies"—the portraits of the various mistresses he had had in six years of campaigning. It says something for their charms that he remembered them at such a time.

Captain Roeder, still attended by the ever faithful Sergeant-Major Vogel, fared worse than usual during this stage of the march. Momentarily separated from his companion he was surrounded by Cossacks who at once began to rob him. Suddenly, however, they stopped, staring at the Hessian Order of Merit pinned to his breast. Then, having relieved him of his torn fur coat and pages of his diary that they probably mistook for military information, they rode away, leaving him unharmed. Sergeant-Major Vogel, emerging from hiding, explained the reason for the captain's miraculous escape. The Cossacks had mistaken the Hessian decoration for the Order of Vladimir and supposed their victim to have been honoured by the Tsar.

After this incident the pair plodded on towards Vilna, living on a supply of biscuits they had taken from a barrel found by the roadside. Roeder and Vogel must have been early arrivals; they got off with eight days' supply. That night, December 8th, they found shelter in a house but it was soon on fire and they had to scramble out into the snow. In the panic Roeder lost the cords and rosettes of his hat and because his nerves were at breaking-point the trifling loss irritated him more than his physical sufferings. The two men arrived at the Smolensk gate of Vilna on the following day and were caught up in a terrible struggle to enter the city amid a mass of struggling fugitives, fearful of missing a ration issue. Roeder went down between two horses and a third horse and rider fell on top of him. He was saved by what he regards as a crowning miracle. One of the plunging horses threw him clear and he landed in an open space and was able to stagger the few last steps towards safety.

For him it was the end of the road. Frostbitten, exhausted, half-starved and suffering terribly from recurrent dysentery, he realised that he could go no farther and resigned himself to becoming a prisoner.

.   .   .

In a collection of original anecdotes from the manuscripts of Labédoyère, Rapp and others, there is a reference, supported by other diarists, to the bad behaviour of the Vilna Jews at this stage of the retreat. Some of the Jewish population of the city had been roughly treated by units of the Grand Army during the advance and now, seeing the helpless rabble pouring into the city, they took their revenge. Survivors were invited into houses and charged famine prices for food and shelter. As soon as the Russians appeared these were flung into the streets and in some cases murdered. Whether this charge is true or not it is clear that the few thousand men who had made such prodigious efforts to reach Vilna were incapable of defending themselves, even against civilians. Vilna proved no more of a haven than Smolensk or Orcha. Such magazines as it contained were soon pilfered and it was beyond the capacity of

Murat or any other marshal to stop the panic evacuation of the city as soon as word came that Wittgenstein's men and Platoff's Cossacks were storming into the town. All who could walk rushed out on the road leading to Kovno and the Niemen. The French reoccupation of Vilna had lasted twenty-four hours.

There were many, however, who could march no farther and in a sense these were the more fortunate, for once the Russian High Command arrived the officers at least were reasonably well-treated. There is no record that they were rounded up and caged, or formed into convoys to be driven back into Russia. Roeder, one of 242 officers taken at Vilna, was even allowed to occupy private lodgings so long as he was prepared to feed himself, and something like this seems to have been the lot of the seven generals and 500 N.C.O.s and unwounded men overrun by the Russian advance. In addition, however, there were 5,500 sick and wounded lying in the hospitals. It is virtually certain that a large majority of these poor wretches never returned to France when peace was signed in April 1814.

2

The French left Vilna as they had entered it and as La Maréchale Oudinot described them—'Soldiers without chiefs, chiefs without a command.'

Russian units made half-hearted attempts to break in almost as soon as the main body reached the shelter of the walls and the spirit of panic spread to all but Ney, his gallant remnant, and a few units of the Old and Young Guard who were still ready to sally out and keep the Cossacks at bay. There was one such action on the edge of the town, where an officer and thirty men drove off an attack, and later the same day there was a more organised stand on a hill east of the city, where some Grenadiers, Chasseurs and Bavarians beat off an attack with two pieces of artillery and a few volleys of musketry.

In the main, however, the spirit of aggression and conscious superiority that had carried the Grand Army into every corner of Europe since the defeat of the Prussians at Valmy, in 1792, had now disappeared. Generals, officers and men had but a single desire, to put the Niemen between themselves and the Russian army, to leave once and for all this vast land of desolation and death. Murat was already on the road to Kovno and during the night of the 9th most of the stragglers followed him, without any organised attempt to divide such stores as were available in the town. Ney, still in no hurry, took up his quarters in a large house, augmenting his rearguard with sixty grenadiers who had been wounded at Smolensk during the advance and had now reported back for duty. This band of about 120 men drew their strength from Ney who was warned by a German general to leave at once. Pointing down into the courtyard where the rearguard were clustered round their fires Ney said, 'With men like that I am not afraid of all the Cossacks in Europe!' A drummer of the Guard told Bourgogne, 'If my hands were not frozen I would sound the charge!' Frozen or not he stayed close to the last fighting remnant of the Grand Army.

Marbot got into the town on the 9th and was shocked by the disorder prevailing. General Marion (he was to be one of Ney's judges at the fatal court martial after Waterloo) broke open some of the storehouses and distributed food and clothing, but most of it was left for the Russians. The men it could have saved were already gone. Marbot saw others roaming about the streets knocking in vain upon doors and asking to be taken in and most of these who could go no farther congregated at the already overflowing hospitals where there was shelter but insufficient food for the patients already there. The cavalryman estimates the number of helpless invalids left in the town at 20,000, including eight generals and 200 officers, but this is a guess and Roeder's figure seems nearer the mark. One of Marbot's officers, a young lieutenant with a first-class record, was so affected by all he had seen during the last few days that he lay down in the snow and could not be roused.

Marbot also speaks of the brutal treatment meted out to survivors by the civilian population and says that, on entering the town, indignant Russian officers hanged some of the murderers. On the following day, the 10th, the survivors of the 23rd Chasseurs rode out towards Kovno, the sick, wounded and dismounted troopers travelling two men to a sledge, drawn by troop horses.

Bourgogne, who arrived in Vilna the same day as Marbot, confirms many of his observations but, as always with the sergeant, farce was treading on the heels of tragedy, and he had a number of adventures in the brief period he spent in the city. The most encouraging of these was another encounter with his friend Picart who, as usual, had a store of flour about him and gave the sergeant his share. Both Picart and Bourgogne took part in the sally outside the town which kept the Cossacks at a distance, and then returned to see what could be found in the way of provisions.

Bourgogne's luck did not desert him. Picart introduced him to a Jew who sold him a bottle of brandy and when Bourgogne asked how Picart came to be on such friendly terms with the family the old grenadier told him that, while staying in Vilna during the advance, he had passed himself off as Jewish and had even attended the synagogue. This amused Bourgogne so much that he split his frozen lips laughing at the ruse.

That same night Bourgogne, foraging for himself while awaiting the promised ration issue, chanced upon a bakehouse to which he and another sergeant gained entry by announcing themselves to be generals. It was already full of officers but by now it was almost impossible to distinguish a man's true rank. Everybody was in tatters and most uniforms were badly scorched. In addition, under thirty degrees of frost, everyone was wearing any kind of garment that afforded protection against the cold.

Bourgogne and his friend descended to the cellar of the bakehouse where they found the bakers asleep and seven white loaves in a basket. Helped by a major-general, they took them all and after they had gone the officer was nearly murdered by the inhabitants. After this incident there was a lively piece of bargaining between the guardsman and two Jews over an exchange of Russian banknotes for gold. The bargain having been clinched Bourgogne went to the Jew's house for a promised café-au-lait, but what he drank there poisoned him and brought on a bout of colic. While he was asleep his bread was stolen but, lucky once more, he was able to buy some rice to help him along the road to Kovno.

By now, however, the sergeant was in a very bad way. In addition to colic he had a frozen foot and a frozen finger on his right hand. He made a makeshift boot from a piece of sheepskin and set out after the column. Behind him was Ney's rearguard, built up to 300 officers and men. It was all that interposed between the tail of the column and the Russians. Not far along the road the last of the stragglers ran into serious trouble. A column of Cossacks and Russian cuirassiers dashed in between them and the rearguard and Bourgogne, together with some Hessians (probably the survivors of Roeder's unit), were involved in a bloody scuffle on a piece of rising ground. Bourgogne saved himself by diving under a waggon, but the Hessians were cut to pieces.

It was here that the sergeant witnessed the astonishing encounter between one of his old friends, a guardsman called Daubenton, and a drunken Russian cuirassier, ending in the despatch of the latter, despite the fact that the Frenchman was severely hampered by the presence on his shoulders of Mouton, the regimental dog.

Mouton, who had been with the regiment since 1808, and whose adventures during the last four years would provide material for a saga, had frostbitten paws and Daubenton, willing to risk his life to save the animal, had put him on his shoulders and tied him to his knapsack! In the fight with the horseman the dog pulled Daubenton to the ground and during the struggle the dog received a number of sabre cuts aimed at his master. From the protection of the waggon, however, the Frenchman shot the cuirassier at close range but another straggler took the horse and Daubenton went after it, leaving Bourgogne in charge of the dog. The sergeant was less sentimental than his friend. He left Mouton in the waggon. It was all he could do to shift for himself.

The survivors of this encounter were saved by the brisk arrival of Ney's rearguard who, hearing firing, came up at the double. The Russians fled but several horses were captured. Of their prompt rescue Bourgogne writes, 'I shall never forget the Marshal's commanding air at this moment, his splendid attitude towards the enemy and the confidence with which he inspired the unhappy sick and wounded round him. In this moment he was like one of the heroes of old time. In these last days of this disastrous retreat he was the saviour of the remnant of the army.'

The column had now arrived at another fatal obstacle, the ice-covered hill of Ponari, a short distance west of Vilna. It was here that the remainder of the Imperial treasure train foundered.

The value of the treasure hauled thus far has been put as high as seven million francs, a good part of it in gold. It is astonishing that it had travelled as far as this when so few horses were available to replace those who died of exhaustion, or were slaughtered for food. The icy ascent, however, proved its terminus and at once there was a mad scramble among men of all ranks to save what could be saved, and perhaps enrich themselves in the process. Men who could hardly walk loaded themselves with money and later attempted to change handfuls of the heavy five-franc pieces for single pieces of gold. There were few takers. All but a minority were beyond the summons of avarice. Bourgogne had about him 800 francs in gold and 100 in five-franc pieces but he was far more concerned with his ailments, his hunger and his verminous shirt than with the chance to make money and was fortunate to find a box containing two hats (which he exchanged for a drink of wine) and a trunk containing four new shirts.

The man with whom he traded the hats was an old comrade, a newly-commissioned officer called Prinier, whom he met walking against the mainstream of fugitives in an effort to rejoin the army. When Bourgogne told him that no army existed Prinier demanded to know the source of the firing he could hear down the road. Bourgogne told him it was Ney's rearguard. 'Then I'll join the rearguard!' Prinier said, and hurried back along the road to Vilna.

Shortly after this Bourgogne received the welcome news that survivors of his regiment, among them some of his oldest comrades, were not far ahead and he made superhuman efforts to overtake them. He was successful and was again welcomed into the ranks as one who had returned from the dead.

Mabot's chasseurs were now mingling with the rearguard. At night they made a laager with their sledges and built their fires inside the circle. Ney, and his second-in-command, General Marion, often came to warm themselves and it was on one of these occasions that Marbot learned the truth about the ransacking of the Imperial treasure on the hill at Ponari, quoted by De Ségur (whose account of the retreat was to do so much to rehabilitate Ney's reputation after the Restoration) as an instance of gross indiscipline. Ségur, says Marbot, did not know the full facts. The waggons were emptied on the orders of Ney, who saw that the money could not be taken any further. Naturally he preferred to see it in French rather than Russian hands. Many of the rearguard justified his trust. On their return to France a substantial part of the pilfered treasure was returned to the army paymaster by the men who had taken it.

3

One party of fugitives was making rather better progress towards the Niemen. This was the small family group surrounding the badly-wounded Marshal Oudinot, who were travelling in two carriages ahead of the main body. Notwithstanding his rank and injuries, however, Oudinot had to share the same privations as other officers and men.

Having surmounted the icy hill at Ponari the carriages sped along the snow-covered road at a spanking pace, travelling far more swiftly, says the Maréchale, than they had advanced eastward in the dust and heat of summer. To a man lying propped on a mattress, however, the intense cold and the jolting must have been terribly distressing, and when night fell the group sought shelter in a large shed, all that remained of a roadside building. Unluckily for them this miserable shelter had been commandeered by a section of General Loison's staff, on their way towards Vilna to reinforce a division that no longer existed, and although Oudinot's party claimed a place round the stove on the grounds that the marshal was dying, it was only with the greatest difficulty that they were squeezed into the group of officers so tightly packed that nobody except the injured man could sit or lie. As men died they were dragged out, but others took their place and the press remained as great. Oudinot's wound was inflamed and Doctor Capioment, who was in attendance, had the greatest difficulty dressing it because his fingers were numb. During the night the fire burned low and no one was willing to brave the terrible temperature outside in order to get wood. At length the doctor went out and returned in triumph with part of a cannon wheel. The marshal's party had brought provisions—wine, poultry, bread and ham, but the portions were frozen so hard that they were all but inedible. The cold, however, probably saved Oudinot's life, preventing the ever-present danger of a nineteenth-century wound, putrefaction. This had killed his friend Marshal Lannes after an amputation in hot weather on the Danube in 1809.[1]

As soon as it was light the party set off again, the Maréchale fearing the worst. 'Shut up in our carriage, between grey sky and the white ground,' she says, 'we felt as though we were wrapped in our winding shrouds.' Every blackened chimney and every isolated pine tree she saw as a Cossack, and the cold that day numbed the powers of speech and thought. As darkness fell they turned off the road and found hospitality with a priest, who not only had a stove but a dish of potatoes. On the third morning, December 9th, the marshal's wound was again giving trouble and had to be dressed in a Jew's cabin, but the poultices froze in Doctor Capioment's hands.

That night they reached Kovno and found shelter with an old friend, Baudecour, the military intendent, who had just learned that his only son had been lost in the retreat. After that, beyond the Niemen, it was comparatively easy going, and eventually they reached safety. Within five months Oudinot was leading his men into action again on the plains of Saxony.

Behind them Ney fought, doggedly, tirelessly and with the deadly fatalism of a man who is a slave to duty. By now he had perfected a technique of retreat. Towards the end of a day's march he would find a defensive position, a knoll, a wood or a small ravine, close his ranks and light fires. Such food as was available would be cooked and the men given five hours' rest. About ten he would follow the army's route under cover of darkness, halting again at first light and repeating the process all over again. He was now commanding his fourth rearguard since Krasnoi and it was melting away like its predecessors, from 2,000 to 500 from 500 to fifty.

Just ahead of him, sometimes within sight of him, went Bourgogne and something approaching 10,000 stragglers, men with frostbitten feet, with half-healed wounds, with double hernias, men who were sunk in despair but somehow kept moving, stopping only to warm themselves at half extinct fires and roast a slice of horseflesh, or make a saucepan of "horse-*brouillé*." One survivor has left the prescription—chunks of raw horseflesh saved from the last bivouac, a shako full of melted snow, and two to three cartridges in lieu of salt. The result was a jet-black broth but it kept many of them alive and hopeful of seeing France again.

Bourgogne's bottle of brandy, bought at Vilna, came in useful when he was turned away from a fire and told to light his own. He passed the bottle round and won a place in the circle. He also managed to cook his rice without a saucepan, using his shako as a basin. Along the road he overtook Quartermaster Rossi, of his own regiment. Rossi's feet were badly frozen and he had given up hope of reaching home. There were, however, men worse off than he for at one bivouac the two stragglers found three men who were unable to march another step. Most of their toes had dropped off and their feet were blue, as though mortified.

At the halting place that night both Bourgogne and Rossi, who had now caught up with their comrades, decided that they had reached the limit of their endurance and talked of distributing their loot among companions with a better chance. After a night by a good fire, however, they set out again, each helped along by their friends, and now that Kovno and the Niemen were almost in sight a better spirit began to prevail among the ranks. Over and over again the Sergeant-Major called a halt and sent men back for someone who had fallen. Bourgogne, however, was not without a conscience. He realised that men like himself and Rossi were narrowing the chances of tougher men like Grangier, and after being helped down an icy slope by his friend, who used his bayonet as a peg in the ice, Bourgogne insisted that the others pushed on and left him to take his chance. They did so but left a Piedmontese grenadier called Faloppa, to keep him company.

As it turned out Bourgogne was the stronger of the two and they encouraged one another as they fell further and further behind. At a point where they could look back along the road they had travelled they saw a strangely moving sight—Marshal Ney and his band herding stragglers forward, as a dog drives sheep. Bourgogne fell into a shallow ravine and would have died there had not a trooper of the Imperial Guard listened to his appeal to be dragged out. Bourgogne asked for a hand and the man laughed. 'I have none!' he said, displaying the stumps of his fingers, 'but you can seize hold of my cloak!' The sergeant did so, using not only his hands but his teeth, and was thus hauled on to the road again. The trooper told him he had lost his fingers on the far side of the Beresina and since then had been in far less pain than before they dropped off.

In the meantime the Piedmontese soldier showed signs of breaking under the strain. They marched together, a man without fingers, a man with a frostbitten foot, a man who was becoming insane under the stress of the demands made upon him. When at last, on the night of the 13th, the trio staggered into Kovno to find shelter in the house of a peasant already billeted with four Germans of the Kovno garrison, Guardsman Faloppa was seen to be dying and soon afterwards he did so in the presence of his hosts.

At first light on the 14th firing was heard in the streets and the Germans forcibly conscripted the wretched peasant, dressing him in Faloppa's uniform and arming him with the grenadier's musket. Outside General Roguet was using brute force to round up the straggling groups of survivors and drive them on to the bridge. From the street came the sounds of shots, cries, curses and the thud of Roguet's baton as he struck at laggards. The peasant's womenfolk, paid a few francs by Bourgogne to watch over Faloppa, began to wail, but when General Roguet saw the Lithuanian in French uniform, and herded him into the street with the rest, they had no reason to counterfeit grief for the man was swept along with the others, protesting in a language that nobody could understand. Waiting to re-cross the Niemen Bourgogne had an opportunity to check the strength of his regiment. From 2,000 it had dwindled to sixty.

Even so, it was a far better muster than the majority of units that had crossed this same river five months before. A captain of the Tirailleurs of the Guard could only produce a lieutenant and one private. All the rest were dead or prisoners. The entire corps of Prince Eugène was billeted in four houses!

That same night Marshal Michel Ney, marching with about forty men, entered Kovno by the Vilna gate. Almost as soon as he arrived the nominal commander of the army, Marshal Murat, King of Naples, left the town, heading for Gumbinnen and Koenigsberg, in Prussia. Since taking over from Napoleon at Smorgoni on December 5th his contribution to the retreat had been nil. His one aim was to get back to his kingdom as soon as he could, stop his wife issuing decrees in her own right, and see if it was possible to come to an arrangement with the coalition of France's enemies that would ensure his throne against the collapse of the Empire.

One should not judge him too harshly, as Napoleon was to do when he learned of his conduct. Warfare, to Murat, was not a creed but a game, and the rules of the game, as Murat understood them, were limited to cavorting about a battle-field in fancy-dress and engaging in sportsmanlike tussles with opponents conducting the business under the same rules. He was utterly unfitted to command a rear-guard although no one could match him during an advance. He was also more deeply involved in politics than any of his contemporaries and had the additional handicap of being husband to a coldhearted, greedy, scheming harlot, without a harlot's generous impulses. He did not lack courage. No one could point a finger at a man who had led eighty squadrons against entrenched artillery at Eylau and, more recently, at Borodino. What he did lack was stability, compassion and the dedication of a man like Ney. It is curious that, for virtually the same offence both men were to face firing squads in less than three years.[2]

It should also be recalled that men like Davout, Lefèbvre, Eugène and Mortier crossed the river in Murat's company and it would be idle to look for cowards in that direction. To them the campaign was over, a disastrous, bloody desperately bungled failure. Their obligation, as they saw it, was to rally what men were left, sort them out, and get them to the nearest garrison town where they could rest and refit in anticipation of a Russian invasion of the west.

Yet Ney remained, to defend Kovno if it could be defended, and to give the fugitives time to get the sick and wounded across the half-frozen river, where alternative frosts and thaws had pushed the ice into jagged peaks and treacherous hollows.

.   .   .

There were 700 Germans in the Kovno garrison and Ney at once enrolled them in his rearguard and manned the walls, already garnished with about twenty-four pieces of artillery. The Cossacks were not long in pressing an attack. At the first discharge of gunfire most of the Germans fled, throwing away their muskets and scrambling for the river. Patiently Ney collected another group and fought on, sometimes firing a musket himself, but now the Russians were beginning to encircle the town and threaten his retreat, so he moved towards the bridgehead, attended by General Gerard and four private soldiers.

By now, as the winter's day drew to a close, all who could walk or be carried by comrades had crossed, some in an orderly manner, a majority in the wildest confusion. A few of the hardiest had crossed the broken ice but the bulk went by the bridge, Bourgogne and his sixty guardsmen among them. The sergeant got across safely but just beyond the bridge he slipped on an ascent and rolled back to the banks of the Niemen. It was as though St. Nicholas, patron saint of the Russians, was loath to let him go, and it was only with the greatest difficulty that he regained the bank near a waggon loaded with money that was being systematically pillaged, even while the roar of battle could be heard from the far bank. Bourgogne was offered his share but refused it. He did, however, exchange his useless musket for a good one while its owner was preoccupied with collecting forty-franc pieces. Sergeant Grangier, his loyal comrade came back to look for him, calling 'Come along *petiot* (little 'un), follow me!'

That night, thinking the worst of their troubles behind them, the group turned aside and took up quarters in a small farm where a man was killing a cow. 'This,' says Bourgogne without irony, 'was a good sign and so we turned in!' It is a fitting comment on the last stage of a 550-mile tramp, performed on a diet of horseflesh.

As the rump of the Grendadiers-Fusiliers made their evening soup the last shots of the campaign were being fired on the other side of the Niemen. Ney had organised yet another rearguard, adding to his general and four privates, thirty stragglers, French, Italian and German, who were there because of personal devotion or by chance. The group thus numbered thirty-six and they passed the bridge at nine o'clock that same night. The last man across was Ney, walking backwards, and firing the muskets that others had thrown down. On reaching the other side he threw the weapon he was carrying into the Niemen and plodded off through the woods towards Gumbinnen.

The next day, December 15th, a haggard, red-bearded man in a nondescript uniform knocked at the door of a doctor's house in the town that happened to be occupied by General Dumas. 'Here I am!' he said, and when Dumas asked the identity of his visitor, 'Don't you recognise me? I'm Michel Ney, the rearguard of the Grand Army!' Dumas stared at the ragged, dishevelled figure, too astonished, perhaps too impressed to reply. 'Ask someone to get me some soup,' Ney said, irritably, 'I'm damnably hungry!'

CHAPTER ELEVEN

'STAIRS ARE NOT MEANT TO BE TAKEN FOUR STEPS AT A TIME!'

Napoleon at Fontainebleau, January 1813

1

GEOGRAPHICALLY, but only geographically, the great re-treat was over. Russia and Lithuania were left behind and the line of march for the men who had recrossed the Niemen now led through East Prussia to the fortress towns of Koenigsberg and Danzic, or across the pro-French terri-tory of the Duchy of Warsaw to the Vistula.

Six months before a Frenchman, or a French ally, could have wandered these regions in comparative safety. His uniform would have ensured such help as the inhabitants could give in the way of food and shelter. Now all was changed. The plains and forests of old Poland and Prussia concealed almost as many dangers and hazards as the provinces of the Tsar in the east. The Grand Army had marched 550 miles to find sanctuary, time and leisure to refit and re-arm, food for the starving survivors, shelter and medical attention for the sick, but another terrible dis-appointment awaited them. Here was little shelter and less food, except for the few units still marching in formation, or men of the rank of colonel and above with the addresses of personal friends in their pockets. The only way a non-entity could obtain assistance was to buy it. For those who had thrown away their loot, or hurried on their way when forty-franc pieces were there for the taking, there remained nothing but sly hostility and a choice between pushing on or surrendering to the Cossacks.

Politically the whole of western Europe was in the melt-ing pot. Many of the Poles were still loyal but their leaders were beginning to realise that their chance of obtaining freedom at the hands of Napoleon had gone for ever. The remnant of the Grand Army was in no position to help any minority. It was as much as it could do to struggle onward to the nearest depot, hoping to reform on the line of the Vistula, or the Oder, or perhaps even the Rhine.

Further north, in Prussia, Pomerania and Sweden, or to the south, where lay the eastern dominions of the House of Habsburg, French prospects were equally bleak. Schwartzenberg, whose Thirteenth Corps had been playing war games with the Russians for the past three months, had lost contact with the Grand Army and made no move to re-establish it. In Vienna Chancellor Metternich, who was to restore to Europe the status quo for something like another century, was already casting about for a means of bringing his sovereign, the Emperor's father-in-law, into an alliance with the more active of Napoleon's enemies.[1] Within eight months he was to succeed. France would then be faced by the most powerful coalition ever arrayed against a single nation; Russia, Prussia, Austria, Sweden and Great Britain. In the meantime—such was still the power of Napoleon's name—Schwartzenberg continued to act cautiously. Unobtrusively and without fuss, he withdrew to the west and re-entered the Habsburg territories. Sir Walter Scott says of him that he and the Russians had been practising field-day manoeuvres with one another ever since June and this is an accurate summing-up of the rôle the Thirteenth Corps had played in the campaign. Schwartzenberg had been in the field for seven months now but his forces were intact.

In the north affairs took a more dramatic turn. Marshal Macdonald, the half-Scottish commander of Napoleon's Tenth Corps who had been left to watch St. Petersburg and Riga when the French advanced to Moscow, had long been aware of the fact that he could not trust his men, almost all of whom were Germans. He had retired on Tilsit but now, receiving news of the disaster, he began to edge further west. One of his divisions, commanded by the

Prussian General Yorck, defected with all ranks, and entered into a tacit agreement with the Tsar's representatives to stay neutral so long as Prussian territory was respected. Later, when the time was ripe, he promised to join the Russian invasion aimed at toppling the French Empire and even sent a letter to Macdonald explaining what he had done and why.[2]

Publicly disavowed by his sovereign, the King of Prussia, Yorck was none the less secretly applauded for his conduct. Certainly nobody in Berlin believed the fiction that representatives of the court were on their way to arrest and court martial him for mutiny.

Prussia, in fact, was now stirring in every city, town and village. As yet there was no open aggression, but the Tugendbund, or League of Virtue, was active among the students and junior officers. Patriotic ballads were being sold and sung and Lutzow's night-riders were in the saddle, so that no isolated French soldier could walk among the Prussians without the likelihood of getting his throat cut. Day by day, almost hour by hour, the whole eastern buttress of the French Empire began to crumble and veterans of the Grand Army who had grown fat in German billets for the past six years found themselves surrounded by potential enemies awaiting the moment to strike.

That moment could not be far away. Kutusoff had not yet ordered a general advance across the Niemen but thousands of Platoff's Cossacks had crossed the ice and were roaming the plains and forests in small, loot-hungry bands. French stragglers were still being cut down or taken prisoner and the cry of 'Cossacks!' was heard in French bivouacs at all hours of the day and night.

After hurrying out of Kovno and leaving Ney to cover withdrawal with a general and four privates. Murat, still nominally in command of the army, had made for Gumbinnen, in East Prussia, and here he held his first Council of War. It was a shabby, indecisive affair and broke up after a fierce quarrel between Murat and Davout as to what steps should be taken to reorganise the mob of fugitives and present a bold front to the enemy. Murat openly proclaimed his extreme dissatisfaction with his Imperial brother-in-law, implying that he saw nothing wrong in doing his best to save his own throne in faraway Naples. Davout, who had always hated the dashing cavalryman, was scandalised by this cynical view and told Murat he would see that his words were passed on to Napoleon as soon as possible. At this Murat's nerve faltered. Seeing that he was likely to get no support from dour fighters like Davout, Lefèbvre, Ney or Mortier, he made his own decision. On January 16th, when the wreck of the army had reached Koenigsberg, he pleaded illness, threw up his command and rode south-west for Naples, making the journey in almost record time. Not only Napoleon but the rank and file were disgusted by such a flagrant act of desertion at a time when each marshal should have set an example to the men under his command.

Leadership of the broken rabble passed to the conscientious Eugène, Viceroy of Italy, a man of a very different stamp. Eugène did what he could to restore discipline and morale and, to some extent, he succeeded. At least the sick and wounded who had dragged themselves through so much snow and ice were given what hospital treatment was available while active survivors were regrouped and reorganised into ranks capable of fighting another battle.

Learning of Murat's desertion Napoleon sent his sister's husband one of the most scathing letters he had ever written to a man who had shared his triumphs in Italy and Egypt. *'I am not going to tell you how displeased I am with your conduct, which has been diametrically opposed to your duties. It is due to your weak character as usual. You are a good soldier on the battlefield but off it you have no energy, and no character. Take warning by an act of treachery, which I attribute to you... I don't imagine you are one of those who think that the lion is dead ... the title of King has turned your head; if you want to keep it behave yourself, and be careful what you say!'* Napoleon then made sure that the entire country was notified of the

King of Naples' failure to live up to the high traditions of the marshalate. Confirming Eugène's command he published his reasons for the choice in the *Moniteur*, the official French newspaper. '*The King of Naples, being indisposed,*' ran the barbed comment, '*has been obliged to resign his command ... which he has transferred to the Prince Viceroy. The latter is more accustomed to the management of important trusts.*' It was, perhaps, the greatest insult one soldier could offer another.

On January 19th, three days after Murat had ridden away, a spurt of Prussian hostility almost overwhelmed Davout in Koenigsberg. His carriage was mobbed by a hostile crowd but he had not acquired the soubriquet of Iron Marshal by letting demonstrations of this kind impress him. He jumped out, seized a ringleader by the scruff of the neck, ordered him to be tied to the carriage, and silently resumed his journey.

Towards the end of the month rumours of the desertion of Yorck and Schwartzenberg became certainties and Macdonald retired to Danzic. On January 12th Cossacks entered the Grand Duchy of Warsaw in force; less than a month later they were at the gates of the capital city.

2

For many of the survivors the final stage of the retreat now became a desperate game of bluff and speed. Among them were those three indestructibles, Marshal Oudinot, Colonel Marbot and Sergeant Bourgogne. Their adventures multiplied as they travelled west to the banks of the Vistula.

Oudinot's coach journey from Vilna to Koenigsberg was a minor epic and his devoted wife, nursing him along every yard of the route, tells one of the most graphic stories of the retreat.

Heading for Gumbinnen after crossing the river well ahead of the main stream of fugitives the two carriages soon became separated, the rearward one, containing the

Maréchale's uncle, being delayed by a breakdown. That night the leading carriage turned off the road and sought sanctuary in the château of a Lithuanian countess, with whom Oudinot was acquainted. The hostess welcomed them but warned them on the doorstep that typhus was raging inside the house and that seven people there had already died of the scourge. Preferring typhus to a night in the snow the marshal's party stayed until morning, setting out early and reaching Gumbinnen on December 11th, three days before Ney crossed the Niemen. Here at least there was food and they were served with soup, beefsteak and potatoes. 'What a banquet, my children!' exclaims the Maréchale in her memoirs.

Between Gumbinnen and Koenigsberg other fugitives began to overtake the party and unwounded officers who called to pay their respects to the wounded marshal were received as deserters and ordered to seek the heads of corps on the Vistula. It was a bold man who told Oudinot that the army no longer existed. He would not entertain such a thought and sent every Jonah about his business with a flea in his ear, growling at his own inability to mount a horse and lead another column into action. To one colonel, who continued to sniffle bad news at his bedside, the Marshal said, 'For heaven's sake man, blow your nose!'

His wound, notwithstanding the hardships he had to endure, continued to heal. Stage by stage the family party made their way to Brandenburg, Danzic, Berlin and ultimately to Mayence. Wherever they went they were treated with respect, except at one town in Prussia where a jubilant mob celebrated Napoleon's defeat under the marshal's window. They met other survivors on the journey, among them General Pajol, who had typhus, and General Rapp, whose ears were badly frostbitten. They crossed the Oder on ice so thin that it cracked and split under the carriage wheels but at Berlin Oudinot's son Victor, left behind in Vilna, caught up with them and celebrated the reunion by buying the Maréchale a pretty muslin gown of British make. How it had evaded the Berlin Decrees and found its way into a German shop window is not explained. 'Our New Year surprise,' says the Maréchale, 'was the 29th Bulletin, which we read in Berlin!' They reached home safely after a series of adventures that would compare favourably with those of a runaway couple in the pages of medieval romance.

Marbot's last lap was smoothed to some extent by the wonderful discipline he had been able to preserve among his chasseurs. He alone speaks well of the German population, recording that he was kindly treated en route but that billets in warm houses after so many nights in icy bivouacs had a harmful effect upon the men. A great number of the survivors who had weathered the blizzards, were taken seriously ill after returning to more normal conditions and among those who died as a result of the transition was the heroic General Eblé, the ageing officer who had superintended the building of the bridges over the Beresina. Lariboisière, of the artillery, also succumbed to the effects of the change from conditions of extreme hardship to that of comparative comfort.

Marbot's unit, still in fighting trim, continued its march westward on sledges as far as Graudenz, on the Vistula, but here, because of a partial thaw, the sledges had to be abandoned and each trooper had to pick his way across treacherous ice. As a further thaw seemed certain, and it was essential to put the river between themselves and the advancing Russians, the regiment took its chance and all but one man got across safely. The next day the ice melted so that for the time being they were safe from attack.

Marbot's conduct throughout this campaign was admirable and it is pleasant to learn that he received Imperial congratulations. In February a parade-state was demanded and he made one out, reporting 693 officers, N.C.O.s and troopers fit for duty. Napoleon, on receiving this figure, rejected it as an error and asked for a correct total. Marbot sent in another 'state', showing the same figure, and after General Sebastiani had reviewed the regiment and checked every man by name, it was seen that the 23rd Chasseurs was the strongest cavalry unit in the army. Marbot had the satisfaction of having done his duty superbly well but watched, with mixed feelings, every colonel commanding less than 400 mounted men sent on leave!

.   .   .

Captain Roeder, the Hessian, was now spending his first weeks as a detainee. Compared with the lot of latter-day prisoners-of-war—indeed, compared with that of men still struggling to reach the Vistula—his situation was by no means desperate. Wars had not yet reached that point of refinement where captive soldiers are herded like cattle behind barbed wire and left to rot in mind and body until hostilities end. Most officers had a good chance of exchange or parole, and once the tide of war had rolled away to the west, carrying with it the bitterness of the invaded for the invaders, even the N.C.O.s and men were not, for the most part, visited with much cruelty beyond that of neglect. They were obliged, however, to shift for themselves and Roeder tried to improve his situation by giving French lessons while his Sergeant-Major, the worthy Vogel, earned his bread as a tailor.

It was only from the civilian population that the French left behind in Vilna received barbarous treatment and Roeder says he saw many robbed and beaten up in the streets. Vogel, the indispensable, found and looted a magazine full of French uniforms, but he and Roeder were wise enough to convert two Imperial Guard outfits they found into civilian suits which afforded them an excellent disguise. The Cossacks raided the magazine the following day but by then Vogel and Roeder had fully equipped themselves and even had weapons, razors and gloves, in addition to shirts, waistcoats, boots and caps. Roeder, however, was still suffering greatly from dysentery and was as thin as a beanpole.

On December 22nd the Tsar arrived in the city but still the two Hessian soldiers remained at large, paying their landlord with bales of cloth taken from the warehouse.

Numbers of officers, some of them German, were being transported back into Russia and none, as yet, were being released on parole, for it was assumed any who returned to France would at once be sent to Spain to fight against the British, now Russian allies. Roeder's position as a German, however, had certain advantages. Prussia was on the point of joining the coalition against Napoleon and a corps of German officers was being recruited to take part in the climatic struggle that would begin as soon as the weather improved. Roeder managed, after many disappointments, to get an appointment with the Duke of Wurttemburg, by whom he was promoted major, but on being asked to join the volunteer battalion he declined on grounds of ill health. He did, however, get some pay from the Duke and it came just in time, for he and Vogel were penniless.

.   .   .

In the meantime Sergeant Bourgogne was discovering that the passage of the Niemen did not necessarily ensure a safe return to France.

The knowledge came to him within a day of setting out from his first billet west of the river. Again falling behind the line of march on account of his violent colic, he was cornered in a wood by a trio of Cossacks, but when they were on the point of taking him a skirmish close by alarmed their loosely tethered horses and the plainsmen left him to recapture them. Bourgogne took the opportunity to strip and wash himself with handfuls of snow, discarding his tattered shirt and breeches and regaining the road barelegged and in desperate straits.

His astounding luck continued. He found an old Chasseur with a spare pair of breeches and bought them for five francs. He also took some gaiters from a dead Grenadier of the Dutch Guard and at the next halting place bought ten spoonfuls of rice for fifteen francs, by no means the highest price paid for a few mouthfuls of food on that interminable journey. Before setting out on his next day's tramp Bourgogne gave one of his spare shirts (found in the portmanteaux near the hill of Ponari) to bandage an Imperial Guard gunner who staggered in with more than twenty lance thrusts and sword cuts after an encounter with Cossacks. On December 16th, the fifty-ninth day of the march from Moscow, he reached the town of Wilbalen, where Murat and the remnants of the Guard were installed. For the time being he was safe from capture.

Yet even now his odyssey was incomplete. There were sentinels at every house and over and over again he was turned away, although half-dead from cold, hunger and exhaustion. At length he met his old comrade Picart, with whom he had travelled as a straggler on the road to Orcha, and Picart had found a way to ensure shelter. He had sewn a colonel's epaulettes on his shoulders and was treated as a field officer by the men detailed to guard the houses against stragglers. Welcoming Bourgogne he produced the inevitable bottle of brandy.

Sergeant Picart is perhaps the prototype of every professional soldier in every army up to modern times. He could meet and surmount any hardship, any deprivation, any obstacle encountered during a campaign. He was brave, self-contained, a first-class marksman and possessed of limitless reserves of ingenuity and animal cunning. In Picart we glimpse the professional survivor of every human upheaval. He is the time-serving legionary who marched with Caesar, the fourteenth-century mercenary who harried France under freebooters like Sir Robert Knollys in the Hundred Years' War, and the old sweat of the British Army, who somehow survived the murderous battles of the First Ypres and Loos, in the First World War. There was nothing he would not attempt in his determination to survive in comfort. Nothing could defeat or discourage him, not cold, Cossacks or a line of march cluttered with the corpses of less resourceful men. He had marched with the Republican Army down into Italy in the whirlwind campaigns of 1796 and 1797. He had trudged across the Sinai desert to the walls of Acre and back again to beat the Turks at Aboukir. He had fought Austrians at Marengo,

Austerlitz and Wagram, Germans at Jena, Russians at Eylau and Friedland, Spaniards, Portuguese and British in the Spanish peninsula. He had robbed, cursed, danced, sung and bayoneted his way across a continent and back again. Yet there was never a time when he had not, secreted about his pack, an emergency reserve of food, plenty of cartridges and money in gold. He could conjure liquor, rice and flour from a desert or a charred hut. He was never defeated and he never despaired.

It was Picart who saved Bourgogne again, feeding and resting him, and telling him gleefully how he had helped himself to Imperial treasure on the hill of Ponari. It was Picart who, once more posing as a Jew, revived the spirits of Bourgogne and other survivors by welcoming them into his billet and striking bargains with his supposed co-religionists. Then, with Sergeant Grangier and three others, Bourgogne set out for Gumbinnen on a hired sledge, defeating an attempt on the part of the drivers to ditch them and make off with their belongings. It was a good way of getting over the ground, particularly as all five men suffered from frostbitten feet but the motion made Bourgogne seasick!

En route they met with surliness sometimes amounting to hostility and were often grossly overcharged for a night's lodging. When they disputed the bill of a statuesque Prussian landlady she said, 'Poor little Frenchmen! Six months ago that was all very well—you were stronger, but today things are different! You are going to give me what I ask or I will keep my husband from putting the horse in the sleigh and have you taken by the Cossacks!' They gave her what she asked and on their departure she spat in Bourgogne's face.

They passed the six-year-old battlefield of Eylau and looked with interest at the cross commemorating the deaths of twenty-nine officers and 590 other ranks of the gallant Fourteenth of the Line, a regiment surrounded and wiped out to the last man defending their eagle in the 1807 campaign.[3] They were turned away from another village where, back in the summer, a handsome young Chasseur had seduced the wife of the burgomaster, stirring up hostility for the French on the part of the menfolk. On December 23rd they reached Elbing, where there was a longish halt and Bourgogne had the luck to be billeted with an angel of light, the wife of a French hussar who had been discharged with wounds. Landlady and servant took a great fancy to the tough little Grenadier and in addition to feeding and cosseting him they gave him a bath. Scrubbed clean, and with his beard and whiskers trimmed, he was unrecognisable when his friend Grangier called for him the next morning.

On New Year's Day he was sufficiently restored to attend an uproarious, Irish-style wake, in the house where Picart was billeted and on the following day he met, to his intense surprise, two men of his company, left behind on the banks of the Beresina who had wandered alone for over a month. He also encountered an old comrade who was still carrying some of Bourgogne's Moscow loot and was thus able to make his charming hostess a present of one of the valuable rings he had saved from the great fire.

The Russians, however, were now moving westward at an accelerated pace and it was essential to rally the wrecked battalions behind the Vistula. With the roar of artillery in their ears the few survivors of the Grenadiers–Fusiliers crossed the river in the early days of January, Grangier commenting grimly on the Prussians and Picart, who had just threatened to bayonet one, planting a well-aimed kick in his behind as he fled. As they marched the guardsman sang his favourite song:

> *'Ah! tu t'en souviendras, la-ri-la,*
> *Du depart de Boulogne!'*

They had survived to fight an array of nations at Lutzen, Bautzen, Leipsic, Dresden and, at fall of curtain, on the plateau of Mont St. Jean outside Brussels. They were to live in legend as long as men talked and wrote of war.

.   .   .

Far away to the east, in the squalid city of Vilna, Roeder the Hessian Lifeguard was still a free man and could even indulge himself in Russian vapour baths. His thoughts were now turning more and more to escape from this hateful land and he cultivated the friendship of an egregious officer, half-spy, half-tout, who promised to spirit him and his faithful sergeant-major over the frontier into Prussia or the Duchy of Warsaw.

Day after day Roeder flattered and picqueted this man, and at length they made their try, the Hessians getting as far as Swedish Pomerania where they ran headlong into a web of red tape and petty officialdom that resulted in their imprisonment at the town of Stralsund. Here, bedevilled by military and bureaucratic bullies, they languished until May, but at length won free and travelled onward to the Elbe, which the French were preparing to defend against the combined forces of the Tsar, the Prussian General Blucher and the French ex-marshal, Crown Prince Bernadotte of Sweden.

At last, on June 23rd, Roeder reached his home in Göttingen, where he had long been given up for dead. In the late afternoon of the 30th he was engaged in writing up his diary when he heard the rush of small feet and was overwhelmed by the affections of his children, Carl and Caroline, who searched his pockets for presents. Then Sophie, his wife, came in. 'To her,' concludes the diarist, 'I had only myself to give.'

Not long before a similar family reunion had taken place in Mons between Major Marbot and his wife, the Major having at last been given the leave withheld him because he had been such a painstaking father to his regiment. It was a year since he had seen her and they met while Marbot was recruiting in Belgium, then part of the Empire. 'It was a great pleasure,' says this estimable man, 'to see my wife again and for the first time to kiss our little Alfred, now eight months old. It was one of the happiest days of my life.' It was indeed, particularly when he recalled how, far out on the left wing of the Grand Army the previous summer, he had nearly met his death on the day his child had been born.

. . .

In the brightly lit palace of the exiled Bourbons, the man for whom men like Bourgogne, Marbot and Roeder had marched and fought and suffered was working far into the night to build another Grand Army in a matter of weeks. Perhaps the most astonishing single achievement of his career is that he succeeded.

The conscript class of 1813 was called up and the class of 1814 anticipated, a levy of half-grown boys, few of whom knew how to load a musket. Veteran officers were dug out of garrison towns; the country was scoured for horses. The gun foundries worked day and night shifts. Three thousand gendarmes, thousands of sailors and battalions of National Guardsmen were called upon to fill the gaps made by the men who had left their bones along the roads from Moscow to the Vistula. Before the first day of spring one in every three of the male population in France between the age of seventeen and forty-three was in uniform.

Reviewing the remnant of a regiment of the Imperial Guard at Trianon in January, Napoleon had paused in front of the young Baron de Bourgoing, later to become a senator and peer of France. He was one of thirty survivors of a regiment that had crossed the Niemen 1,500 strong six months previously. Napoleon asked the young lieutenant's age and was told it was twenty-one. 'That was the age of the whole regiment,' the Colonel commented, bitterly, 'and it was the young who suffered the most!' The twenty-one-year-old veteran took advantage of the moment and asked to be promoted captain, giving as his reason that after his recent experience, he felt capable of commanding a company. Napoleon was on the point of granting the request, as he almost invariably did when a direct approach was made to him by a junior officer or a private who had given proofs of loyalty, but the Colonel pointed out that De Bourgoing had only served three months as a lieutenant. The Emperor smiled. 'Stairs are not meant to be taken four steps at a time!' he said.

It was advice that he should have applied to himself when he set out to federalise Europe in the first years of the century.

CHAPTER TWELVE

'MY LOSSES ARE REAL BUT THE ENEMY CAN TAKE NO CREDIT FOR THEM'

Napoleon writing to the King of Denmark and Norway,
January 1813

1

THE campaign was over. Its results, embracing the fall of
Napoleon and the collapse of his Empire within another
sixteen months, were to influence the policies of Western
Europe down to this day, and perhaps on into the twenty-
first century. Never again was Russia to be discounted as a
semi-barbaric and remote autocracy in the chancellories of
more progressive neighbours. Always, in the minds of
statesmen and strategists, she was to remain the great im-
ponderable, the bear who could be badgered but never
ignored, the great vacuum into which armies could be
sucked, never to reappear. The balance of European power
was tilted in Russia's favour during the early winter
months of 1812; it was to remain tilted, notwithstanding
Russia's long, slow climb to modern status, and the emer-
gence of the United States as a first-class power. Only one
man foresaw this more than a century and a half ago and
he destroyed himself putting theory into practice. As if to
underscore the lesson of 1812 Adolf Hitler put the same
theory to the same test in 1941; with an identical result.

'*That war,*' wrote Napoleon at St. Helena, '*should have
been the most popular of modern times. It was a war of
good sense and true interests; a war for the repose and
security of all. It was purely pacific and preservative, entirely European and Continental. Its success would have
established a new balance of power and would have introduced new combinations, by which the dangers of the time*

present would have been succeeded by future tranquillity. In this case ambition had no share in my views. In raising Poland, which was the keystone of the whole arch, I would have permitted a King of Prussia, an Archduke of Austria, or any other to occupy the throne. I had no wish to acquire any new acquisition and I reserved to myself only the glory of doing good and the blessing of posterity.' Was he speaking in all sincerity, or was he engaged in the task that occupied the final years of his life, the creation of a legend? Nobody can be quite sure, but there are many in high places today who would be prepared to give him the benefit of the doubt. But here is superb irony. Today Russia herself faces a comparable situation. In October 1964, China, the great land mass to the east, exploded her first nuclear bomb. The seats of the imponderables have shifted to Pekin.

.   .   .

It remained to count the dead and here again the truth is elusive. French losses are naturally based on the total of men engaged and, as we saw at the beginning of this narrative, estimates of French forces crossing the Niemen vary enormously, all the way down from 600,000 to 320,000. It is the same with the losses. One can only strike a balance between those inclined to exaggerate in their efforts to denigrate Napoleon, and those who did their utmost, in the interests of the Legend, to minimise the figure. Of the latter group Marbot's figures are a good example.

Marbot's arithmetic was only as good as his loyalty. In the areas where he had direct access to the muster rolls there can be no question but that he was honest and truthful. Of his own regimental losses we have a detailed statement. He began to campaign with 1,018 all ranks, augmented by an additional 30 troopers while the 23rd Chasseurs were at Polotsk; this brings his total fighting strength to 1,048. Of these 109 were killed, 77 captured, 65 maimed and 104 missing. In February 1813 his regiment fielded 693 officers and men.

But Marbot, as we have seen, was an exceptionally zealous and efficient officer. It is a very different matter when he tries to assess the general figure, based on a parade-state shown him by General Gourgaud, an aide-de-camp of the Emperor. Here he was either misled or biased. Giving a total invading force of 325,900 (of whom 155,400 were French) he claims that 60,000 men of all ranks recrossed the Niemen at the close of the campaign. According to him, 93,000 of the French contingent were missing but of these, he declares, about 30,000 returned as released prisoners of war in 1814. Final losses are therefore given as a mere 63,000.

He is in error somewhere. The highest figure of survivors returning across the Niemen in December 1812 has been put elsewhere at 50,000, and even this is almost certainly an over-estimate. Some witnesses of this stage of the retreat put it as low as 10,000, three parts of them stragglers representing every national group in the Grand Army.

The French historian Thiers is far more forthright. He asserts that Napoleon lost approximately 100,000 in battle, 150,000 in the retreat, and 100,000 prisoners, a grand total of 350,000, or more than actually took part in the campaign according to Marbot.

The Russian losses were never calculated, but the authorities made a careful count of the number of corpses buried or burned in those provinces crossed by the invaders during the advance and retreat. In 1813 burial parties are reported to have disposed of 430,707 men and 230,677 horses, but these totals include both sides and probably numbers of peasants who died of starvation or exposure after their homes had been burned. A study of the muster rolls of various French units in the spring of 1813 inclines one to favour Thiers' estimate. Regiments of 1,000 plus had dwindled to squads, and even among units of the Guard nine out of ten men failed to answer roll-call at rallying points like Elbing and Koenigsberg.

To arrive at any accurate guess of the losses sustained

one must first subtract the corps of Schwartzenberg and Macdonald, both of whom deserted without being fully engaged.[1] This would reduce the total number of the invading force by approximately 50,000. Then another factor has to be taken into consideration. The corps of Oudinot and Victor, while heavily engaged in the fighting against Wittgenstein and on both sides of the Beresina, did not suffer the losses of corps that actually reached Moscow and had also lost heavily on the field of Borodino. Even so they were greatly reduced, sufficiently so for Napoleon to regard Marbot's parade state as fiction.

Perhaps the best way to arrive at a final figure is to divide the invasion force into three parts—deserters, flank guards and the Moscow contingent. The deserters, almost exclusively Prussians and Austrians, incurred practically no losses, reducing the original invasion force to about 275,000 men, exclusive of camp-followers. The combined flank guards of Oudinot and Victor, when they rejoined the main body at Borissov, numbered about 25,000 so that by the time the crossing was made the Grand Army, flank guards and main body joined, probably amounted to about 65,000 effectives, many of them walking wounded but still capable of beating off attacks.

In the terrible march from the Beresina to Vilna, when the temperature fell to thirty degrees below zero, at least half this force melted away, proportionately more than were lost between Vilna and the Niemen, where the temperatures were bearable and the sick and wounded had been abandoned in the Vilna hospitals. This means that about 30,000 gained the western bank of the Niemen but of these not more than a third had set foot in Moscow. The majority had not penetrated further than Smolensk. Using this method of assessment the total figure of men lost in six months campaigning is around a quarter-million. Of these perhaps 20,000 returned to their homes in 1814. By any standards the wastage during the campaign was devastating, immeasurably higher than in any other Napoleonic campaign or, for that matter, in any war ever waged on the continent of Europe in modern times. Not until 1914 were men's lives to be sacrificed on this scale.

For the remainder of his life Napoleon was to blame these losses on the weather, giving no credit at all to the dogged Kutusoff, to Wittgenstein, or to the reckless Tchichagoff, to say nothing of the courage and hardihood of the Russian soldier. It was unworthy of him. Undoubtedly the frost was the most punishing of his opponents but a factor that is not always taken into consideration is the breakdown of supplies. Well-fed and warmly-clad men could have weathered the retreat. A few of the hardiest did, against all odds, but the majority perished as much through starvation as from snow and ice.

In a letter written to the King of Denmark and Norway, on January 5th, 1813, Napoleon goes out of his way to emphasise the ravages caused by the snow, and its effect upon horses unaccustomed to these temperatures. He says that the loss of horses meant that the infantry marched without the protection of cavalry and that this led to the taking of many more prisoners than would have otherwise occurred. He is probably right but it was preposterous to claim, in the same letter, that he had not lost a gun or a flag, or to add, '... my losses are real but the enemy can take no credit for them'.

Throughout the campaign the French rank and file fought magnificently, but so did the Russians, both in withdrawal and advance, so well indeed that they were able to boast during the Campaign of France just over a year later, 'Father Moscow is coming to pay a call on Mother Paris.' The call was duly paid. By April 1814 Cossacks were riding down the Champs Elysèes and astute Bonapartists were using the good-natured Tsar to mediate between themselves and the revengeful Prussians.

2

It had happened with the inevitability of a Greek tragedy and yet, to men accustomed to view Napoleon as the most powerful man in the world, with terrifying speed. In October 1812, he was looking down on the ruins of Moscow and dictating terms of peace to the Tsar; by April 1814 he was hurrying south under an assumed name and in the uniform of an Austrian officer, slipping through towns and villages unheralded and unrecognised.

It is beyond the scope of this narrative to tell what took place as a direct result of the Russian campaign but a brief mention of the events of 1813 and 1814 will illustrate how rapidly the Napoleonic edifice collapsed once its fabric had been shaken by the disastrous march to and from the old Russian capital.

From May 1813 until early November the same year, France was engaged in a titanic struggle to hold the eastern bastion of her Empire. Despite early victories, often against great odds, the new Grand Army was thrust back over the Rhine and here, in the New Year, the troops of the Coalition followed it into France.

For four more months Napoleon continued the fight, 60,000 men and boys grappling with half-a-million invaders. Napoleon even continued to win brilliant tactical successes but by early April his bluff was called and the allies marched directly on Paris. It fell without a blow. Then, faced with an ultimatum from those of his marshals still loyal to him, the Emperor abdicated and was hurried off to Elba. In less than eleven months he was back to fight and lost Waterloo. By autumn, 1815, he was at St. Helena, a petulant, used-up man of forty-six, dying of cancer of the stomach. In the five and a half years he spent in exile he thought and wrote a great deal about the Russian campaign but, to the end, he never apologised for it as a political gesture. In the military sense, to some extent, he did, admitting that he was in command and must therefore accept full responsibility for what occurred up to the moment he left the army at Smorgoni on December 5th.

It is intriguing to speculate what might have happened had he taken Ney's advice and stopped at Smolensk, or even Vitepsk. He could have wintered at either town, keeping in day-to-day touch with his outlying corps, and with Europe as a whole. Such a decision might have given him another three or four years in which to consolidate but it would not have induced the Russians to accept permanent domination of Europe by the French. Even before he set out for Moscow he was losing the war in Spain, and neither Prussia nor Austria would have remained quiescent indefinitely. Britain, exercising complete control of the seas, would have fought on for as long as was necessary and in the end, possibly by 1817, the combined power of the autocracies would have triumphed. Even had he succeeded in dominating them during his lifetime, the French Empire would have crumbled within a year of his death for there was no one in France big enough to succeed him and at the time of his final overthrow his heir was only four years of age.

So that it might be argued that the Russian campaign accelerated rather than caused the postponement of the bourgeois revolution that Napoleon, consciously or not, represented. For a possible outline of what form this revolution could have taken had Napoleon succeeded in enforcing a long peace upon Europe one must look further back than 1812, to moments such as the Peace of Tilsit, in 1807, or the invasion of Spain in the following year. His one real hope of grafting the fundamentally progressive forces of the French Revolution upon the stiff, backward-looking, unimaginative autocrats of Europe, reposed in taking things slowly and working step by step, in the manner of a craftsman rather than a wrecker and to ask this of a man of Napoleon Bonaparte's character and ability is to ask the impossible. How could a professional soldier who had conquered Northern Italy in a month be expected to exercise the patience of a Talleyrand or the serpentine statesmanship of a Metternich? Whatever he did he had to do on the instant; that he achieved so much in a period of sixteen years (1796–1812) is astonishing, far more so than the fact that he lost all he had gained in less than three years. Perhaps the truth of the matter lies in the fact that he was a man born into the eighteenth century with a twentieth-century brain.

3

When Napoleon died at the age of fifty-one, in 1821, he had already outlived four of his closest associates during the advance and retreat—Marshals Ney, Murat, Bessières and Duroc, and also his principal enemy, Kutusoff, the old fox of the North.

Kutusoff did not live to see the triumph of Russian arms in the spring of 1814. Strongly opposing the invasion of the west up to the last moment of his life, and more than content with having fulfilled his promise to expel the last French invader from Russian soil, he died soon after the Tsar's forces crossed the Niemen in January 1813. Nominal direction of the Russian forces passed to the hands of the Tsar himself but the actual responsibility for directing the 1813 campaign was Schwartzenberg's who had, as close advisers, men with first-hand knowledge of Napoleonic warfare, chief among them Bernadotte, Crown Prince of Sweden.

Bernadotte was the only French marshal to retain the prizes he had gained during his rapid ascent from barracks to throne. He lived on, greatly honoured, until 1844, dying as Charles XIV of Sweden, and his direct descendants continue to reign in that country.

Two men who played very prominent parts in the campaign on the French side were dead before the third anniversary of recrossing the Niemen came round. One was Michel Ney, hero of the retreat, the other King Murat, hero of the advance. Both were executed by firing squad, the first in Paris, for his share in the Hundred Days, the other in Calabria, after the failure of an attempt to regain the throne of Naples.

The execution of Marshal Ney created a great deal of resentment among his old comrades and an equal stir among his enemies, but the execution of Murat passed almost unnoticed. Both faced death with the dignity and courage they had invariably displayed in the field; both trials made a mockery of justice. Ney was condemned by men who, in some instances, had committed the identical crime for which he died and others who were unworthy to shake him by the hand. Murat was shot down by the hirelings of what A. G. Macdonnell rightly calls 'a miserable, cowardly and corrupt government'. Chief witness for the defence at Ney's trial was his old comrade Davout, whose loyalty to Napoleon had survived every test and who never did bow the knee to the Bourbons. To the hour of his death, in 1823, he remained aloof, taciturn and inflexible, a Bonapartist to the last.

Thirty-four wounds received in action did not prevent Marshal Oudinot, the gallant commander of the Second Corps, from enjoying an active old age. He died in 1847, aged eighty-one years. Bessières, Commander of the Old Guard, and Duroc, the popular Palace Marshal, were both killed in action during the 1813 campaign and Berthier, Chief of Staff, died as a suicide or, just possibly, the victim of an accident. He fell from a window at Bamberg while watching a Russian column pass below. It was just seventeen days before Waterloo and this was the only campaign the Emperor had fought since 1796 when Berthier was not present as Chief-of-Staff.[2] Victor, the man who refused to relieve Ney as commander of the rearguard on the road to Vilna, became an active royalist and a betrayer of old comrades. He died, unregretted, in 1841, a year after Napoleon was brought back from St. Helena and laid in his marble tomb at Les Invalides. Mortier, whose proverbial good spirits had triumphed over the Russian climate, was killed by a bomb thrown by an assassin at King Louis-Phillippe, in 1835.[3]

Alexander, Tsar of All the Russias, did not fulfil the promise of his young manhood. He liberated Europe, or rather he made it temporarily safe for the ruling dynasties, but he did not carry out his original intention of liberating his own serfs. He died in December 1825, four and a half years after the death of his great adversary.

And the others, the humbler men whose experiences form the basis of this story? The majority survived into old age and, in many cases, achieved a modest prosperity. The worthiest of them, Marshal Marbot of the 23rd Chasseurs, continued an active military career into his late fifties, when he was again wounded in the knee, this time in a French expedition in North Africa. His memoirs, written in exile (he was another irreconcilable) attracted the notice of Napoleon who left him 100,000 francs in his will and bade him 'continue to write in defence of the glory of the French army'. He died, greatly honoured, in 1854, at the age of seventy-two. As A. J. Butler, English translator of his memoirs comments, 'Few men of that age seem to have left a more creditable record.'

Bourgogne, who had cheated death a thousand times on the road from Moscow to the Vistula, continued to elude him until 1867, when Napoleon's nephew was reviving the tarnished splendours of his uncle's reign. From time to time he met and recognised his old comrades, men he had encountered at many a bivouac and along innumerable stretches of that long, frostbound road. He was always surprised to see them alive and in good health and doubtless they too were surprised to see *le petiot* plump, rosy and law-abiding. In the notes at the end of his book Bourgogne records some of these encounters. One was with Quartermaster Rossi, whom he left behind with badly frostbitten feet, and the two met by chance in the Hotel de Provence, in Brest, nearly twenty years after the great retreat. Their mutual recognition intrigued the other guests, who insisted on a recital of their adventures in Russia.

These men, the Bourgognes, the Rossis, the Picarts, the Grangiers, could still be found in every town of France on into the middle of the nineteenth century, and a few of them must have survived to witness the Prussian occupation of Paris after the French defeat in the Franco-Prussian war. They were scarred, martyrs to rheumatism, and not a few of them lacked a limb. They had survived several revolutions, two empires and two restorations, but the long procession of notabilities who passed in and out of the State apartments of Paris between 1815 and 1871 made no impression upon them. Their loyalty had been given to the man who had led them across mountain ranges, deserts and snowbound plains and it was never shared with his successors. They remembered the time when they had marched and cursed and looted along roads leading to almost every capital in Europe and as they sank into obscurity they clung to their martial pride and the memories of unimaginable triumphs. It is to these forgotten men that this book is dedicated.

THE SOURCES OF THIS BOOK

THE sources of this book are innumerable, comprising as they do the fruits of forty years' reading of the period 1789–1815 embracing the Revolution, the Consulate and the eleven years of the Empire. They can be divided, however, into three main streams; the histories, the personal memoirs and the commentaries. Both historians and commentators have drawn very freely from the wealth of memoir that flowed from European presses during the long peace that followed Waterloo. In writing this account of the Great Retreat I have gone to the same sources.

The early histories I consulted to reconstruct the main features of the advance and withdrawal include those of Thiers, Joseph S. C. Abbot, Sir Walter Scott, John Lochart, W. M. Sloane and G. M. Bussey, all published more than a half-century ago, some within a few years of Napoleon's death. More recent authors to whom I am greatly indebted are Sir Bernard Pares, Professor of Russian History, for his excellent *History of Russia* (Jonathan Cape), a standard work on the subject, the more recently published *Napoleon Bonaparte, His Rise and Fall by* J. M. Thompson, F.B.A., F.R.Hist.S., another very scholarly and extremely readable work, published by Blackwell in 1952, and Emil Ludwig's world-famous work *Napoleon*, published in Britain by Allen and Unwin, Ltd., in 1927. These are by no means the only reliable sources on the campaign but they are all the work of painstaking historians.

In the second, third and fourth decades of the nineteenth century hundreds, possibly thousands of people compiled memoirs relating to the First Empire. Most of these, however, dealt with civil spheres and were written by court officials, politicians, civil servants and sometimes members of Napoleon's domestic staff. For all that a number of professional soldiers did write of their experiences, sometimes in the form of diaries and jottings and with no thought of publication, sometimes autobiographically and for publication. It is upon these important sources that I drew without stint. The material they provide is accurate, moving and graphic.

Pre-eminent among them are the *Memoirs of Sergeant Bourgogne*, possibly the most detailed and striking record of a campaign ever compiled by a non-commissioned officer in any army, and also the fascinating account of fifteen years in the field by Baron de Marbot. Bourgogne's book has been admirably translated by the Hon. J. W. Fortescue and was first published in England by Heinemann in 1899, since when it has been re-issued by Peter Davies and Jonathan Cape, in 1926 and 1930. Bourgogne fought in the 1806 German campaign and was continuously in the field until captured in 1813, but it is only of the Russian campaign that he writes. The happenings of that terrible experience seem to have been indelibly printed on his mind, so that he makes only passing references to his service in Spain, Poland and the Danube area. It is a magnificent account, all the better for its simple style projecting a man who thought of himself as wholly unimportant.

Marbot's heroic story is equally impressive, although from a different standpoint, for Marbot, an officer from the beginning of his service, and successively the aide-de-camp of many marshals, takes a modest pride in his achievements. He is fully entitled to do so; he survived fifteen years of almost continuous service, and was wounded many times in the performance of deeds that would have made him the most decorated junior officer in the Allied Army of the First or Second World War. In his account the Russian campaign takes its place among all the others but, one way and another, the *Memoirs of Baron de Marbot* is the most enthralling book I have ever been privileged to read. It was translated by Arthur John Butler and Cassell's issued a pocket edition in 1929.

Perhaps the most famous account of the campaign was written by the Count De Ségur, a high-ranking officer, whose book caused a tremendous sensation and reaction in favour of Marshal Ney when published soon after the Second Restoration. Less well known, but written with honesty and charm, is the account of the Duchess of Reggio, Marshal Oudinot's devoted wife, compiled by Gaston Stiegler, and first translated into English by Alexander Teixeira de Mattos. It was published in London by H. Henry and Co. in 1896.

Fortunately for the military student eye-witness accounts of the Napoleonic campaigns are still coming to light, even after a century and a half. Helen Roeder, descendent of Captain Roeder of the Hessian Lifeguards, edited and published her ancestor's graphic diary as recently as 1960 and the book, issued by Methuen and Co., is a remarkable contribution to the military history of the period.

Delving much further back into history I was fortunate to find a two-volume book entitled *Memoirs of the Public and Private Life of Napoleon Bonaparte,* compiled from 'original anecdotes from the MS of Count Labédoyère, M. V. Arnault, Counts Rapp, Montholon, Las Cases, Gourgaud and Ségur'. It was first published by George Virtue, of London, several generations ago, and is a kind of anthology of Napoleonic soldiers. Rapp, of course, wrote a great deal about the campaigns seen from the standpoint of an aide-de-camp, whereas Gourgaud, Montholon and Las Cases shared part of Napoleon's exile on St. Helena. General Gourgaud actually saved the Emperor's life at Brienne, killing a Cossack who was on the point of attacking him.

Another fruitful, if somewhat biased source, are the lengthy memoirs of Bourrienne, once Napoleon's secretary, who tells his story in four volumes. As regards the Russian campaign Bourrienne relies mainly upon De Ségur, but a generous contributor to his notes on the retreat was Labaume, who was on the staff of Prince Eugène, Commander of the Fourth Corps. There are also *Napoleon's Letters,* translated by J. M. Thompson, and published by Dent, in Everyman's Library. One could spend years studying the vast correspondence of Napoleon, and in checking facts relating to the Russian campaign I used not only Thompson's admirable text but *New Letters of Napoleon*, omitted from the edition published under the auspices of his nephew by Heinemann in 1898.

The literature on Napoleon is immense, probably larger than that dealing with any other figure in ancient or modern history. Every year, almost every month, something is added to it and recently a large number of specialist commentaries have been produced. Highly recommended in this field are the following: J. B. Morton's *Marshal Ney* (Arthur Barker), Macdonell's witty *Napoleon and his Marshals* (Macmillan), Jean Savant's *Napoleon in his Time* (Putnam), P. W. Sergeant's *The Burlesque Napoleon* (Werner Laurie), and James Kemple's recently published *Napoleon Immortal* (John Murray), dealing with the Emperor's health, a much disputed subject.

All these books are well worth buying and reading and most of them can be bought or traced without difficulty. I am greatly indebted to every author mentioned in this bibliography.

NOTES

1. Charles XII, King of Sweden, was the great adversary of Peter
the Great in the early years of the eighteenth century. His invasion
of Russia in 1708 has similarities with Napoleon's inasmuch as he
began by conquering Poland and setting up supply bases before
advancing on Grodno with 33,000 superbly trained troops. The Tsar
retreated, employing approximately the same tactics as Bagration
and Kutusoff. but his situation was the more perilous because, at
that time, he was facing four separate rebellions within his realm.
Tsar Peter tried hard to negotiate with the Swedes, but Charles, an
extremely obstinate man, rejected his overtures and made an
alliance with Mazeppa, Hetman of the Dnieper Cossacks. Committing the same error as Napoleon, he advanced too far from his bases,
descending the Dnieper and surviving the exceptionally hard winter
of 1708/9. In the meantime the Tsar crushed the various rebellions
and was able to attack Charles at Poltava, on July 27th, 1709. The
battle began at four a.m. and continued until eleven a.m. The
Swedes were disastrously defeated, the king and his Cossack ally
escaping almost alone. That night Peter proposed a toast to captured Swedish officers, 'My teachers in the art of war'.

2 and 3. When Napoleon abandoned his plan of invading Britain
in the early autumn of 1805 and launched the Grand Army south-
east against the Austro-Russian armies based on Ulm and in
Bohemia, Prussia neglected to join the Coalition against the French.
Russia and Austria were routed at Austerlitz. The following year the
King of Prussia committed the supreme folly of challenging Napoleon singlehanded, without waiting for new Russian forces to come
to his assistance. In the hill-country of Thuringia Napoleon's main
army clashed with part of the Prussian force at Jena. The Prussians
were completely overwhelmed and their remnants pursued with the
utmost vigour. In the meantime, and on the same day, the detached
corps of Davout, hastening to the scene of operations, found itself
confronted by the main Prussian army, led by the King and the
Duke of Brunswick. The French numbered 27,000, the Prussians
60,000, but the latter were completely outfought and Brunswick was
killed. Marshal Bernadotte, whose corps was within eleven miles of
the battle, took no part in the action. For this brilliant success
Marshal Davout was created Duke of Auerstadt, the village where

the engagement took place. Davout's divisional commanders, Generals Gudin, Friant and Morand, were known in the Grand Army as The Immortals.

4. Talma was probably the most celebrated actor in France at this time. Born in 1763 he made his debut in Paris as Seide, in *Mahomet*, and his acting career continued throughout the days of the Consulate and Empire. Napoleon greatly admired his work and frequently watched his performances. Talma died in 1825.

5. Suvorov's escape from Switzerland, in September–October 1798, was one of the most astonishing feats in military history. The French, under Masséna, had defeated Russia's Austrian allies and occupied Zurich. The French mountain fighter, Lecourbe, held the top of the St. Gothard pass. The Russian general had no alternative but to escape over the mountains into the Grisons and this he did, crossing three ranges in single file with some 15,000 starving men, many of them barefoot. Half-frozen, marching through mountain mists, and sleeping where night fell, the Russian column escaped owing to the superb leadership of Suvorov and Bagration. (For a detailed account of this march see Sir Bernard Pares' *History of Russia*.)

CHAPTER TWO

1. The outstanding success of Wellington's strategy in Portugal had been generally recognised in European military circles by 1812. Retreating on Lisbon in the face of a greatly superior force under Marshal Masséna, in the late summer of 1810, Wellington fell back on an extremely complicated system of defence works at Torres Vedras, a network of fortified posts, breastworks, felled trees and stone redoubts. It was, as Masséna saw at a glance, impregnable and after wintering in exterior lines the French were obliged to fall back on Spain. There was undoubtedly a school of thought in the camp of the Tsar who were eager to imitate this strategy at Drissa, but the policy was not pursued, partly because the Grand Army's thrust at Moscow made it unnecessary but also because the Russian aristocracy was not, on the whole, in favour of defensive tactics.

2. Vandamme's most celebrated riposte was given after his capture in the pursuit that followed Napoleon's victory at Dresden the following year. Taken before the Tsar, and charged with excesses against civilians in Germany, he is reported to have said, 'At least I did not kill my own father!', a reference to Alexander's share in the murder of his predecessor.

3. Davout's reputation for rapid marching was equal to Napo-

leon's own. As a strict disciplinarian he was able to exact some astounding marching feats from his rank and file. In order to be present at the battle of Austerlitz, fought on December 4th, 1805, when the ground was laid with snow, Davout marched his corps a distance of seventy miles, from Pressburg, to take up a position on the right wing of the Grand Army, and covered the ground in forty-four hours. At that time, and under those conditions, this was a feat unequalled in the annals of the Grand Army or, indeed, of any modern army. He arrived in time to play a vital rôle in the victory. (See A. G. Macdonell's *Napoleon and his Marshals*.)

CHAPTER THREE

1. Bernadotte's betrayal of his compatriots was never forgiven by the veterans of the Grand Army. Although an excellent soldier he was never much liked by his colleagues. There is no doubt that he was motivated by personal jealousy of Napoleon (he married Desirée Clary, whom Napoleon had once courted) and in joining France's enemies he had hopes of succeeding Napoleon as Emperor of the French. The Tsar encouraged him in these hopes when they met at Abo to discuss an alliance. He owed his position as Crown Prince of Sweden to an act of kindness to some Swedish prisoners, in the Prussian campaign of 1806. A Gascon by birth, he had been a sergeant-major when the Revolution broke out in 1789 and rose swiftly by merit in the field. He was dismissed after the battle of Wagram, in the Austrian campaign of 1809, where his Saxon corps was routed. This did not prevent him from issuing a bulletin congratulating them and the act infuriated Napoleon, who sent him from the field. Soon afterwards he accepted the offer to become Swedish Crown Prince and his negotiations with the Tsar were based upon his renunciation of a claim to Finland in return for Russian help in conquering Norway. His direct descendants continue to rule Sweden.

CHAPTER FOUR

1. Baron Von Stein, a Prussian patriot, played an important part in the overthrow of Napoleon. Emil Ludwig describes Stein as a man of exceptionally high principle, who never ceased to resist French dominance of Prussia. As a diplomat at the Prussian court he survived the overthrow of his country in 1806 but in 1808 Napoleon, aware of the danger of Stein's influence, banished him from his

homeland. It was a reckless act. Stein went to Russia and played a vital part in encouraging the Tsar to resist Napoleon. 'He was the only man at the Tsar's court with no axe to grind,' comments Ludwig, and as such his influence was decisive. He never ceased to counsel the strategy that led to the destruction of the Grand Army. (See Ludwig's *Napoleon*.)

2. The Malet Conspiracy, of October 1812, is one of the most remarkable pieces of bluff ever practised upon an established government. Malet, a zealous republican, had seen active service in the Revolutionary Wars but had been imprisoned as an irreconcilable during the Empire. On the night of October 22nd he escaped from the Maison de Santé where he was detained and with forged documents, purporting to announce the death of Napoleon under the walls of Moscow, took command of 1,200 National Guards, released two other conspirators from La Force, and arrested Savary, the Prefect of Police. Orders that he issued were blindly obeyed by responsible officials and various detachments of troops were sent to arrest other notabilities and take possession of strategic centres, but an official recognised him in the presence of General Hulin. Still bluffing, Malet offered to show Hulin proofs of his authority, but as the General preceded him into a private room he fired a pistol at his head. He was arrested and detained until enquiries could be made. He and fifteen others were subsequently executed. (See Vol. III, *Memoirs of Bourienne*.)

Chapter Five

1. Eugène's father, Alexandre de Beauharnais, who married Josephine in December 1779, was guillotined during the Terror, shortly before Robespierre was overthrown by the Thermidorians. His mother, who was lucky to escape the same fate, subsequently became the mistress of Barras, one of the Directors, who passed her on to Napoleon in 1796. When the Directory ordered that all arms should be surrendered Josephine handed in her late husband's sword but Eugène, then fourteen, made a personal call upon General Bonaparte to ask for its return. Napoleon was greatly impressed by the boy's earnestness and it was probably through this chance encounter that he met Josephine, whom he married shortly afterwards. The close friendship between stepfather and stepson continued for the remainder of their lives, notwithstanding the divorce.

2. Pauline Fourès was the wife of a junior officer who evaded the order that no women were to accompany the Egyptian expedition by dressing herself as a soldier and boarding a transport. Napoleon

became attracted to her during his stay in Cairo and later despatched her husband on a mission to France, knowing that he would be captured by the blockading British navy. This in fact occurred, but the British, aware through their spies of what was taking place ashore, freed him and he returned to headquarters to find his wife established as the General's mistress. He at once divorced her but the liaison did not survive Napoleon's return to France, although he gave her a generous allowance and she subsequently made a fortune importing timber from Brazil. Learning that Josephine, in his absence, had been seduced by a disgraced army contractor, Napoleon determined to divorce her but Eugène, aided by his sister Hortense, successfully interceded on her behalf. The divorce was postponed for nine years. (See *The Love Affairs of Napoleon*, by J. Turquan.)

CHAPTER SIX

1. Leonidas Polk, a prominent churchman, became a popular general in the Confederate Army during the American Civil War. After taking part in many actions he was killed by a shell at Pine Mountain, during Johnston's retreat in the summer of 1864. As a churchman Polk was denied the use of language available to other commanders such as Major-General Cheetham whose battlecry was 'Give 'em hell, boys!' The Bishop General is said to have encouraged his troops by shouting 'Give 'em what General Cheetham says, boys!' He was much loved by the Army of Tennessee. (See *The Story of the Confederacy*, by R. S. Henry, published by Grosset & Dunlap, and *The Army of Tennessee*, by S. F. Horn, published by Bobbs Merrill.)

2. Ney's devotion to duty during this campaign was acknowledged by all ranks, and by Russian field commanders at the time, but it was not until the Second Restoration that Frenchmen as a whole recognised his extreme gallantry. The publication of De Ségur's account made a great impact upon the public and there followed a marked reaction in favour of the man who had been shot for his share in the Hundred Days. Some of Ney's old comrades, however, behaved despicably towards him after Waterloo. St. Cyr ordered his court martial (he was ultimately tried by the Chamber of Peers) and Marshals Victor and Marmont voted for the death penalty. On the other hand Marshal Davout, who considered Ney's trial a flagrant breach of the amnesty he had arranged, fought hard to save him, and Marshal Moncey, having flatly refused to serve on the court martial, wrote to the King in the following terms:

Where were his accusers while Ney was fighting on so many fields of battle? Did they follow him? Did they accuse him during twenty years of toil and danger? If Russia and The Allies cannot pardon the conqueror of the Moscowa, can France forget the hero of the Beresina? At the crossing of the Beresina, Sire, in the midst of that awful catastrophe, it was Ney who saved the remnant of the army. I had in it relatives, friends and finally soldiers, who are the friends of their chiefs. Am I to send to death him to whom so many Frenchmen owe their lives, so many families their sons, their husbands, their relations?'

For this letter Moncey was expelled from the Chamber of Peers and imprisoned in a fortress.

3. General Marion, who was Ney's comrade-in-arms during most of the retreat, and whose life Ney saved at Pleszczenitsky, was one of the signatories of Ney's sentence. (See Macdonell's *Napoleon and his Marshals.*)

Chapter Seven

1. Sergeant Picart was one of the best marksmen in the Imperial Guard and won prizes at the butts. Proficiency with the firearm was not rated highly in the Grand Army. Very little time was devoted to target practice and consequently only volley firing proved destructive in the field. This was true of all European armies at the time, with the single exception of the British, whose individual marksmanship was greatly respected. General Moore, training what ultimately became the nucleus of Wellington's Light Brigade, had devoted much time and trouble to this aspect of training with the result that drafts to the Peninsula produced men like Rifleman Tom Plunkett of the 95th Foot, who shot General Colbert through the head at extreme range during the retreat to Corunna.

2. There were a great number of wolves running wild in the Russian forests at this time but few of the survivors mention them, although there is an instance of infantrymen shooting a bear for food. It would seem that, with so many corpses and partially dismembered horses to feed upon the wolf packs kept clear of active men.

1. Wounded thirty-four times during the Napoleonic and Revolutionary wars, Oudinot created a record in this respect. His constitution must have been a remarkably good one for he survived until 1847, dying in his bed at the age of eighty-one years.

2. In his letter to Maret, written at Zavinski, Napoleon gives Partouneaux's number as 3,000, not 2,000. This might be a slip but perhaps he did not allow for the few hundred of the rearguard who took the river road and thus succeeded in rejoining Victor's Corps at the Studienka ford.

3. General Sir Robert Wilson is the best (indeed, almost the only) British eye-witness of the retreat. He was attached to Kutusoff's forces as an observer and was clearly a chivalrous opponent of the French for later, after Waterloo, he saved the life of Marshal Soult by warning him that he was proscribed and Soult was able to escape into the territory of Berg, thus avoiding Ney's fate.

4. Marshal Victor, after playing his part in the condemnation of Ney, was employed by the Bourbons to investigate the behaviour of French officers who had supported Napoleon during the Hundred Days. He remained an active Royalist and would not attend at the Invalides when the body of Napoleon was reinterred there in December 1840. Two of the marshals involved in the Russian campaign did attend, Oudinot and Grouchy, the latter having been made a marshal in 1815. Soult and Moncey were also present at the impressive ceremony. Victor died in 1841.

CHAPTER NINE

1. On June 16th, 1800, two days after his narrow victory at Marengo, Napoleon wrote to the Emperor of Austria in the following terms:

'On the battlefield of Marengo, surrounded by sufferers, and in the midst of fifteen thousand dead bodies, I implore Your Majesty to hear the cry of humanity, and not to allow the offspring of two brave and powerful nations to slaughter one another for the sake of interests of which they know nothing. It is for me to urge Your Majesty because I am nearer to the scene of war, and your heart cannot be so keenly affected as mine.... Let us give peace and repose to the present generation. If future generations are so foolish as to fight—well, after a few years of war they will learn wisdom, and live in peace with one another.' (See *Napoleon's Letters*, translated and edited by J. M. Thompson, F.B.A., F.R.Hist.S.)

2. General Mouton, Count of Lobau, was one of the most distinguished senior officers in the Grand Army and lived to fight in its final battle at Waterloo. At Aspern-Essling, on the banks of the Danube, in 1809, he and General Rapp saved that part of the army on the left bank by retaking the village of Essling and holding it against five determined counter-attacks by the Austrians. The situation of the French on this day invites comparison with their position on reaching the Beresina. The bridge of boats, on which the advanced corps depended for reinforcements and ammunition, was first destroyed accidentally by drifting tree trunks and later, designedly, by a floating mill launched by the Austrians upstream. Only by clinging to the ruins of the two villages could Masséna and Lannes, with part of the Guard under Bessières, avoid being thrown back into the river. They managed to hold on for two days and were eventually withdrawn to the island of Lobau. Later they crossed over lower down and won the decisive battle of Wagram.

3. Marshal Macdonald had to fight his way back across the Niemen and his adventures during late November and December were a retreat from Russia in miniature. Acting on his own initiative he withdrew first to Tilsit, then to Koenigsberg and finally to Danzic and Berlin. A very honourable man, he found it difficult to believe that his Prussian subordinates would desert in the face of the enemy and ignored many hints. At length, awaiting his rearguard under General Yorck at Tilsit, he was handed a letter which made that general's intentions abundantly clear. He at once began a skilful withdrawal and rejoined the remnant of the Grand Army at Elbing (See *Memoirs of Marshal Macdonald*, translated by S. L. Simeon and published by Richard Bentley and Son, 1893.)

4. In the event it was not until the end of the following year that the British and their Spanish and Portuguese allies crossed the Bidassoa and entered France. By that time Napoleon's main army had been defeated at Leipsic and had fallen back on the Rhine, crossed by the Coalition troops on New Year's Day, 1814. Marshal Soult continued to fight on in south-west France and only surrendered when news of Napoleon's abdication reached him in April. At this time the Grand Army and Soult's Peninsular veterans were contending with the armies of seven nations.

5. On making contact with Murat, Marshal Macdonald drew up and forwarded an excellent plan aimed at holding the eastern sector of the Empire against a Russo-Prussian assault, advising that all troops be concentrated on the Oder while there was still time. Murat, concerned only with returning to Naples and saving his crown, forwarded the plan to Napoleon but issued no directives. As

a result many good French troops were isolated in fortresses and surrounded as the invasion moved westward. Macdonald justly concludes that the entire course of the 1813 campaign would have altered in favour of the French had this obvious counter-measure been taken. (*Memoirs of Marshal Macdonald.*)

CHAPTER TEN

1. During a lull in the battle of Aspern-Essling Marshal Lannes sat down on the edge of a ditch, pondering the death of an old friend, General Pouzet, who had just been killed by a cannon-ball. His legs were crossed and a three-pounder shot, ricocheting close by, struck him where one leg was thrown across the other. The knee-pan of one leg was smashed and the back sinews of the other, for most people a mortal wound. Lannes, however, had recovered from several serious wounds and his constitution was exceptionally good. Surgeon-General Larrey, senior surgeon of the Grand Army, advised amputation of the leg with the damaged knee-pan, another doctor amputation of the other; Doctor Yvan, also in attendance, advised no amputation. As Larrey was the senior surgeon his wishes were carried out and Lannes was taken to Vienna. The heat and dirt of the battlefield proved too much for him and he died nine days later, almost certainly of blood poisoning. A man submitting to an amputation in a Napoleonic campaign had less than a fifty-fifty chance of recovery. (See *Memoirs of Baron de Marbot.*)

2. Murat was caught in the toe of Italy after his hopeless attempt to imitate Napoleon's return from Elba and rally support against the restored King of Naples. He was condemned by court martial and shot in a matter of hours, his dominant characteristics, courage and vanity, demonstrated to the end. He asked his executioners to spare his face and aim at the heart, and he fell holding portraits of his treacherous wife, Caroline, and their children.

CHAPTER ELEVEN

1. After the victories of Lutzen and Bautzen, in May 1813, an armistice was concluded and Napoleon was offered generous terms. He refused them and on August 12th Metternich succeeded in bringing Austria into the field against the French. Schwartzenberg commanded the largest allied army and the strategy agreed upon was to

avoid a general action against a force commanded by Napoleon personally and defeat the French in detail. It proved successful.

2. See Notes 2 and 3, Chapter Nine.

3. The last stand of the 14th of the Line at Eylau, isolated on a small hillock in the midst of the Russian army, is one of the most celebrated actions in the Napoleonic wars. Several officers were killed trying to reach the 14th and give orders for its retirement but when, at length, Marbot did make contact it was too late and the major in command, giving Marbot the regimental eagle, told him the remnant would die where it stood. Marbot himself escaped by a miracle. His mare, Lisette, bit and kicked her way back to the French lines after her rider had been paralysed by a cannon-ball passing through his hat. The horse dropped dead and Marbot was stripped and left on the field. His clothes were recognised, he was found and restored to health.

CHAPTER TWELVE

1. Although mostly composed of Prussians, almost all of whom deserted by the end of the year, Macdonald's Corps also contained a division made up of three Polish regiments, one Bavarian regiment and one Westphalian regiment. This division remained loyal and enabled him to achieve his withdrawal to Danzic. His staff was French throughout the campaign.

2. A certain amount of uncertainty continues to surround the death of Marshal Berthier, on June 1st, 1815. On Napoleon's abdication he agreed to serve under the Bourbons and when Napoleon returned from Elba, and the Royal Household made ready to flee to Ghent, he was in command of the Royal Guard. He was therefore called upon to escort the king to the frontier, a duty he faithfully carried out although he was extremely anxious not to be mistaken for an emigré and asked Macdonald to announce the reason for his "flight" in the newspapers. On reaching Ghent he went to Bamberg to fetch his family and it was here, while standing on a chair to look down on a column of Russian troops advancing to support Blucher and Wellington, that he fell to his death. Many claimed that a bad conscience had driven him to suicide but it might well have been a straightforward accident.

3. Mortier was the eighth and last Napoleonic marshal to die a violent death. In 1835, when he was attending King Louis-Philippe, an Italian called Fieschi threw a bomb at the royal party. The king was unhurt but Mortier was killed.

INDEX

Abo, 243

Acre, 24, 51, 64, 220

Alexander I, Tsar of Russia, 13, 17, 18, 19–20, 30–3, 34, 36, 38, 48, 54–5, 58, 59, 71, 84–5, 87, 88, 134, 143, 180, 218, 223, 230, 231, 233, 234; death of, 235; 242, 243, 244; quoted, 32

Anabert, General, 64, 70

Aspern-Essling, battle of, 51, 64, 123, 184, 187, 248, 249

Auerstadt, battle of, 26, 64, 241

Augereau, Marshal, Commander of Eleventh Corps, 28

Austerlitz, battle of, 16, 17, 18, 24, 30, 32, 54, 55, 56, 64, 123, 221, 241, 243

Bagration, Prince, 33, 34, 39–40, 42, 43, 44, 45 46, 53, 54, 67, 70, 241, 242

Balachov, General, 14, 20

Bamberg, 234, 250

Barclay de Tolly, 33, 38, 41, 42, 45, 47, 52 et seq., 58, 61

Bautzen, 222, 249

Beauharnais, Alexandre de, 244

Beauharnais, Eugène de, Viceroy of Italy, Commander of Fourth Corps, 25, 27, 63, 65, 67, 69, 80, 83, 88, 91 et seq., 94, 95, 99, 102, 112, 122, 123, 126, 127–9, 130, 133, 135, 140, 156, 170, 174, 182, 195, 207, 208, 214–15, 239, 244–5

Bennigsen, General, 61, 123

Beresina, river, 45, 87, 103, 110, 112, 120, 121, 130, 138, 142, 143, 148, 149, 152, 155; crossing during the retreat, 158–70; 171, 175, 176, 177, 179, 184, 187, 195, 207, 217, 222, 229, 248

Berlin, 41, 216, 217, 248

Berlin Decrees, the, 18, 19, 216

Bernadotte, Crown Prince of Sweden, later Charles XIV, 56, 85, 184, 223, 233, 241, 243

Berthier, Marshal, Chief of Staff, 13, 22, 29, 34, 44, 59, 77, 83, 88,

95, 112, 123, 125, 134, 156; death of, 234; 250; quoted, 77

Bessières, Marshal, Commander of the Old Guard, 13, 28, 29, 59, 69, 81, 92, 93, 112, 114, 123, 125, 233; death of, 234, 248; quoted, 69

Blucher, General, 182, 223, 250

Bonaparte, Napoleon, Emperor of France, 13–14 et seq., 19–21, 22, 23–4 et seq., 30, 32, 34, 35 et seq., 39, 41–4, 46, 47, 48, 49, 51, 52; at Smolensk (Aug., 1812), 53–9; at Borodino, 60–71; at Moscow, 73–89; 92, 93, 94, 95, 96, 98, 100, 102–3; at Smolensk (Nov., 1812), 107–13; 120, 121 et seq., 128–30, 133, 134, 135, 140, 142 et seq., 156, 158–63, 171, 172, 173, 174; journey to Paris, 178–91, 208, 212, 214, 217, 219, 224–5 et seq.; death of, 233; 235, 241 et seq., 250; quoted: 13, 14, 20–1, 22, 34, 39, 43, 49, 51, 54, 62, 65, 71, 73, 75, 77, 79, 84, 88, 120, 125, 140, 147, 149, 158, 160–1, 172, 179, 187–8, 189–90, 211, 214–15, 225, 226–7, 230, 235, 247–8

Bourbons, 98, 177, 181, 224, 234, 247, 250

Bourgogne, Sergeant, 24, 36, 46, 48, 61, 68–9, 71–3, 75 et seq., 79, 82, 86, 89–91, 96, 100, 105–6, 107, 113–16, 125–7, 130, 131, 132, 150–6, 164–7, 169–70, 175, 177–8, 195–6, 199, 200–3, 205–7, 209–10, 215, 219–22, 224; death of, 235; 238; quoted, 71–2, 73, 82, 86, 100, 105–6, 107, 113, 132, 151, 154, 175, 195, 202, 210

Bourgoing, Captain de, 120, 224

Borissov, 103, 121, 130, 143, 144, 145, 148, 149, 151, 155, 156, 157, 160, 161, 162, 165, 167–8, 173, 229

Borodino, 34, 35, 60, 89, 93, 97, 98, 102, 107, 122, 125, 136, 151, 208, 229

Bourienne, 239

Jarkovoa, 100

Jena, battle of, 16, 18, 24, 26, 43, 64, 221, 241

Jerome, King of Westphalia, Commander of Eighth Corps, 28, 34, 42–4, 58, 190

Josephine, former Empress of France, 19, 128

Jourdan, Marshal, 185

Junot, General, 34, 44, 57–8, 95, 105; quoted, 44

Kalouga, 74, 89, 91, 93

Kamen, 49

Koenigsberg, 107, 184, 208, 211, 214, 215, 216, 228, 248

Kolotskoi, 98

Kovno, 15, 16, 17, 88, 108, 109, 147, 156, 192, 198, 199, 200, 201, 205, 206, 207, 208, 209, 213

Krasnoi, 51, 121, 124–6, 127 *et seq.*, 133–5, 138, 143, 148, 151, 160, 161, 164, 195, 205

Kutusoff, General, 33, 34, 35, 54, 60, 61, 65, 69, 74, 80, 85, 86, 87–9, 93, 99, 103, 112, 121, 123, 124, 126, 130, 134, 138, 142, 143, 161, 182, 184, 194, 213, 230; death of, 233; 241, 247

Laubaume, 67, 72, 82–3, 174, 239; quoted, 67

Labédoyère, 175, 197, 239

Lambert, General, 145

Lannes, Marshal, 59, 204, 248, 249

Lariboisière, death of, 217

Larrey, Surgeon-General, 249

Latour-Maubourg, 64, 70

Lauriston, General, 85

Lecourbe, 242

Lefèbvre, Marshal, 29, 102, 123, 125, 151–2, 156, 158, 170, 182, 208, 214; quoted, 152

Lefèbvre-Desnouettes, 182, 186

Legrand, General, 118–19, 163, 165

Leipsic, 174, 222, 248

Lepel, 64, 70

Lisbon, 181, 242

Lobau, 248

Loison, General, 204

Longchamps, General, 126, 131

Losznetza, 149

Louis XVI, King of France, 18, 151

Louis-Philippe, King of France, 234, 250

Lukulen, 120

Lutzen, 222, 249

Macdonald, Marshal, 28, 87, 103, 118, 184, 212–13, 215, 229, 248, 249, 250

Mainz, 190

Malet Conspiracy, the, 100, 113, 191, 244

Malodechno, 173, 176–7, 179

Malo-Jaroslavitz, 89, 92–3, 107, 112, 122

Marbot, Major, later Colonel, 25, 36, 57, 85, 116, 119, 120, 136, 144, 145, 146, 152, 158, 162, 167, 174, 175, 193, 194, 195, 199–200, 205, 215, 217–18, 223–4, 227, 228, 229; death of, 235; 238, 250; quoted, 119, 158, 194, 195, 223

Marengo, battle of, 24, 44, 64, 181, 189, 220, 247

Maret, Duke of Bassano, Minister of Foreign Affairs, 56, 117, 120, 147, 171, 172, 184, 185, 187, 192, 193, 247

Marie Louise, Empress of France, 19, 51, 63, 71, 87, 191

Marion, General, 64, 70, 118, 199, 203, 246

Marmont, Marshal, 56, 63, 185, 245

Masséna, Marshal, 33, 57, 64, 131, 242, 248

Mayence, 216

Mazeppa, 241

Mestivier, 62

Metternich, Chancellor, 98, 212, 232, 249

Mickalevka, 100

Milan, 41, 73, 150

Milhaud, General, 86

Miloradovich, General, 99, 124–6 *et seq.*, 135–6, 142

Minsk, 42, 43, 120, 121, 142, 147, 161

Mojaisk, 72, 93, 94, 97

Moncey, Marshal, 245–6, 247; quoted 245–6

Mons, 223

Montbrun, 64, 70, 87

Mont St. Jean, 222

Morand, General, 64, 70, 242

Mortier, Commander of Young Guard, 29, 59, 79–80, 81, 86, 89, 95, 102, 112, 113, 123, 140, 151, 156, 208, 214; death of, 234; 250

R. F. DELDERFIELD

R. F. Delderfield, born in London in 1912, has been writing for publication and stage presentation since he was seventeen. His most recent play, *My Dearest Angel*, about Queen Victoria's courtship, is to be seen this year in London, but he devotes most of his time to historical biographies, military studies concerning the First Empire, and novels on provincial life. A noted lecturer on the art of war from the Norman Conquest through the 1914-18 period, Mr. Delderfield is considered an expert on 15th-century warfare, but his particular fascination has always been the Napoleonic era. His books on the personalities of Napoleon, his family and, particularly, his fighting marshals have been translated into many languages. His principal historical books published in the United States include *Napoleon in Love* (1959), *The Golden Millstones* (1965) and *Napoleon's Marshals* (1966). His Devon saga, *A Horseman Riding By*, one of the longest novels ever published in Britain, will appear in the United States this year.